Tears On The Wind

by
Alma G. Stenger

Alma G. Stenger

TEARS ON THE WIND

Copyright 1996

by Alma G. Stenger

All Rights Reserved.

Printed in the United States of America.
by Morris Pub. Co., P.O. Box 2110,
Kearney, Nebraska 68848

No part of this book may be used or
reproduced in any manner whatsoever without
permission except in the case of brief
quotations embodied in critical articles or
review.

Cover Illustration by: Dustyn Tallman

All bible quotations are from The King James
Version.

LIBRARY OF CONGRESS DATA

LCCN # 96-069053

ISBN # 1-886364-01-X

SAN # 298=4034

Published by:

RABETH PUBLISHING COMPANY
201 South Cottage Grove
Kirksville, MO 63501

To obtain more books, see Book Stores
or order from:
Rabeth Publishing Company
Attention: A. G. Stenger
P. O. Box #171
Kirksville, MO 63501
Enclose $ 14.95 + $2.50 S&H

I lovingly dedicate this book to all victims of abuse, and to all those who care enough to understand and help those victims.

ACKNOWLEDGEMENT

I wish to thank my dear daughter, Vicki Lloyd, who diligently put more of the elbow grease into this book to bring it to complete fruition, and to my son-in-law, Tom Lloyd, who was patiently supporting her throughout the entire time, and offering his computer knowledge. To give appreciation to my grand-daughter-in-law, Cindy Lloyd, for her expertise in polishing the entire mess.

I'd like to commend Pastor Jim Collins, from Kirksville MO, for his kind overlay critique, and the way he plowed through "TEARS ON THE WIND" in the manner befitting his calling, for he certainly must care and listen to bruised souls of victims of varied abuse on a daily basis.

My gratitude is extended to my publisher Betty Quigley. To others not mentioned by name who helped Vicki and me in encouragement-- even a friendly pat on the shoulder. GOD BLESS YOU.

AGS

PREFACE

As Alma described some of her experiences to me, I was reminded of a song Billie Holiday sang called "Strange Fruit": "Southern trees bear strange fruit. Blood on the leaves, blood at the root." This song was written to protest the violence against African Americans in the South as epitomized by lynchings. In <u>Tears On The Wind</u>, Alma writes of family oppressions and domestic violence that leave their blood marks as well. Her traumatic memories are the fruit borne of a strangely twisted family tree.

Even Alma does not know how the roots of this tree grew so violent, abusive, and destructive. From reading her life story, it seems to me that the extreme poverty of the Depression Era, the socially condoned practice of ridged, authoritarian parenting and male dominance, and even the "fire and brimstone" fervor of rural Southern religion all fed those roots. I do not know if the mountains of western Arkansas were more deeply scarred than the rest of America from the devastation of those times or not. I do know that this area was hit hard, very hard. Towns were devastated, families disintegrated. Many people were lost to hopelessness and despair. Their spirits hardened, becoming bitter and cruel.

Today, I practice as a clinical therapist in the area of Arkansas where Alma was raised. The hardness is still with us as is the poverty and violence. The mountains of western Arkansas remain heavily wooded with family trees much like Alma's.

If Alma had not already written this book, my first words to her would have been to "write, write, write it out." Many more books like Alma's need to be written. In this way the survivors of abuse can begin a selective harvest to remove the dark woods, opening space for sunlight to pour in and grow new and healthier family trees.

God bless the "wild spirit" Alma found inside herself to defy her abusers and survive. Remember, that not all of the trees of Arkansas grow darkly. There was the giant oak that saved Alma as a child and had a bit of God in it, too. Many Arkansans performed acts of kindness for Alma and she has not forgotten them. I am deeply ashamed for my state that more was not done for her but I have to remind myself that social workers, therapists, and other helpers were few and far between back then.

Tears On The Wind is not easy reading so be prepared. Alma's fragmented memories sometimes lack a time sequence. You will not always know when or where you are, when someone strikes. This lack of structure will leave most people feeling uneasy, disoriented. I do not think it is intentional technique on Alma's part but it works very effectively to put the reader in the same state of mental confusion Alma must have felt. Be prepared for your own experience of shock and anguish.

Because of the years between us, I cannot rescue the child Alma was. I can affirm with her, though, that she was a good child and she is cherished in this world. Peace be with you, Alma.

                              Lida K. Simpson, LCSW
                              Waldron, Arkansas

At fifty-two years of age, I know and realize how much the younger years mold the child, affecting every aspect of his personality including his parenting skills. I may have been spared being an alcoholic or a drug addict, but I still fight what I call the demons or the bad seed.

I feel my children have been spared but only by the love of Jesus Christ and taking back our homes as Christian homes.

Mothers and daughters need more protection and I feel it is everyone's responsibility. They should never have to suffer as my mother has. A child should never have to fear for their mother as I did for mine, more than I ever feared for myself.

We hope this book will give readers the courage to get involved, or save someone from abuse, save a child, or step out of an abusive situation.

My mother is the strongest person I have ever known and we have a special bond, she saved me and protected me the best way she knew how. I have a hard time with those who have hurt her so much and wish there had been more I could have done for her.

In my own father's case, it was alcohol, but my grandfather, what makes a person hate so much?

I asked my mother to write this book and felt she could come through some healing but soon realized as I typed and edited page after page was almost more than I could bear. I know God is the only reason she is alive today.

God Bless the Readers
Vicki Lloyd

Foreword

I keep thinking over my life, and wonder why I feel so much pain, regret, and grief when there are so many more people who have suffered more abuse, and their scars are more extensive than mine. I have one hitch. I can't turn off the regret, the grief. Why can't I turn it all off and get on with things as I know I must? I'm too old to be unable to understand some major facets of life, for crying out loud. I'm too old now to not know how.
Aren't I?

All of us are constantly looking back upon our lives, the important events that form our thinking, that mold our personalities, that allow us to succeed in life or prevent us from the success that we know our intellectual abilities can take us, if there just weren't the stumbling blocks a sizeable percentage of us have. The stumbling blocks of fear, pain, and the most crucial one, lack of self-esteem, or self- image. If children are not encouraged to go for it, or praised when we go for it and win, or at least do well, we can become discouraged, and perhaps half-heartedly go for the ring, or maybe not even attempt to go for it at all.

I hold no degrees in psychology, but I'm a first hand recipient of overt physical and verbal abuse from family members. Believe me when I tell you, I was not a passive onlooker, one who can go on to something else after viewing something disagreeable on a screen that does not explode my head and my heart. Oh, no. My head exploded, my heart exploded into broken pieces, my back hurt from the whipping, and a bloody nose from an angry hand branded my brain, my memory. It only took a moment to discontinue my full potential for the rest of my life. What dreams can a 6 year old child have of the grand future? Who will be there to guide and nurture that child? Who will see the potential, and perhaps the talent, and bring it to life for the child, taking him on to the final mile of success, the capacity of grabbing with happiness and a job well done, the gold ring? The parents? You would think so.

I wanted to go on, to do better, but by the time my poor, dysfunctional family got out of the low-ring social status they had always been in, I was seventeen and without the counseling I so desperately needed. There wasn't such a thing as a medical doctor, and who in our neck of the woods ever heard of a counselor, or therapist for emotional and behavioral disorders? I was about half wild anyway by that age.

I didn't know it consciously at the time, but I was on a big collision course with what I know best, and was used to all my life. Another potential abuser was breathing down my neck even if I was not aware.

I needed my Protector desperately, but I really wasn't listening.

* * *

PART ONE

To this day I can't shake off the feeling that if I had gotten lost as a child, or later, no one would have cared enough to look for me.

"For the pastors are become brutish, and have not sought the Lord: therefore they shall not prosper, and all their flocks shall be scattered."
Jeremiah 10:21

Chapter One

It seems as if I have been sick most of my life. Why or how I have survived I will never know. I was basically born perfect, and my mother has told me I was the easiest birth for her, the best baby, and the happiest. I also was very active and inquisitive. She said I learned to roll across the floor before I learned to crawl, and sometimes ended up in the most unusual places, like back under pieces of furniture and in corners.

So far so good.

My memories up to age five are now somewhat vague and to my knowledge I was not sickly. The only adverse memory was of my sister two years older than I; the memory of keeping out of her angry reach, and her bawling noises. Bettye was not a happy child and I always felt she resented me terribly. Both of us wore Buster Brown haircuts, Bettye's hair being dark brown in color, mine almost white, giving me the nickname "Cotton Top". When I was six and Bettye eight, she cut one side of my hair off with scissors above the ear, leaving me looking as if I had been caught in a lawn mower. We were both soundly spanked for that, I think, by Mother.

In that same year of my young life, I remember the first of a series of childhood physical punishments by my father. In this first case a blow to my face with the back of his hand left me with not only a bloody nose, but inability to breathe or catch my breathe properly. I was knocked off my feet and taken completely by surprise. To this day I don't know exactly what I had done, except get too close to him when he was working with some crystal radio parts. Times were very different then, the early thirties; years of no work for people, depression, and long lines of hungry people waiting for free food at soup kitchens. In the midst of this, a long drought settled on the land. Places of business went bankrupt. There was no economy to speak of. The devastating years of Wall Street crashes became an introduction to the Depression. The Dust Bowl era hit the Mid-west and South- west parts of the country, leaving ghosts of a proud people with barely crusts of bread and the once lush, waving fields of green turned into dull scenes as bare as landscapes of the moon. People changed. Sparkling bright eyes turned into dull sunken things hardly recognized as the once happy people. Tired of not being able to feed their families, and with hope gone, hoards of men deserted, becoming wandering bundles of rags sneaking under the cover of darkness onto freight trains that carried them away like wisps of vapor. It was the time of the hobos. Back at home, the deserted ones fought for life and were buried in dust-covered graves.

Into all this came a new president of our gasping country, crippled and an aristocrat, with an empathy for the lives of the citizens, and best of all with a plan to save us all from the dying economy. The plan was in a package termed "The New Deal", consisting of various working projects of which one was the W.P.A., Works Progress Administration, providing work for all employable people.

My father, in all of his so-called pride, refused to sign up for W.P.A. jobs, or commodities given to the people, because it smacked of welfare. It wasn't until I was 13 years old that Mother insisted he sign up for commodities at least, and so they both went to Fort Smith, 30 miles north of our town of Hartford, and came home with basic foodstuffs and articles of clothing. Everybody was doing it, and I wondered silently why my father objected so strenuously.

When I was seven we picked up and moved to another small town here in Arkansas. Lavaca. Oh! I could climb the big oak tree in our new front yard and see a tiny, shiny sliver of the Arkansas River, if the river was high. Dad would go out in the surrounding areas looking for work, driving his own put-together model T Ford with his tool kit in the back. Mostly he tried things on his own, though. He always had good tools, and making cherry wood furniture was one job he could put artistic touches into.

Next he built himself a sawmill at the edge of town providing clap boards for the local coal mines for shoring pegs of cave studding. I'll say this for my father--he was good at what he did. But he became discouraged easily. That was a drawback. All in all during his lifetime my father had been a garage mechanic, a comic strip and design artist, a mattress refurbishing co-owner, a carpenter, a school teacher, a shoe repairman, sawmill operator, roofer, writer, and a journeyman machinist that he finally stuck with later in life that provided him and Mother a decent living. But success didn't come for us children in time. We kids were hungry, wormy, and certainly feeling the stresses that dad and mother were feeling.

It is with reluctance that I write this narrative, for bringing back the memories of episodes in my life does not evoke warm feelings of nostalgia. On the contrary, I view them with some dread and a lot of sadness, pain, and a sense of betrayal. A shiver runs through me and I then rise to the battle with the anxiety that almost always comes with the memories. Being sick is one phase of recollection that brings out feelings of fear. I actually begin to breathe faster and the heartbeat picks up, for it is so real to me now. I've often wondered if the mere thought could throw me into a painful migraine on the spot. As I write this I feel the awful, open wounds, so must stop and push these things back into a dark place in my mind, to continue it later. The door to the hiding place must stay closed until I've gained strength again.

We called our mother "Mama" until we were in our teens and "Mom" became fashionable. "Mama" was for children or so we thought. It wasn't until I grew to be middle-aged that I referred to her as "Mother". To me "mother" is more adult, less loving, more formal, and yes, more distant. I slacked- off references to "my mom", and also "Mom" to her deliberately. I do not like to touch her or kiss her.

I do not like her and I am sad. Poor Mama was either depressed and crying, or ecstatic and singing; however, she cried more than she sang. She really wanted to be more than what she was and certainly felt she deserved more than what she got.

My heart cries in deep loneliness when I think of her. She was a sensuous woman, and from some of the things in her speech over the years, she led me to believe that she felt that producing unwanted children was her punishment for her obvious delight in lovemaking. On the other hand she had PMS stretched to the max, and I will always remember her bloody rags soaking in a large dish pan of water removing the great stains before she boiled them to be used over and over. We were usually too poor to afford sanitary napkins. She cried and had temper tantrums, slinging things about bemoaning her faith as common white trash. We went about our allotted chores at times suffering her anger if we did something wrong. She yelled, cried more tears, and slapped us when she was in one of these moods.

I do not recall my mother ever reading to us children, or of me actually sitting on her lap, ever. My older sister recalls that Mother constantly had my baby sister on her lap, fiddling with her curls. I don't recall loving hugs, and never kisses. I could only feel impatience in mother, if she held my hand when I was small, leading me perhaps in town, or in a crowd. Her parents, my grandparents, were not demonstrative people either, so I suppose her withdrawal had something to do with that. This day is November 1994, I left my mother after a visit to Pinewood Nursing Home in Waldron, Arkansas. Wanting to do all I can to make her life more cheerful. She will soon be 95 years old, has no diseases, but is quite frail, and again today asked me to move down with her to care for her. As usual, I declined and she went through her pout. Her years of manipulating of us, not only of me, does not work any longer. She never fails to be the actress to the hilt, as she tells me not to go. The tears come to the faded eyes, and cause red rims, and she waves a limp arm.

"I love you, sweetie. I love you, darling," the voice says as a sob catches in her throat.

I feel disgusted as I go through the ritual of giving the car horn two toots and wave at her behind the large glass windows. I feel disgusted because she is not genuine, and she never ever called me names of endearment when I was growing up and needing them. I've only now heard her pay this much attention to me, because I am the only person left to visit her, bring her the needed items she asks for, and listen to her hate and belittling of the other residents.

Dear Lord, forgive me, but it is too late for her to call me loving names.

Tears run down my face as I coast down the hill to a stop sign. I know that if Peggy came back, or Bettye took more interest in her, she would dismiss me with a wave of her hand. But they want nothing to do with her, and now she knows it. I am it. My mother, having terrible mood swings, would scream how dumb I was or laugh at my being so skinny and ugly. She switched me across the back of my legs, and slapped my face so many times I lost count. What ticked her off?

One day I came into the kitchen where the delicious smell of chocolate cake filled the room, and my stomach lurched in hunger. I also knew what might happen, as it had at other times, so was ready to make a quick dash for the door just in case. Sure enough she took the cake from the stove oven, set it on the table and proceeded to turn it upside down on top of a plate. It tore into pieces, and she let out a scream of extreme anger, and began to throw the cake, pans and spoons on the floor, against the wall, out the window, and all other directions.

Bettye and Peggy disappeared. I almost tore the door off its hinges getting out.

Sobs of anger followed inside the house. I did not want to be anywhere near her until all this had blown over.

My mother could never make a cake from scratch. She was good at pies, puddings, and cookies, but never cakes. Had she listened when first learning to cook? For had she been more patient, she would have done fine. She always seemed to have dumped the cake out of the pan before it had sufficiently cooled. Grandma Michael, who was the ultimate in cooking, should have taught her. Mother could not compete with Grandma. After she cooled off, and no more noises and sobs came from the house, we knew she then was down on her knees picking up the cake pieces to arrange them on the plate, then make frosting to pour over the broken pieces.

This happened time after time. Why didn't she quit attempting to make cakes, if she couldn't learn the basic fundamentals of cake-making?

I do understand why Mother wanted to make us cakes. She obviously thought the next cake would turn out good, much like a gambler saying he would win the next card game.

Grandma lived on a farm where there was lots of food products. She had plenty of fresh eggs, cream, and butter to cook with. Poor Mother didn't and she should have really never tried the same procedure time and again.

We kids never laughed at Mother. We felt sorry for her.

Mother was a pretty woman, and when dress hemlines went up, she had lovely legs to show. She was proud of her beauty and was always neat and clean. She loved to show off. She came from farm people who always had plenty of food, but it took backbreaking labor to keep the farm going. With a big family of six sons and three daughters, Grandma and Grandpa had plenty of help. Even as the babies came, the oldest children cared for the little ones. To hear some of them talk, Grandma, a strong woman, would give birth and almost immediately head for the fields, leaving the infants in the care of Mother and her oldest sister.

Mother was twenty when she married my father. I didn't understand why she chose him, but I've heard that with the many boyfriends Mother could have chosen from, she picked an "outsider" nobody knew too well. She was crazy about him.

Dad had told Mother and the Michaels that he would take good care of her and they would start married life in Dustin, Oklahoma, the home then of his family, the Mays. They would have their own apartment downtown. Mother told me at the time of Dad's death, that he lied to her. There was no apartment and no job for him. She was appalled at the condition of the place she was taken where the whole family would live together. She did not want to continue to work on the farm of her own folks from dawn to dark, milking cows, wading in deep snow by lantern light, hoeing and picking cotton, and always canning and cooking, and smoking meat. It was endless work, but when she saw the Mays' unkept small place, she felt she had made a big mistake.

She constantly cleaned, scrubbed dirty laundry on a rub board, mopped dirty, bare floors, cooked and tidied-up. She even took some insults from Grandma May and was forced to put up with the lazy antics of Dad's two younger sisters. Then when she discovered she was pregnant, her temperament could handle no more. She demanded for Dad to take her back to Barling to await brother Herb's birth.

Dad was not comfortable working for Mother's parents, but tried to stick it out until the baby was born. Grannie May, who was a renown mid-wife in her younger years and a nurse as well, arrived with Grandpa May to help with the birthing.

Labor was agonizing for Mother, and in some way Grannie managed to accidently infect Mother during the birth. Days later, Mother began running a high fever and things didn't look so good. Grandpa Michael bundled Mother and the baby up in his new Maxwell touring car and took them to the farm nearby, then called a doctor out to look at Mother. Dr. Honeymichael washed his hands thoroughly, closed off the bedroom, and started his examination. She indeed had a bad infection in the womb, and Mother said she was given shots on a daily basis for sometime, and medications. This was May of 1921, and she could not remember what kind of shots she received. She began to recover, and was up and about two months later. She called Herb "Baby James" for the first year of his life.

But where was Dad? He couldn't do farm work or take orders from J.F. Michael and his boy, so packed a bag and left saying he would find a job and place to live for his family.

Grandpa May told Dad he wanted Herb to be called Herbert, after his brother, so mother was forced to give up her son's name "James". She was angry at Grandpa May for being so forceful and at Dad for being too weak to stand up to him. The little family stayed in Barling long enough to add Bettye Lou to their number, then back they went to the May family who now lived in Nowata, Oklahoma.

There I was born.

My life began in Nowata, Oklahoma just before Halloween in 1925. That must have been a terrible scream for Grandpa May, who was part Cherokee Indian, and looked it. Unlike Bettye, my hair was white, and my eyes were a light blue- green. Grandpa teased Mother about the "ice man's kid" which threw her into a tantrum and caused her to sulk for days. I was a chatter box, giggled all the time, seldom walked when I could skip, and was chubby until about five years old. Mother has told me these things through the years, so I will believe her. I was happy and sang songs I heard on records; old 78 thick celluloid records played on a cranked phonograph player. Grandpa began calling me "Dear old Gretch" even though I was little. Perhaps, he liked me a little bit. My father began teaching me songs, two kinds, church and not so church, and I could memorize verses he called reciting. I was too young to be self-conscious, so used gestures, facial expressions and a few, little, unsteady dance steps.

I don't remember these things or the following, even though there are quick and short flashes of a primitive memory. I used to guess that because the stories were told by mother so often, I would only think I remembered snatches of memories so long ago. Of course, I am telling only what has been told me at this time. Even Grannie May backed her up on it.

Mother invited the preacher for Sunday dinner after church. My father was bragging about my musical talent, so after dinner I was asked to sing a song for the pastor; just any song would do. I did not hesitate, or hang back, but proceeded

to belt out any song with gestures and body language to boot:
"Show me the way to go home.
I'm tired and I want to go to bed.
[Mother's face turned white]
I-I had a little drink [hic] about an hour ago,
And it went right to my head.
[Stagger about like a drunk]
Where ever I may roam,
on land, or sea, or foam,
you can always hear me singing this song.
Show me the way to go home."

I finished and waited for applause, Mother's face was still pale, the preacher sat quietly, and my father sported a grin. Then I got a few limp claps.

I would suspect I was then quietly hustled out of the presence of the dinner guest, who passed along this form of entertainment long afterwards among his parish, no doubt with a smile on his face. This doesn't sound like much to us today as having a shock to the mid-drift; but, it could have caused a scandal sixty-some years ago in a small town. I've often wondered if my father taught me that particular song for that one purpose, just for the Baptist minister, and it was he who clued me in to sing that song. You see, Dad was a Methodist, as were his parents. He really didn't like Baptist preachers, and wasn't seen inside one of "those" churches, except for funerals or otherwise forced to be there. At least not in the early years. If boy scout meetings were held in a Baptist church, or Presbyterian, then he would be there. He was an Eagle Scout to the max during his teens.

My confusion came in when I was six and we lived in the peanut house in Slatonville, Arkansas. This was when my bubble burst for real, and I was thrown into a whole different world; the one that began with my first memory of abuse. What changed my father from a doting father who taught me songs and verses and was proud of me into the monster I quickly started learning about?

From Nowata we drifted up to Anderson, Missouri and

Carthage for bridge construction Dad always seemed to go back to in those happier days. I still have a few memories connected to these places. I remember a little wool bathing suit with a white mesh-like bib Grannie May gave me. I almost drowned in a river near Anderson where Dad had pitched our tent for the summer while he worked nearby. Mother said I was being swept down when Dad went in and got me out. I wasn't told if I had been punished.

In Carthage, Mother had to tie me to a tree to keep me from running off.

We lived in a rooming house near a busy street and the railroad tracks. I'd been rescued by a train engineer while I played with the pretty gravel between the rails. He set me up asked "Is this your baby, lady?" She said she yelled out in horror, even though the train had been stopped to take on water. Immediately a new rope was purchased.

I was certainly busy. Before that I disappeared in the middle of the night. A storm was upon us with claps of thunder and lightning streaks close by. Neighbors were called out and lanterns glowed throughout the area. Behind our rooming house was a pasture and beyond that a fence enclosed barn. They found me there in my white nightdress near the stall of a cow and new born calf, with only lightning for me to see by. They asked me why I had run off and I told them to see the baby cow. This only tells me I was not afraid of the dark. Or I was determined to see that calf. Did I get a whipping for this? I don't know. These are my mother's tales.

One thing strikes me that sounds like sadism on Dad's part in another occurrence. I had formed a habit of running to meet Dad when he came home from work and anxiously take his dinner pail. He always left a little something in his pail for me everyday, day in, day out. He must have gotten real tired of this and so needed to break me of this habit. One day I gleefully ran to meet him and he held his pail high until we got inside the kitchen. He then gave me the pail and unsnapped the two hinges opening the lid. Inside was a nest of red, squirming hairless, baby mice. Quickly I dropped the pail, and jumping up onto a dining room chair, screamed until I was almost hysterical, while my father laughed his head off. I do not remember this, I don't think, so I do not know how Mother felt about the "joke", even though she told the story.

Later I sulked, but the joke worked. The lesson was successful for him. I can almost be certain that this child lost some respect and trust for her father. In a split second the damage was done. But it worked for him. I guess that is what mattered.

When Dad's work on the bridge at Carthage was finished, we headed down to Barling, Arkansas and lived in the tent down by a creek. The summer was still with us, so it was pleasant enough for us three kids.

The tent was of canvas, big as a medium-sized room, and Mother used a rug as flooring. Furniture consisted of everything that would fold and pack in a 2-wheel trailer that was pulled by an open top, model T Ford, one seater and small flat bed. We kids rode in the back. The chuck box was the only thing we couldn't fold, but Dad was real good at balance placement.

I don't know what kind of job my father found in Barling, which was a very small town near what is now Fort Chaffee. Jobs were not too plentiful and within a short time would become almost impossible to find. I wouldn't begin to guess.

In 1930 blacks mostly lived in communities that were more populated with their own race, at least off to one side of the town of whites; but, where Uncle Jonah Brooks came from I couldn't say. To me, not quite five, he was a novelty. I thought of him as a dark man. He also was fun.

Dad must have been "self-employed" at something or other because he hired Uncle Jonah as his helper. He was older than Dad, was courteous to everyone, and laughingly teased me.

One day he teased me into anger. I screamed at him, "you leave me alone you nigga." Why I wasn't in the tent with mother, I wasn't told. Dad picked up a small rope, grabbed me by the arm, jerked me about, and began laying on the rope.

Uncle Jonah, put a hand on dad's arm, saying, "Please, Mistah Tom, don't whup her. She is too little to know what she said." I was made to apologize to Uncle Jonah, and he patted me on the head, grinning his acceptance of my apology. I'm certainly not proud of that, but I was exhibiting some trouble with my temper at that age. I can make guesses, but I might not be correct in my guesses. But, where did I get the word "nigger" if not directly? I picked it up listening to talk from the people around me. I had total remorse for sometime, but Mother said Uncle Jonah made it easy on me. I did discover she called the black people "nigras", the old Southern pronunciation, no doubt passed on from her mother's folks from Alabama, and her father's from Tennessee. Left- over garbage from the plantation days.

After that I had fond admiration for Uncle Jonah, because of his strength of character, his gentleness, and because he forgave me. He would lead me up to the small grocery store run by some of mother's Bullington relations, my little hand in his big one, me skipping to keep stride. Once there, he would buy me some of the messiest candy the store had, so Mother told me, and he would lift me high up on his shoulder, and I would ride all the way home. Mother would scold him for ruining my clothes, and he would laugh and pretend he didn't know I was all sticky and messed up. I think I loved him. Something inside me tells me I've missed him all these years.

Finally I found out Uncle Jonah had a family, a wife and children, when he brought Mother some "shortnin' bread" his wife made just for us. I never saw them that I remember. Mother said there was only him and his family, out somewhere at the edge of Barling, and only he was seen about. His family was invisible.

Recently, my mother told me that the Jonah Brooks' family had attained high prestige with the town of Barling, was involved in civic duties in the fifties and sixties, and managed to send the children to colleges. In the thirties, his little children weren't allowed to attend school there; but, somehow, and I don't know how, they got their education.

Uncle Jonah was an exceptional man. I would have been lucky to have been his child. I'm told Uncle Jonah and his wife were laid to rest in the white cemetery at Barling.

Uncle Jonah, a forerunner of my own uncles to be fill-in dads, held my hand. Not my own father. And you know, I don't know where my sister Bettye was all these times.

When fall came upon us in 1930, we moved into a house there in town. I turned five in October of that year, and the following January, on Mother's birthday, little, sweet, sister Peggy was born. I remember her and the absolute miracle of this tiny bundle of a doll with the dark hair and enormous eyes. I adored her. I don't remember Herb being about much, anymore than I do Bettye. They went to school and my other memory of Bettye was Easter evening 1931, when Bettye played the piano with two fingers and I sang. We were presented two papier-mache' bunny rabbits with candy eggs in a basket on their backs. That I do recall still, in a dim fashion.

Bettye and I were taught more music, songs for church mostly, by mother's childhood friend, Willie Smith, a pretty woman who always seemed to be sitting at her piano and making music. So, the inspiration to sing was not to be ignored. Miss Willie taught us to sing duet, with Bettye soprano and I was taught to harmonize. We loved it. Too bad it didn't last longer there. We waved bye--I wonder if I cried at all--to Uncle Jonah and Aunt Parrie, our cousins, and Willie Smith. Dad couldn't stay put. He was like a nomad, always with grandiose ideas and plans that never panned out. His greener pastures seemed to mean moving about in circles.

His family grew, and so did his frustrations.

Some people come into your life for only a short minute, or two, touching you, making a difference and leaving you with a good memory that would always be brought up during your many years by a nice trigger of some sort, thereby keeping the people, however faceless, alive and bright in your memory. How do we know whether this kind of gesture is no accidental happening, and how do we know that we are made kinder ourselves by it throughout our lives? It could be on purpose, to show us the better side of people and life, and so we pass it on, and on, over the years as in a chain reaction. Our hearts don't forget all brief kindnesses. Mine didn't.

Mrs. Walker lived past the Richardson place in Slatonville where the school bus stopped to deposit Herb, Bettye, and me, tired and weary from our day in school. The sun would be low in the southwest sky in the winter as we three trudged slowly home, a lonely and long way for young children.

Herb always walked ahead, Bettye close behind him, and I being only six, followed up the rear...a long rear. We usually cut across Mrs. Walker's cow pasture to shorten our distance; but, we tried not to intrude too closely to the house. We were cold, shivering, and we were always hungry.

This particular day was colder with a chilling wind and the pasture was wet and soggy, our thin shoes made more inadequate by the seeping wet we felt inside, and the soles making us aware of every rock we stepped upon. Soon we were at the shortest distance from the side of Mrs. Walker's house. Thin wisps of smoke curled out of the rock chimney on the roof.

Suddenly, a kitchen window was raised, and Mrs. Walker's face peeked out at us. She smiled and motioned for us to approach. Herb, being in charge, walked over to the window, Bettye and me following. She held a plate in her hands and she asked, "Would you children like to have a piece of nice gingerbread?"

Oh my goodness, would we ever! Herb, the nice gentleman he always was, thanked her, and told Bettye and me to thank her. We did and she placed the dark, moist squares in our grubby hands. I have to smile, I'm sure, as Mrs. Walker told us to be careful crossing Riddle Creek and waved bye to us.

Today, I smile when I think of Mrs. Walker and her kindness to a bedraggled trio of children. I'm sure that wasn't a single good deed of hers, but it was a gesture of a good person also kind to everyone. An action like that simply doesn't come out of the blue. It is of the heart.

The non-supervision of children is a complete lack of

concern for them. I speak of caring when I use the term non-supervision. In those days of square-box school buses that collected their scampering cargo which picked up small children to high school age in outlying areas before the sun came up, and brought them back in right before it sat on the horizon, it is a wonder some of the smaller and weaker children didn't collapse in exhaustion.

Teachers, bus drivers, and siblings, cared for the children, and so many of us were so dirt poor we had insufficient clothing and certainly not enough to eat, and there wasn't much anyone could do. If we got sick during the day, there was no one to care for us, or transport us to our parents back in the woods. There were no telephones, no way for any messages, except for the kids in town. The Peanut House was a long way off for me one Monday at school in the first grade.

I didn't feel well, and hadn't for a few days, so my unthinking Mother had given me a dose of Black Draught Sunday night. She must have forgotten. I used to go to school all day. Whatever her reason, the die was cast.

It was winter and we wore gray looking, long underwear under our clothing with seats in the back for use of the toilet. The laxative began to cramp my belly directly after lunch. I raised my hand holding up two fingers to signify I needed to do a bowel movement. Mrs. Reid gave me permission, and I quickly ran out to the large two-roomed stinking toilet, one room for girls, the other for boys, I struggled with my clothing, finally getting the bloomers down, and the long-john flap down and relieved myself mightily. There wasn't anything similar to toilet paper, so I couldn't clean myself. it took me forever to get the clothes back into place and trot back to my room. A little later another spasm gripped me, and again I raised my hand, extending the two fingers. Mrs. Reid chose to ignore the hand, so I sat in my little desk seat and relieved myself, again, in those long- johns. Immediately Mrs. Reid discovered her mistake. My classmates were gagging and trying to move away from me. I was so mortified I couldn't move for the rest of the afternoon. I sat in my seat, in my waste until four o'clock when the buses were being loaded. It had been almost three hours, and I was an uncomfortable little wretch. I was crying silent tears of humiliation when I walked stiff legged to board the bus. I kept my eyes down in remorse, especially as the high school kids got on board. When it was discovered I was the stinking culprit, they hastily moved away holding their noses.

Herb and Bettye were so embarrassed, they tried to blend in with the rest of the crowd. As I was the last to go up the steps, the bus driver gave me a scalding look, and said, "go to the back of the bus." There were dissenters who groaned, "no, no, don't send her back here," and "put her off the bus." I sat on the very back seat, and there were empty seats around me. I hung my sorrowful head. Half way home, one of the larger boys challenged Herb, telling him to take me off the bus and walk the rest of the way home. Herb didn't take kindly to being challenged that way, so hit the larger boy in the face with his fist. All bedlam broke loose, and the harassed bus driver stopped the bus and told the two fighters to get off and finish it. They fell off and onto the shoulder of the gravel road, gripped in deadly combat, Herb yelling "you will not talk about my sister," and, "you take that back, you hear! You can't make fun of my sister." He promptly bloodied the other boy's nose, then roughly pushed him up the steps into the bus. There was quiet except for a few girlish giggles once in a while.

There were deepening shadows under the trees alongside the dirt road walking home. Bettye flatly said she would not allow me to get too close to her. So Herb told me to walk farther behind. I did as I was told, the soiled underwear was drying and chaffed my crotch, upper thighs, and my bottom so badly, every step I took was agony. A couple of times I ran to catch up, because the darkness was coming on and I was afraid, but Herb and Bettye picked up rocks and threw them to force me back.

Funny thing. I do not remember getting to the house or having to clean up, or if I was punished soundly for my lack of bowel control. I remember the pain of humiliation, being isolated, and condemned. I never brought this up to Mother, but

I have often wondered if she knew she made a mistake, or did she blame me for it, as Bettye put it later, the embarrassment I caused her, too? I'm quite certain though, that I was teased by my sister and my classmates. I wonder how I felt when I had to get back on that school bus the next day? I don't remember.

Chapter Two

Something unpleasant happened to Bettye and me while we lived in Lavaca. We were almost never taken to doctors, even though we both had been given the early life protecting immunization for diphtheria and scarlet fever while still in Nowata, Oklahoma and of course, at the direction of Grandpa May and Aunt Nannie I'm sure. But now at about nine and eleven years, the sickness hit both of us.

We had sore throats, fevers, energy loss, shortness of breath, terrible leg pains, and vertigo, that I remember. I can't speak for my sister, but I remember quite vividly the time spent in bed, Mother applying hot cloths to our legs and cool ones to our foreheads. We were a couple of scarecrows after a while.

Our father's answer to all childhood illnesses was to be given cathartics to purge all invading body problems. So he made us drink a strong solution of spoons of Black Draught mixed with water.

With very little food in our stomachs and our children's bodies, the mixture all but flushed out our entire insides and then some. We were forced to get up from our sick beds and weave our way as quickly as we could to the outhouse, to sit in that ice cold, smelly place purging ourselves. What in the world did we use to clean ourselves? How did we manage at night with no light and no coats, or shoes? I can't remember this at all, and our father never favored a chamber pot under the bed. Perhaps the Lord's angel felt best, I don't remember all of the hardship, or our poor little memories were tucked away in a trunk somewhere where it was dark and not needed. I don't know how Bettye was, but I know I lay on my back lethargic, so weak and if I moved my head just a little, the dirty ceiling would spin, and I wanted to vomit.

Baby Jesus wasn't in my mind at that time. It was only God I was thinking about and was asking, "was I bad?" I felt if I had been bad He would send me to hell-fire. Was the devil making me sick or was God? What a sad child I was. I needed to crawl up in the highest branch of my oak tree now for I wanted to know. But, I couldn't. I was too weak. I hadn't the strength.

Bettye and I were left alone and we lay there. Where was Herb? Was he alright? And, where was little Peggy? I don't remember seeing them. I suppose I could remember just so much and I was focused on my pain at the time. Why Bettye and me?

Getting up and walking after the illness was an experience in itself. I can only speak for myself. The weakness was bad; but the legs, oh how sore the legs were! It hurt to simply stand, and putting my feet down step after step was a shock to my system. Slowly recovery set in, but neither one of us was ever the same again.

What would a doctor have diagnosed at the time, I wonder? My sister and I were up and in school once again. We were always behind in our books for one reason or another, illness or being moved to other places--but we always managed to catch up. There are exceptions as I will inform you about.

Then, the migraines hit with a viciousness that had me in disabling pain and left me with a new side-kick named "fear". I could temporarily hide from the awful pair, but the two managed to find me. To this day, I couldn't kill them. Day would dawn, bringing the pain, the blindness, and the racking vomiting until the sun went down and the cool breeze of night came to release me from the demon.

What was worse the migraine itself or the fear of the inevitable migraine? What would an 8 1/2 or 9 year old answer to that? Well the pain, of course, even if fear gripped me all my waking hours.

I was active, or as it is called now, hyper. I was a sickly, hyper kid. I climbed the trees, I danced, I stood on my poor head, and I could outrun any boy up to half again my age in my school.

I also was beginning to notice a couple of weird things happening. One was I had sudden spells of weakness and leg pains along with dizziness. If I stopped and breathed deeply and heavily, it would be gone. At times I felt I couldn't breathe as well as normally, the other thing was I felt a presence; a protectiveness of something I could not see, or identify. A child's imaginary "friend" perhaps? No. I was too aware of not having proper food, a coat, a doll, or other toys, to imagine an invisible "friend". This was something else indeed.

For thou art my hope, O Lord God:
Thou art my trust from my youth
-Psalm 71:5

Arkansas during the thirties was a hell-fire Bible belt and evangelism that hiped up all the people in the small towns into a religious frenzy would have warmed Billy Sunday's heart.

From what I noticed back then, all preachers were not really "called by God" to minister unto his people, but were, if anything, lacking in proper education and a kindness toward the striving of what the people strained toward- blessed peace in Jesus.

Blessed peace in Jesus. All we poor wanted that. We did not reach for death to release us from our lives' burdens, nor did we believe we would ever sit at feasts at royal tables in this life, but we did believe He was there and one day we would be wrapped in His lovely peace and plenty after we raised to God's glory.

We were the poor people of the soil of the fields, the fruit of the orchards, and coal from the mines. We were teachers, grocers, sawmill workers, and we were the salt of the earth. We needed our Lord.

We needed the preachers to fire us up and give us hope

of a better tomorrow. We got these preachers. Slipshod, itinerant men, almost bedraggled, who decided they had read enough of the Bible to drum out a half-decent living from the dusty little towns where the eager, hopeful faces smiled welcome to the men of God. They would give succor to the near dead hope of the hungry people.

As a child I did not see the kindness on the preachers' faces. I felt there boredom and impatience, especially with the children. Some were young, some were middle-aged, and to me some were down right tottering. The tottering ones had short fuses, gruff manners, and tried to stare down a member of a congregation who had just asked a difficult question he wasn't prepared to adequately answer. Oh well. Not to worry; because, most of the roving preachers were con-artists anyway and could squirm out of an expected small annoyance. They were no doubt accustomed to the uneducated and sometimes childish questions of the back-woodsy people.

I remember my mother taking her turn to make Sunday dinner for the preacher. The ladies of the church took turns, you see, and no way could a poor lady get out of this labor of love, unless her funeral was to be held that very day.

Mother was nervous with us children running about, but we did settle long enough to allow her to not become over-stressed and "flop" a cake or over-cook the very small fryer chicken she probably borrowed from Mrs. Withers, the neighbor nearby. We children were warned about our manners, and told in no uncertain terms not to ask for seconds of anything, especially the chicken.

Visiting preachers eat. A lot. I never saw one to fail. Later, I'd go behind the house, press up my mouth and attempt to mimic the words and gestures of the Rev. We were all relieved when he would leave.

Revival meetings were highlights of small towns, and children were taken to listen to the words of God so we could grow up to be God-fearing just like our folks.

The preachers made up in loud voices what they lacked in expertise, or so they hoped. After all, there actually could be some intelligent people out there, so being loud and adamant, standing under lanterns and sweating profusely, they pounded the podiums mercilessly, and cried out that all sinners were going to hell and burn forever among the other wicked thrown into sulfur and hot brimstone.

The adults shivered in fearful excitement, the ladies' hands clutched their cotton dress collars to still their pounding throats, and the men sat stern-faced to show they were reverent, yet unafraid.

But mercy, what was happening to the children through all this? I could hear some whimpering and squirming and mothers' voices shushing.

It wouldn't have been so bad, if the preachers didn't shatter the top of the podium with their fists, brought down hard to emphasize the word HELL-FIRE. The noise woke up the sleeping babies, already restless with the gosh-awful voices bellowing out to the congregation.

Well, after a whole week of one of these revivals, I, for one, couldn't sleep nights, having some bouts of dreams. Lavaca was the best little town south of Fort Smith to boast of their revivals--to the point of causing a rash of bed-wetting in young families. Fortunately, I wasn't a bed- wetter. I'd be severely punished if I had been. But I was disturbed.

After all, I sang my first song in church when I was five years old, in Barling, and I'd been in Sunday School and Church from birth, I'd guess. So it wasn't as if I didn't know who Jesus was. I was a trifle ignorant about who or what the Holy Spirit was, or to say it in Paul's words, the Holy Ghost. Now, to a little child, and with all the expert teaching I'd had, God the Father was a very old man, our Creator, who had snow-white hair and a long beard, who sat on a throng of pure gold, and carried a long rod so he could frown and hit one, in this case, me, on top of the head when he was bad. Fluffy white clouds swirled about his throne.

Well, I just knew I was headed for hell-fire to burn in agony forever, for indeed, I must be bad, else Dad wouldn't hit and whip me so much and tell me I couldn't do anything right.

Or Mama wouldn't shout, and slap at me when she felt badly. Or, Bettye wouldn't be crying a lot, and hitting me with her fists, and calling me dumb. Sometimes I felt that Mother slapped me and yelled at me because Dad did, and Bettye, being two years older than I, hit me and told me I was ugly and couldn't do anything right, because Dad and Mother did.

Where was Herb all this time? He was suspiciously absent a lot. He was the oldest and only boy. He was out doing boy things. It was only in recent years that I learned he did not like Dad for putting him down all the time, and he abhorred Mother's spoiled attitude and temper tantrums. I was told she ignored him. But more about Herb later. Okay back to the Baptist preacher.

This one special preacher had enough credentials to be hired by the town people to minister their modest church, and officiate over weddings and funerals, counsel the unsaved, the newly saved, and fighting couples, and any and all cases of thievery, and adultery.

I just figure he knew about everything there was to know about God. Sitting high on my favorite limb in the big oak tree, I could see the sliver of the Arkansas River; especially, if the river was high, and I'd think about God. Because I felt He would not accept me with bad thoughts of a sort, I'd practice clearing my mind of any thoughts, so I could perhaps feel He would take more favorable notice of this poor child, and just maybe He wouldn't send me to hell- fire for my wickedness. I needed more information about Him, so I could plead my case. The preacher would know! I hesitantly approached the Reverend, even if he was busy talking to the adults at the church house door. I stood close to him, and timidly looked up at him. When he got a moment, or maybe I made him uncomfortable, something made him ask, "What is it child?"

Better to blurt it out than stutter you silly goose, I told myself, so plunged in. "Who is God?" He self consciously patted the top of my head, and said, "Why God is love, child. Now go along."

I didn't skip happily along. I was disappointed. God is

love, is he? When he hits you on top of the head with a long hard rod, and tells you that you are wicked and will go to hell-fire! Is that love?

I climbed back up to my seat at the top of the oak tree for more cogitation.

Something was stirring in my heart and my little mind struggled to pick up on it. I know I would understand much more when I was an adult. Those around me seemed so wise about so much, so I should be patient; but, patience wasn't one of my virtues. I wanted answers now! My big problem was not being able to find a grown-up who would care enough to explain things to me.

Would God have to wait?

I can only try to explain as rationally as possible the protected feelings I experienced when I was a child. Now I'm an adult, I surely better be able to explain it. After I became aware something was really with me, I clung to it and dared not breathe a word to anyone. Why, I don't know. I suppose for the same reason I did not want anyone to watch me pee behind the house in bright daylight.

I was just an uninformed little girl of eight, almost nine years, but I did want to know about God, and in my little, shy way I'd pray for healing of me when I was sick, make Daddy like me, make Mama be happy, and bring us food. Bettye was a part of me I always told myself I'd grow up someday and get the best of her, and as for her, I was working on my running skills to out distance her to old man moon.

So I'd shinny up the oak tree, sit on my high perch, and if I didn't care if anyone knew where I was, I'd sing "Bringing in the Sheaves" or "Springtime in the Rockies." Didn't matter if I'd mix my songs. Sometimes I'd hang head down from a limb, pretend I was a bat.

I'd always turn my mind to God.

When I was finished mulling over God, I would turn to Jesus. I had more to go on thinking about Jesus, and I wasn't so frightened of him. It was during one of those outside-emptying-of-the-mind episodes in which I'd be concentrating on what I knew so far about Him that I had begun to practice, that I felt peace and comfort. It was almost a psychical touch inside my chest, and I looked to see but I saw nothing. No hand.

Was this my first taste of sweet peace that would sustain me in the coming years of sorrow?

Why did I recognize that there was actually something spiritual happening and I was to gratefully accept it?

I don't remember what happened after that, how long the feeling lasted, or if I was changed by the experience, except to hold this one happening in my memory.

Others followed, especially after the particularly difficult time, and even if I felt no peace as such, I had courage that turned to anger when I was in danger of losing my mind. This anger, I finally discovered later, was my protection from succumbing to the pain and fear; of giving in to it.

Many times, though, I can't remember Him being with me.

I was growing, and after the belt-beating when Mother intervened, Dad didn't try that again. The hand-hitting, knuckles, and hair-pulling continued though, and trips to the farm accelerated.

Climbing up into the tree, sobbing deep down in the belly, and rubbing tears, and hurt parts of the anatomy, was one good way to summoned up a friend. Eyes swollen, I'd gaze off across the river and up into the sky, hoping for Him to bring me peace. Fluffy clouds would pass high over head, briefly blotting out the sun, and the large oak leaves leaned in closer as a shield, or so I imagined.

I did feel frustration that was part of the anger, but after the anger had passed, the frustration lingered on. If Bettye came to the base of the tree to taunt me, I'd ignore her. I'd be very still and try to clear my mind. I'd try two, three, four times. If I succeeded, I'd feel my Protector, and sweet peace again visited me for another greatly needed span of time.

Constant ridicule loaded down the times I spent at the dining table, so swallowing food that was so hard to come by stuck in my throat, and I could barely force it down. Also my

"Dodge Syndrome" was always on alert. I always lost at the table. If I looked up at all to meet the anybody's eyes about the table, I at least imagined all eyes were hostile.

Our meals always started with my father saying the "blessing" that was short, memorized words: "Our Father we thank thee for this food, pardon our sins-----," and I would clinch my hands under the table, and ask the Lord to keep him from that deadly sudden action that would put another bump on my head, or cut my lip with a tooth. If Dad was relatively friendly talking of other matters and I didn't provoke him by dropping a fork or turning over my glass, my faith strengthened in my protector.

When I got through childhood, my protector really kicked in with obvious "savings". I will refer to these incidences throughout this book. They can't be missed.

As a child, even as sick as I was, He was there, quietly guarding me, and poring the courage into me until I got better. If it was summer and the migraine was upon me, I'd lie out under the tree on a canvas cot, still as a mouse, because the pain began really bad if I moved. I just lay there, gritting my teeth, hoping not to cry, because that increased the pain too.

Suddenly there would be a violent shaking of the rickety cot which would almost dump me to the ground, and I would hear Bettye's loud, squawking voice, "Get up! Get up! You are not sick! You are pretending, so you won't have to dry dishes. Get up and help me!"

Thankfully, Mother would call her, and I'd settle back down to try and stabilize the pain and nausea.

As the migraines usually woke me in the summer mornings, and, escalated into gigantic tornadoes of pain, I'd naturally be unable to eat anything all day. As the sunset and the horrid heat lifted, my body would quickly cool down, and I'd go behind the tree or the house and throw up. The pressure of vomiting would nearly take off my poor head. My heart would pump so fast that veins in my neck would bulge. I'd go back and sit on the edge of the cot until I was able to walk a straight line; then, I'd go into the house, weak and hungry, and sit down on the bench at the table.

Mother would say something such as, "you look a mess. Go wash your hands," and put a plate of food down on the table she had saved for me. One night I got split bean juice on a wedge of corn bread. I don't recall other times.

But He was there watching and helping me go on.

You won't find the title "Dodge Syndrome" in any books on behavioral psychology, or hear an expert speaker use it in any books on behavioral psychology, or hear an expert speaker use it in any seminars. That belongs to me, the non-psychologist. It is merely the title, though that is mine alone, but what it means belongs to all abuse-victims. We may not noticeably use it after we become thirty, fifty, or seventy years old, but it remains with us all the same.

I developed my "Dodge Syndrome" when I was at least seven. If truth be told, it happened that night at the Peanut House when I was six. From that night my life was changed. I went off by myself with a toy of some sort, probably a doll, to sit by the rock chimney. And I'd sing. I remember a gray colored cat that was as skinny as I was beginning to be, that followed me about as I played around outside the house.

I would sing the songs Dad taught me in Nowata, Oklahoma when I was about three, and the church songs he taught both Bettye and me when we were five and seven, the ones we sang at Barling Baptist Church.

The only time I felt safe is when Dad was away from the house. Then I could be a little child again, play with baby sister Peggy, or read my Peter Rabbit book. I liked books and colors. At school in first grade at Midland, Mrs. Reed from Hartford was my very first teacher, and we children were reading from the Baby Ray readers. I did like that. There was no kindergarten back then and the Arkansas school system was extremely poor.

When Dad came suddenly into the house I would scrunch down, trying to make myself smaller or scuttle out as silently as I could, so as not to be noticed. If he passed too closely I would feel the back of my neck prickle and I would quickly have this involuntary ducking of the head, sometimes so violently I'd fall off my seat, and he hadn't laid a hand on me. I was becoming too aware of the pain in those deadly missiles that were my father's hands. So the "Dodge Syndrome" was my involuntary reflex action--similar to the automatic knee jerk. I just couldn't help it. As I grew, I got quite good at it. It was much like shooting basketball hoops: You shoot enough, you get good at it. But I wasn't fortunate always. I couldn't always dodge and win.

When I finally confronted my Mother in October 1994, at a time I felt right for her, to ask of some of my memories-were they really true, or were these blown-out-of-proportion bad dreams of a highly sensitive, little child? Her replies startled me. In my growing-up years, she laughed my questions off, but that was then. This was now. I needed to know.

We were talking easily. She was alert, and at times we laughed my questions off.

I asked her, "Do you remember when I was six, and we lived at the Peanut House, and Dad hit me and bloodied my nose?"

She glared in sudden anger. "Yes, when I saw the blood, I wanted to kill him."

"Mom, why was I taken to the farm so much, and for long periods?"

"So he wouldn't hurt you." She was talking low, and her mind was back in time.

"Why did he dislike me so much?" I asked.

"Oh, I don't know." She was becoming agitated, and began crying.

"I've put up with so-o much. How did I stand it, how?"

Abuse births many negative reactions, both physical and psychic, and it has its crippling beginning. Mine began at age six, and my mother confirmed this.

As I look back, my reactions began with surprise, followed by confusion, recognition of danger, shock, feelings of betrayal, guilt, and the big one, fear.

Naturally, the feeling of pain and fear of suffocation, and

the visual blood from the nose helped me realize something was all too true.

In a matter of minutes, I went through the complete list of reactions, as many as I was capable intellectually to compute. I wasn't stupid, but I was after all, just a baby. Why did I remember the dreadful act and be able to determine the feelings quickly happening? Of course, I wasn't aware of what those feelings were called, but by the time I was grown, I knew the words to go with the feelings, alright.

Chapter Three

When I would see my lanky, dark-haired father walking along the road in Lavaca, I wished I could run up to him, grab his hand, skip along with him, and smile up into his blue eyes. But I couldn't. By the time I wished for this I dared not get within striking distance of those quick-as-lightning hands. He wore a blue denim shirt and overalls. His brown hat, that sat rakishly, was like Jimmy Durante's I'd seen in a movie magazine somewhere.

I almost could not have eye contact with him. Without knowing the reason, I felt guilty and withdrawn. The back of my neck automatically tightened, if one of us passed too closely to the other. If I saw him in downtown Lavaca on the short sidewalk that ran along the dusty main street, I would try to duck behind a store or other objects to avoid him. In any case I'd not speak a word to him. I thought if I was forced to speak, a scream would come out instead of any intelligent word, or tears would run like the Arkansas River close by. He would smirk wryly, that pulled his lips to one side of his face, and I would race toward home as fast as my skinny legs would take me. I climbed the big oak tree in the front yard, going as high as I could to the top, and there I would sit so very still for ever so long, at least until my poor little heart would stop pounding so hard. But I wanted to be able to skip along with him, my hand in his, and have him smile down at me. He never did, and I never could.

> *"Fathers provoke not your children*
> *to anger, lest they be discouraged"*
> *Colossians 3:21*

    Mama called us to the table for supper. It was already dark, and she had the "coal oil" lamp in the center, its yellow light casting shadows in the four corners of the kitchen. Mama had painted the stationary cabinet and the table a pea green to match gingham, cottage curtains. The curtains were opaque and shut out the night, for we had no roller shades as everyone else did. Peggy was sitting in the passed-down high chair that was purchased for my brother, Herb. The flip-up tray was long gone, and was no longer needed, and Peggy's little legs were getting longer as she grew. Herb sat in a chair next to her. Dad and Mama each sat at the end of the table, and Bettye and I sat on the backless bench along the other side with our backs near the wall. I was to Dad's right, as I remember it, and I was always in a state of anxiety at the meals, after feeling I would have been more comfortable if I wasn't so close to him. My stomach would curl up into knots, and the muscles in my neck were strung tightly rigid.

    Dad was the boss, the king, the ruler, the punisher; even Mama would give into him at the table, despite her hot temperament. He would stand for no excessive talking or talking at all, no laughter of any sort, no mistakes of any kind. Heaven help us if we dropped a fork or spoon, and demons giggled, if you turned a glass of water onto the oil-cloth that permitted the water to pool and drip off the table upon the floor.

    This particular night everyone must have been tired because it was a solemn, quiet family supper, sit-down group.

    I can't recall the food on the table, or if there were water glasses. I do know we seldom had milk, and Dad and Mama didn't seem to have any ambition to acquire and keep a cow for milk and butter. We never had chickens for eggs and meat either, even though there was a fenced-in piece of pasture with a large shed at the back.

Anyway, the quiet wasn't to last out the meal. Eating came to a dead stop when I must have done something I can't recall now, but as suddenly as a snake's strike he swung the back of his hand across my face knocking me backwards off the bench and causing me to strike the back of my head against the wall behind. I remember lying crumpled in a heap on the floor half under the bench, holding my head. The back of it hurt so. After that, the only memory was dead silence. Even little Peggy was shocked into silence. A dropped pin could be heard.

I have no memory beyond lying in a heap, sobbing out my hurt as quietly as was safe, and wondering if I was so bad. I do not have the idea at all that I received comfort from Mother, certainly not my brother unless he wanted a dose of Dad's punishment, and not from Bettye, who I am convinced, even though brutality is not a pretty sight for anyone, received some delight in my predicament. She would pick at me for days and taunt me about "getting it" for days following that night. "Alma got in trouble. Alma got in trouble," she would say in a sing-song voice until she became tired of it and enough time had passed for something else to happen.

After I was "punished" it did take a few days for me to recover some. I'd slink quiet as a little mouse, if Dad was about, and if the weather was nice, I'd climb up into the safety of the limbs of the oak tree and try to think, to try to get on with me. I'd straddle a limb and make Jacob's Ladder out of the string, one ladder after another, humming along.

I was getting thinner and thinner. I was eating less and less. At meals I would watch the servings of the plates as Dad filled them and passed them about. My servings were undoubtably somewhat smaller than Bettye's, except for Peggy, who was little and didn't require as much. If there was fried chicken, I got one wing, and for years I was led to believe, especially by Mother, that I would only eat the wing. Unless there was a reunion and people congregated to eat, and I was served another good part of chicken, Mother would say,"Oh, just give her the wing. It is all she eats." I would say "That's okay. I can eat this." I was really wanting a good piece of chicken, and I was in stages of starvation for about five years beginning at Lavaca and later Midland.

I was so thin and sickly, the relatives were shocked to see me after an absence of six months or a year. My Grandfather May, Dad's father, and his sister, Vesta were quite vocal in my presence upon our arrival to Nowata for a visit. "She is so skinny------just bones---this child needs good food----are you starving her? Aren't you feeding her?" This went on until my Mother became upset and began to cry.

An uncle of mine showed up briefly in Lavaca and gave me a Three Musketeers candy bar, the 1930's type of candy bar with three separate bars. This was pure candy delight, of soft malty filling, caramel, and the exquisite chocolate covering. I was in heaven. I raced around the side of the house, and sat down to eat my great gift. I ate slowly, savoring each bite, but then something happened, I couldn't finish eating the candy bar, and I was suddenly nauseous. I couldn't finish the complete candy bar. My poor stomach wasn't in any condition for such food---wasn't used to it. I can still feel the disappointment, and I was angry with myself at the time.

Am I not good enough
to be your child?

What an immense burden unfortunate children carry during abuse and all through life to the very end, and many of us older ones often fail to rid ourselves of the effects so drastically and carelessly dealt out by sick, unhappy people, the majority who called themselves parents.

Sometimes now, when forced to bring up all these memories that I write here, the saliva dries out my mouth as strength and defiance die, while momentarily I feel the back of my neck tighten. I stop in the midst of all this to fast forward my memories ahead to the future and my own defenseless children and how close I came to being too free with my slaps and spanks. I shall get to that later.

Consecutive dreams do not invade my sleep as yet, I'm not so certain they won't as the book progresses. Occurrences in my fateful life pick up speed as I enter the threshold of adult life and yet another brute takes over as the number one abuser, while the others take a back seat, and rear up occasionally to certainly let me know they were still there. Why, there are two in there even today, pitching, and I will never be free of abuse until one has gone on and the other one living far away during my life. But that is too close to call, considering my own age and health. My Protector and Comforter is still with me and I understand more about Him now that I am aged, and my patience and understanding out- weigh the hysterical, sad life of a little child.

While we still lived in Lavaca, Mother's relatives visited one sunny afternoon. The house was full with the uncles and aunts, and I especially recall Uncle Jim and Aunt Jess being there among others. Uncle Jim was a successful businessman in eastern Oklahoma, wore nice suits, drove the latest car, and smelled of tweed and cigars. He had no children, and was especially fond of me, I'm told, but I was too big now to sit on his lap and ask to see his gold watch that hung on a gold chain attached to his vest.

After dinner was over, and there was conversation connected to the death of Uncle Will, pipes and cigars were lighted, and I headed for the oak tree, even if I was wearing a dress just for the relatives. I was beginning to dread these family reunions, because after dinner was over, always without fail, Bettye and I were called upon to sing. That is, Bettye played the piano, not too well, I might add, for she hadn't had piano lessons as yet, and banged out cords, and I sang and did some sort of Irish jig to end the song. Uncle Jim always paid Bettye and me, usually a nickel, or dime a piece, after we were through. I really liked Uncle Jim. He was very nice to me, as all my Michael uncles were, but something was the matter with me. I didn't feel well, and was showing a sulky side I wasn't familiar with. Dad called out to me before I could climb the tree. I was trapped! I stood still. He called again. Slowly I went in to the living room where everybody was, and Bettye sat at the piano waiting. My feet were dragging, and there was no spark of spunk about me...not even a smile for Uncle Jim. I felt as if something else had a hold of me, and I knew I was not going to sing or dance, make a silly little spectacle of myself, when I didn't want to. There was no song in my heart, and Dad would certainly kill me. At this point I was going to be defiant. I must have been completely crazy! What was I thinking of? I refused. I was only nine years old and I was scared to death of Dad, and I knew I was disobeying my own father by refusing to go through a short little song and dance for the company. Again, I said "No."

Was I crazy, wild-eyed terrified? Not just yet. Unfortunately, I was really a stupid girl. I suppose I deserved some type of punishment, and I'd suffered his "punishment" plenty of times, but this...this was totally different. I did not understand what it was that was pushing me off the ledge. Later on, I put a childish name on the inner thing causing me to want to defy my abusers. I called it my "Wild Streak." It had caused me lots of trouble, but has helped me out of situations, and prevented me from giving up when I couldn't stand anymore.

The relatives left for home. I sat on the front porch, my feet hanging down, waiting for fate. The dust from the departing car had barely settled when I was called inside in an almost normal tone of voice. Dad was calling now.

As I walked through the front room into the kitchen where he was waiting, I wondered where everyone else was. I didn't see Mama, Peggy or Herb, or even Bettye. There was dead silence. Until I heard his belt buckle....the almost deafening tinkle like no other sound in my world of fear, and I looked up at him. His eyes to me were fire, and rage was twisting his mouth.

I can't remember if he placed me in a certain spot, made me grab the back of the chair, but it really didn't matter at all, because I could never stay in a stationary position after the first stroke of the belt. I knew the belt was doubled, thereby inflicting a truer target, and soon I wasn't aware of the sound of the buckle at all. I'm sure I screamed, for he had warned me to be quiet. How can a little child in awful pain and tremendous fear of being killed prevent screams from happening. They were coming out without any help from me.

Again and again he laid strength into those strikes, from my neck down to my ankles, and then I was aware I was on the linoleum floor writhing about as the belt struck again and again. Now I was whimpering more and screaming less.

Suddenly, Dad was being pulled away and I heard Mama's voice yelling at him to stop, that he was killing me, and that the neighbors could hear.

Dad stopped, told me never, never disobey him again, and left taking the hated belt with him. I had "embarrassed" him in the presence of the relatives. I had committed the ultimate sin of refusing to obey him, my father.

I was an injured little girl, and I don't remember any comfort from Mama. She helped me up, took off my dress and panties and put cold wet cloths on the welts; my back in flames. I could barely stand, and my skinny bones had very little fat to protect me. I don't remember any tears from her. Just a warning that I would stay inside the house. I stayed in for three days, slowly walking stiff-legged about, and I don't recall Dad after the belting anyway soon after that.

October 1994, while visiting my 94 year old mother in a nursing home, I asked her if she remembered this particular belting, she said, "Yes, if I hadn't pulled him off you he would have killed you." I was shocked she had told me that at all, for I needed to verify my memories.

I also asked her before time ran out on us, if she remembered Dad hitting me across the face when we lived at the Peanut House and I was six. Her eyes blazed as she said "Yes! When I saw all that blood, I wanted to kill him."

If my little sister saw all of this, and heard all of this, what must it have done to her, the young mind just four years forming? No wonder she clung to Mother, seldom being out of her sight.

And where did Herb get off to? And Bettye? What about her, who already was beginning to show signs of stress? Bettye who bent over backwards to gain favor in Dad's eyes, perhaps as a survival maneuver? I can't blame her.

My mother had told me that Dad had whipped Bettye once when she was small, and it made her "crazy" enough to frighten him from ever trying it again. I don't recall him ever whipping or slapping her or Peggy, heaven forbid. Bettye fainted frequently, and I feel that Dad hurt or frightened her to the extent that she fainted and he thought he had killed her. Perhaps.

I was fast becoming an unhappy child and when I had to get out of the house, I'd climb the tree, straddle the comfortable limb with no hands holding on, and lace the dark green leaves together. My mind would go away sometimes, far away where I was in a small airplane like Lindy flew, and I'd be off where I didn't know these people I lived with.

> "Brangin' in the sheets,
> Brangin' in the sheets,
> I will come rejoicin'
> Brangin' in the sheets"

Even my singing slowed almost to whispers and sometimes sounded like whimpers instead of songs. I was beginning to sound like the mewing of a sick kitten. Bettye was always in there telling me I couldn't sing, that I sounded like a cow bellerin'. I guess she was right.

I wasn't sleeping well at all, but would lie still beside Bettye, hating the dark of the moon that couldn't light up my nights until sleep came at last, and because I would lie awake after everyone else was asleep and snoring, I was a late riser, if I could get by with it, especially if there was no school. If I had a headache I would miss breakfast and the noon meal.

Bettye, on the other hand, went right into sleep, but was a fitful sleeper, thrashing about, talking in her restless sleep fighting her own demons. Dad snored loudly, which made Mother unable to fall asleep, and I'd hear her in their room trying to coax him to turn over without waking him.

But, I did love that moon, which I felt didn't shine enough. I did not like the pitch black nights. There were no street lights, no front porch lights, and I hated the black panthers with yellow eyes and big white fangs that jumped on top of me and ate me. My "fraidy fears" were emerging, and I couldn't dangle a foot off the bed, or it would be chewed off and I'd never walk again, do a jig again, or climb my oak tree. Lawzy.

As things happened and we became more impoverished, I could not generate artificial happiness or joy. Yet there were times I could laugh and play--and sing.

Dear Aunt Vesta, my father's younger sister, would send her children's unwanted clothing and shoes occasionally to us, and we felt so fine at those times, and I shall always be grateful to her for coming to our aid up through the years. There is always a bright light to scare away the darkness, and she was that bright light. She always squawked loudest with her opinions on how sickly we children looked, too. My cousins' coats and sweaters were gifts from heaven for us. Some did fit big, but the lovely warmth is what I remember.

I often wondered if Aunt Vesta knew of my Dad's abuse, and further, what she thought of it. There are questions I'd like to have asked her about Dad and the relationship with his father, Grandpa May. What I have been told comes second hand, but I can only believe it considering my Dad's behavior.

Grandpa was a tall, strong, United States Marshall of the Indian territory in the latter part of the last century. He was part Cherokee Native American, and English, with a good education, very bright, and almost arrogant to the point I was a bit afraid of him myself. He and Grannie May had six children most of them female. Grandpa wanted a son, and so Grannie gave him David, a child with all of Grandpa's characteristics, strong, bright, brown eyes and black hair, a perfect replicate. The boy was four and Grannie was pregnant with my father when David died in an accident. Grandpa's heart was broken. He adored David.

When my father was born, it was clear from the start

that Dad was no David. He was sickly, scrawny, had blue eyes and brown hair, and resembled the Haynes, her family. He grew into a nervous child, terrified of Grandpa, cried a lot, and wouldn't let go of Grannie's big flopping dresses.

It was evident that Grandpa hadn't much use for Tommy, as my dad was called, and he could deal out hard punishment "trying to make the boy strong." The thing is, Grannie herself, afraid to talk out and take a stand against Grandpa, would comfort Dad nonetheless, and Grandpa called Dad "mama's boy" in his formative years, and made demeaning remarks to him. He would say the "pattern words" of "he can't do anything right" a favorite phrase of the abuser. I had heard some of Grandpa's remarks when I got older and could pay attention enough to remember them. He criticized Dad's penmanship and spelling, both of which to me were perfect, and commented on his slouchy dress. It was clear that he was disappointed in him. Dad never defended himself, to my knowledge.

I've often wondered how changed my father's life would have been if little David had lived. Would he have been such a handsome and brilliant man that my father could not possibly have competed with him, or would David have taken him under his wing and protected the younger, weaker brother? Or would he have been as my older sister was to me and jump right in there with his father to add to the humiliation?

I do not have any information whether Grannie May disciplined her children one way or the other, but I suspect she probably had to in the absence of Grandpa, away so much from his family a large part of the time. His excuse for being away from home so often was that whenever he wasn't on Marshal business and bringing in wanted criminals, he was off with his carpenter tools making a living building homes and cabinets. Ah, yes.

My father was away a lot, also. Herein he emulated his father in a second trait. Of course, the first one was abuse. It was up to me to break the deadly pattern of abuse. Could I do it?

Something I learned eventually was, do not allow your abusers to uncover your fears, or weaknesses, if at all possible, because it will only give them fuel to add to their brutality. They will use those to fulfill their feelings of power, of control. They must feel good by their brutality, for they are actually acting out on vulnerable victims as it was done to them in the past. It feels good to be in control, to be in power, rather than to be the victim.

The schoolyard bully is usually another abuser who is a victim at home, or a weak person who needs to feel powerful over smaller children. You will notice they do not pick on other children who are the same size, or bigger, who are not afraid to bully back.

Also, notice that abusive husbands and fathers do not seem to work their brutish ways on another man or even a woman who appears aggressive to him in any way. They appear to take out their frustrations on their families they feel belong to them, and they are theirs to do with as they please. It is their pleasure to keep them under control. The more fear their victims show, the more relieved they are, the more frequent the abuse happens. Trust me.

If a victim has a sore arm, the abuser will hone in on it, bruising it more, actually causing more pain in a sadistic way. All this time the abuser is working up his own anger and blaming the abuse on the victim by yelling, "See what you make me do? It's all your fault!"

My first husband cruelly hit my shoulder that I could barely move due to a severe case of bursitis. My legs buckled from not only the blow, but also from the excruciating pain. He also kicked one of my ankles where I'd had surgery that required stitches to close, therefore causing massive bleeding under the stitches that necessitated further corrective surgery. The abuser uses something else to give him any excuse to start a beating. Maybe he believes it, who really knows for sure? I use the pronoun "he" throughout this writing, but I make no gender bias, for "he" could very well be "she" as my own case shows, too. That something is telling the abused one that "You embarrassed me. Do you know that you embarrassed me?" Dear me, how many times have I heard this from all my abusers! I grew up with the idea that whenever I got something right, I embarrassed at least one in my family.

> I read *Psalm 118:6 which says:*
> *The Lord is on my side, I will*
> *not fear: What can man do unto*
> *me?*

Man can do real damage especially to a little child, but the Lord is our Healer, His Holy Spirit our comfort, and I curled up on the lap of Jesus, and felt his loving arms about me. Here I felt blissful peace.

I will try and tell this as closely to my memories as I possibly can, and I sincerely feel I must not whitewash my actions that have made me wonder what possessed me to act the way I did. I feel to this day that I had sprouted horns and behaved so badly. I couldn't have been in any kind of proper mind. Sure, I was only nine years old, but I knew right from wrong, however screwed up I was. I am totally embarrassed to tell this, but perhaps it can establish some correlation in regards to harsh treatment over a period of time upon the futile, trapped feelings of a highly sensitive child.

I loved little helpless animals, and never mistreated any of them. I cried over lost kittens, starving dogs, and fallen birds. This was my true nature.

It seemed that some neighbor gave us kids a half-grown chicken, so docile it allowed us to pick him up and carry him about. We named him Chicken Little and loved every whispy feather on his funny looking body. We cared for him and fed him some of our biscuits and crumbs from saved corn bread. When we weren't playing with him, he scratched about under the house, and roosted there nights. There was no way we could foretell disaster would befall him and leave us crying and wringing our hands. We should have known that nothing in our lives was permanent, except hunger, cold, a constant need for the bare necessities, and unhappiness.

Then, one day a half-grown, starving cat came on the scene, and tore our world apart. Peggy was screaming, Mother was frantically yelling, and when I rounded the corner of the house, Mother had retrieved the lifeless body of Chicken Little, blood oozing from fang marks. And there was the cat, trying to retrieve his catch.

I heard Mother say, "the chicken is dead," and I went berserk. I felt this boiling up of anger and grief tearing at me, and I ran and caught the cat who was trying to escape, but I got him in the middle of the dirt road. I grabbed its tail and began to slam it against the ground, over and over, the cat so frightened and unable to get away or escape.

I was unaware of the world around me, except my cries of anger and sobbing, until someone stopped me and told me to drop the cat before I killed it.

I ran to the other side of the house, feeling weak and shaking from head to feet, and I sobbed.

No, we didn't eat Chicken Little, but I'm told we buried him in the back pasture. We would never hear of allowing a starving cat to feed on his kill, or, so the reasoning went, the cat would continue to stalk and kill.

I actually was appalled at my own behavior, was sick for a couple of days, skulking about like some type of specter, and felt I was no better than that cat. I was left alone during that time, and can't say for sure what anyone thought of me and my behavior. No one came to me to explain to me that my actions were out of line, or certainly not why I behaved that way. Not even a preacher.

I was a very bad person. I hated myself. And I was sure God hated me. Would Jesus be mad at me, or would God really punish me? I moped about, no appetite. I can remember, and just plain felt sickly.

Remorse had overtaken me; now I had some time to think after my insides began to settle some.

I was sitting on a canvas cot under trees on the left side of the house, the weather so hot I could hardly breathe, when I felt the softness against my legs. I looked down, and, gosh, there was that scrawny, little ole' gray cat, rubbing against me, purring, and mewing. Automatically, I recoiled, and told the murderer to go away and leave me alone. That day I could not begin to allow it to rub itself against me. I couldn't even touch it.

A couple of days later, I reached out my hand and gingerly rubbed the cat's back. It's yellow eyes looked up into my face and appeared to rest its face on my hand. Only momentarily. But a big lump came into my throat, and tears came. The cat was forgiving me. I knew it, and to me that meant God was forgiving me, and my Jesus wasn't angry at me anymore. Then I picked up the cat and held it close to me, and my hold grew tighter, and the love for Chicken Little was transferred to that cat. That, of course, wasn't to last either.

The way I acted, trying to kill the poor cat--or, was I really trying to kill the cat? It was, to me now, a great big cry for help. I didn't like the world at all, and I was helpless to change it. I had no voice in whether I could be miserable or happy. I was only a kid who needed to burst out of a life of deprivation, abuse, and be allowed to grow in love and attention. I needed my crying times to be fewer and my laughing times more numerous. If only I could have had my mother as an ally, or at least feel she cared about what happened, but she wasn't a very demonstrative person, so I always felt she objected to me entirely.

A short time passed that I kept the cat with me----where was the family?----Why can't I see them in my memories as I'm positive they were fluttering about on the fringes of the memories I had hoped would dim and fade away, but didn't?

Then, suddenly came this male voice out of the blue that startled me as I hugged the cat to my breast.

"Alma, Alma, put the cat on the ground." I looked up and saw a neighbor man standing at the corner of the house, a small rifle in his hands. I stared, then grew afraid as I computed the purpose of the man's intentions.

"Put the cat down."

I hugged the cat closer, and stepped behind one of the

large tree trunks, but I stuck my head out to see him, then pulled it back. "No!" I yelled at him.

Again, "Put the cat down."

"Why do you want to shoot him?"

"Because he got some of my baby chicks, and he can't be allowed to live." I don't think I had time to really think at all about this. As quickly as I tried to hurt the cat, because he killed Chicken Little, I would protect the cat now, who was my friend.

So clutching the cat, I stepped out from behind the tree and loudly said to the man, "If you shoot my cat you will have to shoot me!"

Oh boy, now my mama was on the scene. She did not come to me, but stayed next to the man. She did not attempt to tell me to do as the man said. Instead, she began talking to him, things I can not recall, but felt certain of, as the man lowered the rifle, turned, and left.

Still, there was no one to explain things to me in a civilized way. No one came to me, or touched me. And by this time I didn't expect anything, nor did I want anyone to touch me, to comfort me, or talk to me.

They won, of course.

They allowed me to hug the cat for a short span, I don't know. But one day he wasn't there. He didn't greet me on the back porch and rub against my legs. My piece of breakfast biscuit with a smear of pan gravy I saved throughout the day, hoping he would come, lay limp in my hand.

He never did.

I knew.

I got back up in my tree and grieved for my poor little cat. We were alike. We were both poor, little cats.

"Brangin' in the Sheets
Brangin' in the Sheets"
* * *

I will begin this next traumatic episode by saying that after the belt punishment I was taken to Grandpa Michael's, now located in a place next to the Arkansas-Oklahoma border, a large expanse of fields of commercially and domestic growing foodstuffs that nestled below Sugarloaf Mountain.

But, first I must tell you about Old Boone and Jack, dogs in my life during those turbulent years spent in Lavaca. Old Boone was a yellow, short-haired dog, we were barely feeding that Dad had brought to us when I was six and a half and we lived in the Peanut House. He was even tempered and stayed out of the way much of the time that I remember. He was afraid of the dark and night roaming creatures. His home, like Chicken Little's, was always under the house. For the life of me I don't know what kept him going. He had very little care, yet he was faithful to our family. But, of course he lived about six years only, and we did take him with us as we moved to Lavaca, then on to Midland, where he finally had all the neglected life he could bear, and went out into a grown-up corn field and died. I missed him; his old friendly face, and tongue on my hand.

While in Lavaca, a half grown, part shepherd dog honed in on us kids and decided to stay on, which at the time was great for me with all the terrible luck I was having. He was playful, naturally, and no amount of stove wood throwing by Mother could run him off. He needed a home, and, I suppose, I needed him, or anything passing himself off as friendly and loving. He was with us for as long as it took for me to fall in love with him. He bounced, he would fetch sticks I'd throw, and wrestle with me.

The day I went to the farm my poor heart was broken, and would break again before two days were gone.

When we piled into the bob-tailed, topless, model T Ford, Jack was put in the back with us kids, little Peggy on Mother's lap. Old Boone wasn't taken, and as I clutched a paper bag of a change of clothes with one hand, I put my other arm around Jack, so tickled he was going with me. I patted him affectionately as we left the city limits. We were a few miles out on the gravel road with woods on the other side when Dad stopped the car, went to the back, grabbed Jack by the scruff of the neck and hauled him down onto the road. He gave him a few kicks to chase him away, then he picked up rocks and threw them at him to discourage Jack from wanting to cling to us.

I remember being horrified, and crying, "No! No!" until a cuff to the side of the head forced me to cringe down and put my hands over my mouth to keep out the noise I felt inside my head. Why couldn't I be more like Bettye, or even Peggy, who never made a peep? Even Herb, being so much bigger, and a boy to boot, was silent--if he was there at all.

The car moved on, slowly at first, then faster, the dust boiling up behind, and Jack let out a couple of barks, then tried to keep up. I watched my poor friend, running sort of lop-sided, his tongue hanging out of the side of his mouth--- and, he got farther and farther away, until he was exhausted. The last I saw was that he had stopped, his tail sagging, the body lifeless. He got smaller and smaller, and I couldn't see him anymore, because the tears were running, streaming through the hands over my mouth. I knew he watched us, him standing there in the middle of the road, not knowing what had happened to him.

And I? Well, I was choking back tears, hiccupping sobs that shook my body, but I had to be quiet. My little friend was gone, like other things went for me, and finally I silenced myself, and became quiet. It felt to me a death rigidity, and the hate, and hopelessness of anything good happening ever to me, took over. I was subdued and I felt sick. Out of the sulkiness I grew stronger. It was like a dying.

I hate him.

It would be about a month later that I would hate Mama. It took that long.

I weep now as I tell this, for taking out the memories only makes what happened so real again. I see Jack again so clearly, and wherever he is, I don't want him to think it was my doing to abandon him; that I didn't want him. We were torn apart--two small things of God, the working of his hands-- and, we needed each other desperately. But, then, was Jack meant to only come into my life just long enough to brighten my life, or simply to spark my love, so I could experience yet another episode of heartbreak? My child's brain was beginning to think the latter, and without knowing it, I was beginning to pull away, to not want hugs, and certainly I was not going to give my love to animals. Now I realize that Jack was a fluke. Reason tells me I would not have had him for very long under any circumstances. Not then, not there. The promise was invalid. That was just the way things were.

As we approached the farm I was still having my troubles, but I was not crying. That would come tomorrow after a good supper at the great hands of Grandma and her superb larder and a night's rest. We kids were put to bed early. Now I expect there had to be some talking as to a decision of acceptance on my grandparents part that I be kept with them.

I have no idea what my parents told them the reason for wanting this was, but as I got to my teens, I realized there was some talk of me being, as they succinctly put it, "They don't want you."

Of course, I already knew this, but didn't want to believe it. After all, I was a child, and I did love and cling, so I thought, to my mother.

I still didn't want to believe it when I was told bluntly by Mother that I would stay with Grandma, and, she added, "we will pick you up in a week." My pitiful paper sack with my change of clothes was left in the bedroom, I recall, as the others prepared to leave. I was worried, as poor Jack must have been, as I watched my family get in the car.

I said to Grandma, "When will they come back for me?" She said, almost in anger, not at me but at the car, "Your mama lied! They are not picking you up in a week." With that she went to the kitchen.

I ran out calling, "Mama! Wait, Mama!" and just like Jack did, I ran up to the two-rutted dusty road past the pond, after the model T, crying. The car didn't halt, and it made dust, but I saw Peggy standing up between Dad and Mother, and nobody saw me. I fell face forward in the dust of the road, and cried bitter tears of broken-hearted betrayal.

My grandparents left me pretty much to myself for several days. I didn't talk much and I really didn't know what was to become of me. I know that when the second batch of gut-wrenching sobbing ended, I'd feel sick from it, perhaps have another headache, then do some easing up of the shock of the whole thing.

I did become ill. I didn't eat, was listless, and I started having diarrhea that wouldn't stop until only blood came out, and I was too weak to walk to the toilet and back.

I loved the farm, but I couldn't take any joy at all in the fun-loving happy contentment I'd always experienced before. I loved my grandparents, but they weren't the demonstrative type, and there was an unfamiliar catch in the relationship. Grandma spoke her mind, though, and didn't matter if a bunch of her grandchildren were about, or not.

As I became sicker, Grandma led me into the kitchen and sat me at the table. She said I had the "bloody flux", and I wasn't eating anything. She busily began to pour water into a poaching pan, got a big ole' fat egg from a crock and told me I was going to have a nice egg with butter on it, and some milk she would warm. Poached egg was real good for the "bloody flux", she said solemnly and placed the lovely plate in front of me. Besides, I would be sicker if I didn't eat, and with that, left the kitchen.

Nights were very difficult for me. I'd lie awake in the solid black darkness, clutching covers under my chin hoping the black panthers with blazing yellow eyes would not pad around my bed just waiting until I went to sleep to pounce on me and eat me. Also, I was homesick for Mama and Peggy, and as I thought of Jack, I really cried myself to sleep. The night sounds were soothing, and I recall vividly the lonesome sound of the whippor-will as it called out deep in the woods near Riddle Creek.

I told Grandma I was going to see Uncle Leon, who now lived in the well-known Peanut House. I stayed with him and Aunt Nola, and played with my two-year-old cousin, Nita. After a few days there, my uncle was rubbing off on me, although I'd loved him since I was a baby. I remember eating Post Toasties for breakfast with Nita, and Uncle Leon taking us both to the Riddle Creek swimming place where he encouraged me to dive from a tall rock from the edge. I was beginning to laugh some now, but I still felt my loss and pain. My sadness didn't escape any of them, even though staying with Uncle Leon was good for me.

I had been at the farm for about four or five weeks, and I'm sure Grandpa, Grandma, and Uncle Leon, were getting a mite tired of me, not knowing what to do with me, and I had no clothes, and I'd guess school would be starting. They had to make a decision. I would be sent home on a bus from Barling where Uncle Leon had to go on business. He bought me a sack of candy, and gave me a nickel and some pennies, kissed me, and I was on my way home. The same, worn out paper sack with my extra dress lay on the seat next to me.

This next part gets tricky, and I will tell it as I remember it, just one more hurdle, and I could feel my way, and figure out how I was to feel about my family. From here on out.

I was nervous and a little apprehensive about walking the short way to my house. I was fearful they would shoo me away--run me off. I walked, did not run as a happy child would do to see her mother and family, and they return the happiness. Oh, no.

I didn't go in the front door. Instead, I slowly approached the back door and kitchen. I passed open windows with the sun shining in through the screens, and I opened the screen door, went in quietly and stood still. Mother was standing at the kitchen cabinet busy with something--I didn't know what, I couldn't see, and without even turning around she asked, "What are you doing here?"

I didn't answer, just clutched my sack of candy and clothes sack, and stood staring at her back. She wore a cotton dress...some design on a white background. Now I know she must have seen me pass the open window. I don't remember anyone else about. I don't even remember Ole' Boone, if he greeted me or not.

I stood in the one spot as long as I dared, then turned and went back out, off the back porch, and made a decision hastily. I dug inside my candy sack, and got out the nickel and pennies, wondering if I had enough money to get back on that bus before it left town. I don't know why I didn't follow through. Instead I walked over to the side of the house, starting beating on it with my fist, crying more bitter tears while I said over and over, "I hate you! I hate you."

That day I learned to hate my mother. Why did I want to cling to my family who obviously didn't want me? I already knew I was pushed to the outer fringes of their near-miserable lives, and I felt ostracized, and now felt that the reason was I was certainly defective, and if I was defective to them, it was for sure I was defective to people other than my family.

Maybe I was a freak and couldn't see it, for my eyes were blind. I'd look in the mirror and couldn't see anything except a hostile and somewhat sulky glint about the eyes, and oh, gee, I really was ugly. No wonder they called me ugly. I was ugly.

Chapter Four

I was walking along the street that led from Main Street in Lavaca to the cemetery, nothing on my mind, pushing my toes in the softer dirt of the road. There was some activity about, but not too much busy noises, and the weather was mild enough for me to be barefoot. I was also wondering what I could find to occupy myself. Catching grasshoppers wasn't any fun unless fishing was on the mind. Anyway, I didn't go fishing anymore, even though I had caught great grasshoppers and put them in a pint Ball canning jar. We would take our bait with us when once upon a time Dad took Herb, Bettye, and me fishing in a wooden boat on the slough in the bottoms that ran parallel to the Arkansas River. Nothing but old, mud catfish there, but I'm sure if we caught any cats, we were not too proud to eat them.

I continued on, stopping to listen to birds and hear, maybe either kids' voices that could lure me into playing dolls, or Bonnie and Clyde.

I heard the wagon wheels grating on the packed, hard street approaching Lavaca, but it wasn't until the wagon got closer that I looked up. Even in 1934 Arkansas, the scene I saw was quite unusual. Maybe I have seen something similar in movies after those times, but this one big piece of experience was going to imprint my memory forever.

The wagon was a spring-like, one-seater type with side

boards, open tail gate, and a single tree allowing for a single pair of plow horses. My mind photographed it all then, and as I grew I could identify what I saw. A tall, thin man wearing overalls, and blue shirt with a brown or black hat was walking in a slow stride beside the wagon, the reins clutched in his hands. He kept his face to the front, except once in a while would look over his shoulder to check the little group following behind the wagon.

The small group consisted of four, or five children, an older boy and girl about ten and twelve holding the hands of still younger ones. They also did not look around, but trudged in their best Sunday clothes, silent as little fawns hiding in the grass, eyes on the back of the man, their father.

In the bed of the wagon was a rough, wooden casket the size to fit an adult. They were headed toward the cemetery, and there was a determined look on the man's face.

I did not follow them to the cemetery, but we heard the story soon enough.

Seems a small family lived a few miles out in the woods off Highway 96, never bothering people, and so dirt poor like the rest of us, the children were not in school often. I don't feel I knew the kids at all. The mother was sickly and died from lack of help at all, and the townsfolk never bothered to help them.

After the strange party arrived at the cemetery, the wagon was driven to the back side where the man proceeded to dig a grave for his wife's casket. Some town father went out promptly upon hearing the news, and attempted to stop the grave digging. He told him it was against the law to bury a body in Lavaca Cemetery without buying a lot, and notifying a funeral home, and certainly have a properly signed death certificate by a doctor.

The man never missed a shovel of dirt and never acknowledged the town people. The children stood by the grave, huddled close together, and never took their sad eyes off the father as he dug the grave deeper and deeper. They never cried. They never smiled. They spoke not a word.

Then, the intruding leaders of the town backed off a way and talked in low tones. Then, they left, no other words were spoken, and no other citizen of the town made a showing; no words of condolences, no flowers, no hugs for the children, and certainly no offer of a funeral.

When the wagon left, the father and his children rode up in the wagon, still not looking right or left.

I felt an anger in the man, and pain. The anger appeared to me as aimed towards the town. But after that day, I never saw any of them again, and I wondered what happened to them.

I couldn't sleep that night without restlessness and a couple nights after that. Once more I wanted to talk to Jesus and ask him to take care of the children. I've never forgotten, and I would like to visit Lavaca, and find the mother's grave. How silly of me.

* * *

Another unique form of punishment of Dad's, because those old wooden houses built in the twenties contained no closets in our part of the country, was to put me under a bed, and I'd stay there to cogitate my sinful ways until he felt it was time to come out. If there had been closets, I think I would have hated to be remanded to one of those very dark cubicles. But, of course, to hear Mother tell it, I was always exploring under furniture, when I was a crawling infant, so I wasn't too afraid of close quarters, or even semi-dark ones, with one exception--scorpions, centipedes, spiders, and other roaming bad things indigenous to that part of the country.

I'd lie under the bed, picking at the wire coils of the springs, and hum or sing softly. I still liked my favorite ditty, "Show me the way to go home," and always added it first to my repertoire, for who knew how long I'd be under there?

I liked the Insect Baseball song, where the grasshopper hit the thrown ball, and rounded the bases, and "hit the home base with a hippity-hop." I learned this song when I was about five, most of it lost from memory now, and it had to be seen to be appreciated, for it was an action song with body and hand movements emphasizing the words, ending on a final louder note as the grasshopper hit the home base and won the ball game. I'd "done" this song when I was seven, for the Lavaca High School assembly room students, standing up on a long library table. What I remember most vividly was when I hit my two fists together one atop the other, and a stamp of the foot, to end the song, and I heard the applause. Then I was hustled back to my second grade class. I don't think I ever sang that song again, unless it was for Uncle Jim--for pay too. But during those bleak years in Lavaca, my singing was for myself, for my sanity, almost absentmindedly, and to occupy myself as I lay under the "punishment bed". Even though I do remember this, I feel it, in itself, did not harm me; it was that it seemed to blend into my concept of abuse. The big hurtful things and lesser punishments were simply a part of each other, therefore I perceived them as one and the same effrontery even though my mind did, in a way, categorized each punishment in its severity.

The Lavaca house didn't have a clothes closet to its uncomfortable name, but it did have an attic of sorts. There was a door in a corner of the kitchen that had several steep steps up a dark stair to a small room, also dark, used for storage. Now this child did not like that room, or that stair, or even opening the door leading to the both of them. It suited me just fine to just ignore that door, and pretend the attic did not exist.

The punishment was probably the most threatening to me while we lived in Lavaca, my ages being from seven to ten, and I did learn one thing early on: Never tell anyone, not a soul, not Mother, not Bettye, not even little Peggy--do not tell Dad, to save my soul--that I was terrified of the attic! As young as I was I knew that instead of being put under the bed, I'd be put up the dark stair to the dark room, if they knew my fear. Never, never show your fear, if at all possible. If Dad had thought of it on his own, then my goose would be cooked, and I would have been a blithering idiot quite quickly. My Protector was with me on this one.

Just put me under the bed, Daddy, and I'll make out fine, and I'll sing you this song: Show me the way to go home; I'm tired and I want to go to bed--you can always hear me singing this song--show me the way to go home.

Haircut day was terrorizing to me. I didn't want those silly looking cuts, shingled up the back with bangs and a dumb looking side flap coming down even with the tips of each ear. That was not the Buster Brown hair cut where the back is left long as the sides, but the thirtyish style for girls and most women was a leftover from the Flapper age. I wanted my blond hair to grow long, so I could wear braids, but I was not allowed this. Dad said it was too hard to keep clean, so out came the chair and on the seat was balanced a wooden box, and up I'd go, usually after Bettye, my heart pounding in my throat. It was "blood day".

My terror would build up as Bettye would have her dark-brown thick hair first thinned a little before Dad would start on the actual cutting, so I had plenty time to become a basket case when it came my turn.

He would finish Bettye, then take a brief break while he rolled and smoked a cigarette.

I would be almost in tears while I climbed up on the box, got the cloth about me, and Dad would pick up his scissors, comb, and clippers, and approach. I didn't even like him that close to me, and I had good reason for my terror on these days.

Most haircuts, I remember, were preformed out in the yards, and three haircuts in particular, I will never forget. The first one was an introduction to another form of "punishment", but was called an accident by Dad. He combed and parted the hair, shingled the back, trimmed the bangs, then moved to trim a side flap even with my ear. He cut the tip of my ear, I let out a squall, and the cut was bleeding. He told me, "If you would have been still, I wouldn't have cut you. Now, shut up." I was too afraid to move. He knew that.

Two times in Lavaca, he cut the tip of my ear--I can't remember if there were two rights and a left, or two left tips and a right tip. The third cut was done in front of Grandma Michael's place in Slatonville. Why Dad chose that place and that time I will never know, but for the third time he cut my ear and called it an accident.

Why in the world did he bother to cut my hair at all? As

"punishment", or because I wanted my hair left alone? Even now, although I do not bear scars of the little snips of the scissors, the tip of my right ear itches slightly quite often, and I think of the three accidents as I touch the ear lobe wondering if at least three "accidents" really were accidents. I see that child not too much as myself, but I think, "poor, grubby, little girl."

How significant is it to educate your children of the hazards of child and spouse abuse, and for that matter parent abuse, which is more prevalent than we think?

Even though I have no credentials that would make me more credible in the eyes of the parade of masters and Phds whose hypothesis and theories are based on studies of not only experts down through the years, but their own case studies, I am the study case, and feel strongly I can contribute more to the understanding of the matter of abuse.

It can be so subtle that a casual observer will miss it, for-crying-out-loud. I found the psychological type can be the most crippling and long-lasting of them all. I call this the "nuance" type.

Also, I've noticed in my own case, the "dog pack" chain reaction is deadly. This is exhibited most frequently when demeaning remarks are involved--the verbal killing of the free spirit, which can take a whole lifetime for the victim to feel he is competent more than he isn't competent. But my experience was to have Dad say, "you can't do anything right," and Mother agreeing, "no she can't do anything right," and sister Bettye taking up the chant, "you can't do anything right," and glory be, after a few years of the bombarding ritual phrases, I began to lose confidence in so many easy tasks I was doing before.

The ones needing desperately to be informed about being, or becoming an abuser are the abusers themselves. Sound silly? Where in the world can we begin the education, then?

Non-abusive people do not usually produce abusive children; even so, not all victims of abuse become abusers. Chain reactions from one generation of abusers handed down to the next and so on, if they do not produce abusers, they will certainly produce mental illnesses so that devastated victims may not be able to live in the normal world as we know it.

Non-abusive parents do not need a program involving the education of abuse for themselves as long as there is awareness and the children are taught verbally that abuse is wrong, and abusers have mental and emotional problems. Many of these abusers are potential murderers. They have problems in a seriously screwed-up mind, and many are not able to exercise control at a critical time of explosion, and believe it or not, the victim can't hide from him, for he will seek him out to vent his rage upon him.

Sometimes the abuser will focus on the weakest of his family, and some have a great need to break the spirit of a strong member, even if it takes a lifetime. It is a need to control; to empower.

When a child is sexually molested, that becomes the ultimate shame of a child, I'm told, plus the abuser's vivid threats what he will do to the child or it's mother, or baby brother, keep the child constantly in a vortex of fear.

Of course, severe cases of abuse should be punishable by the criminal courts, working with protection agencies, and the decision for education of the victims instituted, not only to help them emotionally, but to stop the pattern there, thereby, not passing it on.

Breaking the pattern would be my way of thinking, and it should start with a victim before he becomes an abuser--if the abusers themselves cannot be educated, and cannot break the pattern themselves. It would be great if abusers could be rehabilitated, <u>really</u> rehabilitated. With our current awareness making it a criminal offense to beat your wife, your kids, your dog, the stress will be put on the offender so strenuously he will be forced to shape up or be shipped out. He will opt for shaping up, and perhaps some good old education will cut the pattern chain. Who knows?

I went out exploring one day. It was a lazy day with

butterflies flitting about, blue jays scolding of my approach, and small lizards quickly darting behind rocks as I walked the dusty two-rutter road on the outskirts of Lavaca.

I picked up a stick, and trailed it in the dirt, trying to see just how swiggley I could make tracks. I threw the stick away.

I tracked turtles, poked my finger at doodle bugs, and investigated the sudden scampering of a gray rabbit. Then I looked about for flowers. Maybe I could pick some.

There were fluffy white clouds in a clear blue sky, and I saw chicken hawks riding the air currents, making lazy circles overhead. Then, I heard children talking and laughing. Interested, I looked toward the sound, but my vision was obstructed by a curve in the road, trees, and shrubs. I began walking towards the sound. I got to the bend and there up to the right was an unpainted wooden shanty, gray now with time and weather, corrugated tin roof gone rusty, and a sloping porch. I wasn't interested in the house. Where were the children? The voices grew louder as I got closer. Then I saw them. Suddenly I was shy, and became hesitant in my joy at hearing happy children talk, laugh, and play, and I stopped to look for them. Yes, there they were playing around the porch. One little boy was teasing a smaller girl, and there were two or three other children-- maybe one my age, one Bettye's age, girls, and I think, a boy. As I remembered, the boys were in overalls, and the girls were in gingham dresses. They were so caught up in the exhilaration of life and playful fun they did not notice me standing in the road watching them. I remember standing there stock-still until I got the courage to say "Hi" to them. I can imagine it croaked out, but one looked up, saw me, and the rest stood up, staring in curiosity, their black faces a lovely sight to see. A couple of the smaller children scampered in the house, and I was afraid I had startled them.

I was slack-jawed with wonder, for I had no idea the other side of heaven, or Mars for that matter, that a black family lived anywhere near Lavaca. What a break, I thought. I'd missed Uncle Jonah Brooks, and here were people just like him. They must be kind people, or so my mind had built it up that negroes, or "colored", as they were called back then, were kind, friendly people. I'd heard Mama refer to them as "negras", but to me they were life--they were people--they laughed with happy abandon, not slapping each other, or saying hurtful things to each other. There was no hateful name calling.

It seemed they stared at me an awfully long time--ever so long--as I took a tentative step to the side of the road, closer, and stopped, waiting for them to make what I hoped would be a friendly gesture. A woman straight and tall and wearing an apron, came to the open door, and the two little ones clung closely to her, and all of them stared out to where I was.

I said "Hi" again, and one of the older girls looked at her mother, who gave a nod, and the oldest of the children slowly began to walk toward me. They would look at each other and grin to hide their nervousness. Finally they were almost to the road. We stared at each other, me at their unfamiliar blackness, and they at my unfamiliar whiteness. It was a stand off as to who was the most curious. The conversation went this way, I suspect:

"Who you?"

"I'm Alma." Ama I pronounced, leaving out the "l".

"Where you come from?"

"Town."

"You lives in town?" "Yeah, nex to the school. You don't go to school?"

"Naw. We not 'lowed."

"Why not?"

"Cuz we colored."

Then the mother called from the porch for the kids to return to the house. We said "bye" to each other, and they went back, looking over their shoulders every few steps.

I stood there, crestfallen, for I knew from the mother's tone that I would not be welcomed to play with the children. I had been shut out, and I felt it unfair. They didn't need me. They had themselves. A family unlike mine. It would have been nice to go up to their house and play with them, and I felt ever so slightly the unfairness of it; the race difference.

Today, I understand why the mother's tone showed a finality to it. It couldn't happen back in the early thirties. It just didn't happen.

Later, as I returned to the house, I asked the question why the colored children were not allowed to go to school. I was given an unsatisfactory answer, but I did realize as young as I was, it was unfair that colored children couldn't attend school.

When a white person--any caliber of white person--made slurring remarks, and had Civil War names for the negros, from "pickaninnies" to "niggers", and passed these on to their own children as if the colored people were not as good as even the white trash, I almost got sick to my stomach.

After that day, I wandered up that dusty road, and had a child's hope in my heart the children would accept me and allow me to play with them. But, it was a waste of time for me. I know deep in my heart they didn't want to shut me out, but the mother was right, it wouldn't have worked.

"We are all the same in our Father's sight."

Sunday evening Nov. 6, 1994, I attended the Cumberland Presbyterian Church in Mansfield Arkansas, and my heart sang, and the tears threatened to overflow my eyes, because the invited black choir sang from the heart, and the black preacher touched and comforted me. We, all whites and blacks, sang together, stood together, hugged one another, shook hands and talked, and laughed, and loved one another. Thank you Lord.

I wished desperately for the toughness and obvious good health of the Jenner twins, two constantly whirling dervishes with more energy than even I could keep up with. They lived in a large farm house out past the railroad tracks, very near where my father had his small sawmill located. They were older than I by maybe a year, or perhaps were Bettye's age. They were mirror images, and I would have sworn if one had a scratched right knee, so would the other one. I've long forgotten their given names, but I can tell you what I remember they wore on one particular day.

After school in early winter, I went to their place to play. The game we selected to engage in was the old "Annie Annie Over" of throwing a fairly soft ball over the roof top of the house where the catcher would be ready to catch it. If the ball was caught, that lucky person then could barrel around the house to where the thrower was waiting, and chase him down by throwing the ball, the purpose to hit him and score one for that side.

Those girls could throw. It was much harder for me at first, but I started catching on, and was able to get the ball to at least clear the peak of the roof, but I was never able to out-best them.

Their mother cooked supper for a big family, and delicious smells came out from between the cracks of the windows and doors until I would salivate, and get almost weak in the knees from hunger. One of the twins asked me if I was hungry. I said "Yes", where upon, she dashed into the backdoor and returned with a huge wedge of golden corn bread warm and fresh. I walked home slowly, biting into the lovely bread, and savoring every bit of it. I had never had a piece of corn bread that big in my life. By the time I arrived home for supper my stomach was full, and our skimpy supper didn't entice me at all.

Following that, again I walked home with the twins, one on either side of me. I felt at ease with them, and we prattled as we walked along, up past the tracks and I could see my dad and another man busy at the sawmill cutting clapboards for the coal mines, or studs for shoring. I did not wave. I never did that.

The twins danced and hopped about me. They were dressed in identical skirts, red turtleneck sweaters, knee socks, and brown brogans. They laughed, and said they had something for me to do--a game perhaps, I thought--as the red sweaters whirled faster about me, making me dizzy. Then, we stopped in their yard.

"We want you to do somethin' for us," one said solemnly. "Yeah. We do," said the other one, just as solemn.

"What?" I asked.

One walked in front of me and crossed her arms in front of her. "We want you to get a nickel from your daddy down there at the sawmill."

Suddenly my mouth got dry. It was simply the idiotic suggestion that made my spit turn to cotton. Why, surely they were kidding me.

"I can't do that. Unh, Unh." I shook my head.

The other twin joined her sister, and gave my chest a little push.

"Why not?" The question wasn't gentle. "Cause, if you don't, you ain't ever gonna play with us anymore."

I was in serious trouble here, and these big girls were acting like James Cagney in the movies. "I can't. He won't give it to me." I was sure he wouldn't give a nickel to me now, or ever. "Jist tell him your mama needs it for a bag of P&G Soap," spoke up the other twin, her hand pushing me backwards.

"But, but, that's a big lie." I stuttered, getting really nervous now.

The other twin got down close in my face, and her eyes slitted. "If you don't, we will hit you hard, real hard."

They both raised their fists, threatening, my eyes followed the fists.

Her sister hissed, "You better do it, now." With that each grabbed one of my arms, and we began walking toward the sawmill. I could hear the saw going, and the screech as lumber was fed into it.

We got close, and the girls pulled me down behind some bushes. I was warned that I would severely be dealt with, if I didn't come back with a nickel, and they would be watching me closely. Slowly, I walked to the sawmill, and my nerves were about to explode. This was not right. I had two bullies behind me, and my dad ahead of me. Who could hurt me more?-- but I wasn't thinking straight, or I would have chosen to call their bluff, and with no hesitancy at all, refuse to do the wrong thing. But, I kept walking until I stopped near where Dad was working the saw.

"Yeah, what do you want girl?"

"Mama needs a nickel for a bar of soap." I almost choked on the words, the lie, and I wanted to die right there.

Without another word, Dad reached into his pocket and handed me a nickel. I couldn't look at him at all, but then my acting somewhat fearful wouldn't have appeared abnormal to him at all, I suppose.

What I wonder today, is, how could Dad have not seen the flashes of red sweaters behind the bushes? Did he really know?

I gave the nickel to one of the twins, and the two headed toward town, me tagging behind to see what they were up to. They went into a grocery store, and came out with a bag of candy, laughing as they headed back home.

I dragged on home, knowing with all my heart that I would be killed. Dad was going to kill me when he asks Mother about the P&G soap she needed the nickel for, but she actually didn't send me for the nickel. There were too many holes in my crime of lying and thievery. Perhaps a bar of soap cost more than a nickel or maybe the twins knew. I was suffering agony. If Dad didn't get me, Mother might switch me, or worse, God would never forgive me.

My breathing was shallow and quick as we sat around the supper table that night. I just knew it was coming on. It didn't, not that night, or the next day, or that week, that year--never. I was so ashamed of my sins. I only confessed to the Lord Jesus. I could never go to Dad and confess, and I kept the bad thing buttoned down tight in my heart.

After that the twins would pass me going home from school, hit me on the shoulder, or slap my head, and race past laughing as loud as could be. They never asked me to go to their house to play again, and I never really wanted to go, even if it meant I would never taste the best corn bread I'd ever tasted, never again.

I think of the whole thing and even today I cannot believe I actually got away without both my parents knowing of this bad deed. How could they have not known? And why wasn't I severely punished? A nickel was hard to come by for us sixty years ago, and it was bound to come up in their conversation, at least sometime.

* * *

Awareness of things unseen were becoming stronger inside me as the months passed. I wasn't quite ten yet, and even if the migraines came and went, and the shame and need in our poverty came hard for me, I felt I was adjusting somewhat to my life, or, at least, I was attempting to tolerate it.

There were times of a recess, or of the ability to take deep breaths, of singing again, and skipping about, all this between the more harsh times, breaks that allowed my insides to settle down.

Bettye seemed to be hovering more about the house, maybe sewing or trying to feel a closer bond with mother. Little Peggy was getting taller, her legs were long and skinny, but she was not old enough for school yet. Old Boone lazed about under the house, and rather be left alone. Herb was a Boy Scout, and dad the Scout Master, and with these interests going on, I really don't think I'd had a box across the head in some time.

Then, oh rats, I discovered I had ugly warts all over my right hand. They were so offensive, I'd hear, 'ugh,' as a school mate saw my hand as I wrote, or read in front of the class. I hadn't played with frogs, I tried to convince a chum with vigorous shakes of my head.

I tried chewing the warts off and scratching them off, but only got bloody, sore warts, for my pains, so I wore rags around my hand. I could swear they were growing bigger, and more were coming on.

A classmate came up on me when I was re-wrapping the rags around my hand, and told me he knew what I could do to get rid of the warts. I was game for anything, so asked how.

He became conspiratorial in his manner and voice as he dared come closer. "There is this witch---" "A witch!" I screamed out. "Are you crazy?" "Shhh---," he whispered, "not so loud. She is a very old, good witch, who can heal."

"Oh I dunno, I don't like witches."

"If you want to get rid of them warts, go to her."

Finally, I said after mulling the witch over, "uh, okay, I'll do it. Where does she live?"

I was a nervous wreck by the time school let out. My friend wished me luck, and I was on my way. Something had to be done about these warts. As I walked past the witch's house and reached the road that would take me to her house, I was scared and wanted desperately to turn back. The warts pushed me on. As I approached the house, I could see an old woman, a sun bonnet on her head, sitting on a porch swing. She was busy with needle work and didn't look up.

I hesitated as I got to the ditch with a wide board serving as a bridge, but got my nerve back and stood at the gate leading up a path to the steps of the porch. I froze, and frantically wished I was brave. My goodness, a witch, for Pete's sake.

When I did move, a raspy voice gently said, "Child, come here." I still hadn't seen her look up. The voice gave me some much needed courage, and I went up the steps onto the porch. Then she looked up, and quietly said, with her outstretched hand, "Let me see your hand." I stretched my hand out to her without making a sound. Her touch was soft, as she examined it. She lowered her face and mumbled some words I didn't catch, then put a finger on the tip of her tongue, and touched each ugly wart. When she was through, she looked up at me and said, "Go home and wash your hands, and keep them clean with soap and water. Do not touch them anymore than you have to." She picked up her sewing and began to put her full attention on it. Quietly, I backed off, then ran down the steps, out the gate, and home. I had to wash my hands.

I watched the warts shrink, the tall craggy ones smooth off and flatten out. In one months' time my hand was clear. My hands were also kept cleaner than ever before.

The thing I was feeling inside me was the beginning of a

realization that here was something good that I could tap into, even though strong soap and water could be a great healing agent. Actually, I like to think the good witch was a bonafide healer from God, and I wanted to know more.

* * *

There were short breaks in my dark storm clouds that occasionally lifted me up to feel happy, and I'm quite certain those times were appreciated by the others as well. I could get rid of the sulky me, and lose the seriousness to let in a bit of sunshine. Even Betty Lou could enjoy herself although she was showing added signs of nervousness as time passed.

When dad was happy, he could cajole mama into a good mood, but he chose the fewer times of doing things he felt less burdened about. One pleasant thing he liked to do was tool along a road in the bob-tailed, T-model Ford with the sun on his head and the wind in his face. Then he felt free. While on our way from Lavaca to Nowata in the T-Model, dad burst into song. Mama joined in, Peggy clapping her small hands, delighted to see smiles on faces, and soon Herb, Bettye, and I jumped in singing loudly to the fields, the cows, the streams, and mail boxes, as our little car passed.

> "Oh I ain't got a barrel of money.
> Maybe we're ragged and funny.
> But we're rolling along,
> Singing a song,
> Side by side."

I can still feel the warm breeze, hear the song, and feel something inside of me so close to happy good will, that I now feel sadness to think a time as this didn't happen often enough. But it did happen, and I'm so thankful that I am able to remember this much.

I'll tell you one thing, remembering this day and my inner feelings made me feel closer to my family---almost.

A group of us children, all girls, including Bettye Lou, made our way to school close to our house. We were chattering and in constant motion as we stretched ourselves across the road swinging sacks of belongings and lunches, and books, making such a tremendous racket that dogs began to bark and birds flew to trees at a distance, excited by all this activity.

"You girls wait" mother was on the back porch waving a hand. "Wait up for Glenn."

I ran back yelling, "Glennie, Glennie, hurry up."

"Go to sco, go to sco," cried out Glenn, her large head supported on a thick neck was thrust forward, while her slanted eyes were swollen almost shut and her thick lips grinned from side to side. She lolled out her tongue as she tried to run in a stiff-sided gait, anxious to reach us, and concentrating extremely hard to coordinate her chubby feet and legs.

Glenn was a Mongoloid. She was about twelve years old, the daughter of an older couple who lived a way from us. Each morning that the weather was sunny, her mother sent her to school with a sack lunch, and a piece of twine string. She would come by our house and stick like glue to Bettye and me after we moved into the house in Lavaca.

We would go on to school, where we would separate and go to our respective classes. Glenn would tag along with whomever of us she chose. Kids would pass her and say, "Hi Glenn." and go on. Glenn would choose a seat, and the teacher would come in, and after looking the class over, would say, "I see that Glenn will be with us. Good morning Glenn." Glenn would smile a big smile, get her twine string out and start playing with it between her stumpy fingers. Glenn went to recess with us, if not entering actual games, would sit and shake the string, a far off look in her pale eyes. She knew when she wanted to use the toilet, so there was no problem there. The school had decided to allow her to come to school and be present, to be with children, but sixty years ago the retarded didn't have chances to learn, because they were termed "unlearnable," and there certainly were no special classes for her kind, not in a place like Lavaca. But then, Glenn was the only retarded person I'd ever seen that it showed in the construction of the body.

She was lonely, I could see that, the way the look would come into her eyes as she wiggled that piece of string. That sad look said, "I know I'm different, and I'm sad." Sometimes she would concentrate much better than other times, and she would cry in frustration if she couldn't keep up with us kids as we bounced and ran. She knew her thoughts came ever so slowly, and the ability to concentrate was so difficult. And, she would become angry, because she tried so hard.

School would be over, and Glenn would be tired and sleepy, so on those days Bettye and I, and other kids, would take her home to her mother, who would thank us and give us a cookie, it seemed as payment for looking out for Glenn. Before Glenn went to her bedroom to sleep, we kids would tell her "bye" and "see you tomorrow," and be off.

Glenn's mother kept her spotlessly clean, had taught her words, and how to do chores about the house, but in her eyes there was a broken hearted mother. I could see she loved her incomplete daughter very much. And so did we.

My brother Herb was, as I mentioned, almost a shadowy figure in our growing up years. I really regret this with all my heart, but I don't know exactly what I could have done to have had a closer relationship with him. He was four and a half years older than I, and I thoroughly believe he too, was fighting his own battles for some reasonable closure to the demons of hardship we all endured. Bettye Lou, being closer to his age, could have remembered a lot more than I. Perhaps she didn't see a shadowy figure all the time as I did, but I can only speak for myself.

I did not find him, shall we say, friendly, but of course, we weren't striving to be friendly. We were squirming to survive, and I'm also sure Herb found more cheer and friendliness with his school and Boy Scout chums. All I can say is that mostly he was out, away, gone, as he could manage excuses for being gone.

Herb was a slim, dark haired, good looking boy with his grey eyes. When nervous, he chewed on his nails. He kept himself clean, and presentable, the nice little gentleman. He liked to be neat.

By the time I was ten, I felt he simply did not like his family. Heaven knows he had a right to feel as he did. The worst part is I feel he had begun to know our mother, her moods, her selfish ways, her manipulation of her children around her, and her lack of concern for us in our illnesses, and her inability to love.

In Lavaca, when Herb was about twelve or thirteen, he wanted to sell the Grit paper, and, on top of that, Cloverine Salve, a big seller to southern towns people back then. The Grit also was read by the men mostly, so he decided to become the enterprising business man, and buy some much needed things for himself with his earnings; some extra spending money on the side to boot. He needed shoes, a pocket knife, a watch, and if he could stick to it, he could also help the family some.

We were excited for him. A good plan for making money hadn't come our way in a long time, and to think he just might break the tough chain of bad luck since I could remember. Maybe dad would catch the bug and try harder for a better way. Maybe mother wouldn't cry and wring her hands so much if there was something for her to be proud of, her son.

I don't remember dad's reaction to Herb's business venture, especially as it progressed. But, Bettye and I knew mother's reaction of a prize to be given out to the salesman of a certain number of tins of Cloverine Salve sold. Herb had a dream of making life easier by helping himself, thereby relieving the burden from the family. Mother, on the other hand, had other ideas. Mother, the manipulator, began her campaign.

The day was getting close when the maximum number of the tins of Cloverine Salve was sold, and Herb could select the prizes where he would make his choice and fill out the order blank.

As the time grew closer, mother began to work her ways. She got us girls worked up over a set of green glassware dishes that would match her green kitchen furniture and curtains, and linoleum.

Then Herb discovered that he wouldn't be allowed to get the prizes he had worked so hard for. Mother got the green dishes, and never thought a pip about what her son was feeling. She went about the neighbors and at church telling about her son working so hard just to give his loving mother something she needed because he loved her so much.

I can only guess his disappointment, and the crushing blow to his ambition, for I'd guess she probably made plans that Herb continue being the salesman in order that she could have "things". He kept up the Grit paper for a while, then quit که. He never attempted to sell Cloverine Salve after the green dishes came.

I don't know if my brother ever knew ---Bettye and I did---that when we were very hungry, a town businessman's wife offered mother a weekly house cleaning job, whereupon mother promptly refused, saying she wasn't a servant.

My poor brother. I think back, and I weep for him, because he was forced to sleep in icy, little lean-to additions next to the kitchens common in those days, on canvas army cots with barely enough covers to keep a cot warm. His privacy was one thing; his comfort another. He could always set up a hammock between two trees to get out of a small, hot room, but when the weather was so cold that ice formed on the bucket of drinking water in the kitchen, he needed to be kept warm.

Then on those snowy, ice-cold mornings when the whole world inside and out were places no one rather be, my father would start calling out to my brother. "Herbert. Hey, Herbert, get up and build the fire." if we were using a wooden kitchen stove and the pot-bellied, front room stove, he had to build two fires.

At the first sound of dad yelling, I'd be instantly awake, looking about into the early darkness, and listen to Herb's heavy breathing as he rushed into his clothes, and struggled with numb fingers to tie shoes. Poor dear. He had to see that there was plenty of kindling to catch the fires and enough wood in a box behind the stoves. If he forgot the night before, he had a very unpleasant early morning fire building.

I hated these mornings. I hated the winters. Dad usually didn't work in the deep dead of winter, it seemed. He would lie in bed making cooing sounds to mother as they lay cozy in their bed, and call out to my brother, every morning of every winter until Herb left home.

While we all waited for the stoves to heat up the rooms, and the big kitchen stove oven hot enough for biscuits to cook, if dad heard Bettye and me grumbling, or fussing, all he had to do was shake that belt buckle and we would freeze like the ice on the bucket of water.

Some bad mornings I would awaken to the calls, and I'd barely be moving, I was stiff from the cold, for our covers never, ever kept out the bad parts of the winter, I felt this deep sadness, and now I know it was depression.

When Herb reached Eagle Scout at Lavaca, he was about fourteen and a half years old, and for his final merit badge, swam the width of the Arkansas River...it was my father's idea. I never knew he could swim at all. I wasn't invited to watch on shore, but most of the town was present. I've seen that river. It is awesome, and quite dangerous. My brother sure did have a Protector that day, too, wouldn't you say? Who did he really do it for? He did it out of pride...for himself..., but then he had to. Even if he knew he might be swept down the river and drown, dad had already advertised the big event, hyped up the town, got his own time in the spotlight, so my brother probably said, "Well, here goes," and went for it.

I must take another time out here, for the ghosts are bombarding my poor head. I am weeping for the misguided ghosts who were caught up into a situation of life that was painted in only one direction, their whole beings working fast upon the speeding treadmill that wouldn't slow down, or stop long enough for them to get off, and certainly not enabling them to access their miserable direction, or attempt to alter the direction.

My thoughts race backwards, then fast forward to the point I must stand and walk about the house, or go out the back door, to stare with tears in my eyes, across the lake and into the woods behind the lake. How I would love to see some geese go over, perhaps land, but they won't. Only my ghosts are landing and my hurting mind sees their outlines so clearly. More tears come, and I ask my Lord for comfort and courage to go on.

The little girl, Alma, ceases to be me...that small, scared girl of so long ago. She has become someone else outside of me that I can only see her outline, a ghost of a struggling, and confused little girl. But her pain lingers on, and I am inside her again, to feel that pain, and with a shudder I see her future, and the pain becomes unbearable.

I see my father, the bleakness on his face, and an anger that turns to frustration, because he appears helpless. His ghost looks toward my mother, who sits openly crying, and wringing her hands in self pity, who then grabs up the little outline of my baby sister, who sits in Mama's lap only staring out of large eyes. The darker outline of Bettye stands by, her nervous hands fluttering to her pale face, and somewhere in the dark doorway I make out the shadow of my brother, Herb, his expression wooden, and holding a promise for his escape.

As my thoughts are almost physically jerked back to the present, my tired shoulders droop in a sudden relaxation, the air cold on my face. I watch the softly blowing gusts of wind scamper over the surface of the lake, making ripples that die out as they move out farther and farther, and blinking my moist eyes, I return and go inside.

PART TWO

"wherever I may roam"

...my sighs are many, and my heart faint.

Chapter Five

"a child can die more quickly from lack of love than lack of food."

In the lonely hours before dawn, I lay awake listening to the sleeping sounds of the family. Somewhere I hear the ticking of the clock-oh, yes, it was by Mama's and Dad's bed. Few birds were beginning to stir, and make a smaller chatter, and a light breeze stirred the filmy curtains by my bed. I was wide awake, but didn't dare move and disturb Bettye. Her sleep was becoming more restless as the time passed, and I could hear her grind her teeth.

I was awake, because I was somewhat excited over the prospect of moving to another place, where dad explained, he could find better work and make money. We wouldn't be without shoes, or pretty clothes, and have all the food we needed. I was excited, but in an apprehensive way.

Mama was happy, too, singing, playing on the little orchestra piano dad bought her from a bankrupt carnival in Nowata when I was little. She laughed as she stumbled over the keys, instead of the usual temper tantrums she had, banging the keys viciously when she couldn't get it right. She was suckered in again by dad's big daydreams of doing something great for the family, and bringing in lots of money. He always spun his yarns, talking feverishly about great plans that invaded his mind the many idle hours he spent. Yes, mama was happy, believing every word he told her.

We were leaving Lavaca, and moving outside of Midland on the gravel Highway 45 that led to Hackett. He rented a nice little, three-room house, dad said, until he could situate us in Midland. Everything would be alright and much better for us. I desperately wanted to believe him, but I had no faith in his big ideas. I was a gangly ten and a half years, but I'd heard too many stories that never panned out. I could hear him talking to mama nights after we kids were in bed. His plans were big indeed.

With Herb's help, dad moved most of the heavy furniture on a trailer hooked to the back of the car, and on the last load, mama swept out the Lavaca house, loaded us kids, and I'm happy to say, old Boone into the car, and off we went, raising a humongous dust.

When we arrived at our destination, and saw all the thick brush growing in front of a little old, grey, shanty- type house, we girls were stricken dumb. Oh my gosh, there went any shred of grandiose pictures planted in our heads. And I for one, ducked my head in disappointment as we started inside where the rest of the furniture rested. The front porch was slanted and some posts completely gone, and accessibility was completely impossible with the sudden sloping of the land, and the thicket growing there. Obviously, no one had used the old shack in quite some time. Opening the front door was too difficult, so we used a side door. It was still summertime, however late, and the heat wasn't the furnace blast it had been, but I thought it was better than breaking ice off puddles. We girls trudged in with our meager belongings, wondering where in the heck the rest of the world was. I was desperately hoping Old Boone could find a rabbit, squirrel, or field mouse somewhere, but the area looked bleak even with the trees and brush still green. Perhaps the dying corn field next to the house would have something for him. It would be in that corn field that the poor yellow dog would go to die a premature death in the middle of winter, and we girls cried, and mama cried, even though we were impervious to his needs. I feel so sad about him unto this day.

It was squalor, pure and simple, and I truly felt mother

did the best she could under the circumstances, and no doubt continued to hope dad would somehow live up to his promises for a better life. The only true hope I had inside me was that one day I would be grown, and I would do anything I wanted to do, and go anywhere I wanted to go. To a ten-year-old this sounded so hopeful, so right. That may have been the key to my survival, to Herb's, to poor Bettye Lou's, and surely to little Peggy's.

Mother was glued to dad out of her love for him, and their sexuality with one another, but one day, too late, she would feel as I felt, and love for him would begin to turn into something unpleasant to feel, a tarnished thing of no beauty, where loves and dreams vanish into smokeless nothing, and we are left shells. But for her, the time wasn't yet. For me, he would never be my hero, or my role model. I already came to know that he could not be trusted to provide for us. I truly believe he did not know how to provide for a family.

I looked up the road northeast of us, and saw a big white house, sitting back looking so magnificent it took my breath away. "Who lives there?" I asked panting. "Coy Anderson, the man who rented this house to us," Mama said. "He sure must be rich," I commented. She nodded, sagely.

Dad and Herb got the stoves in place, the stove pipes fitted into their outlets, while mama began unpacking the two lamps. We were all busy unpacking dishes, cooking pans, pots, skillets, and coffee pot, and bedding for the two double beds, and Herb's cot-where ever that cot was.

Peggy was five now, so thin her little legs were like sticks, and I must mention at this point, that she slept with dad and mama. Always had. Why wasn't she put in the bed with Bettye and me? Was it because of Bettye's restlessness? I don't think so. I think Peggy was something my mother grabbed onto, much like a doll to take to sleep with her. To me this is an extremely awkward revelation, and I am uncomfortable talking about it, but I would think it certainly wasn't a good position for Peggy.

We started school in September. Midland was four or

five miles away, so we would ride the school bus. Bettye and I wished for clothes, as I'm sure did Herb. Herb was so very particular about his appearance, I'm sure clothes crossed his mind too. Every fall of the year mama would say, "It would be so nice if your Aunt Vesta sent another box." Often she did, but not always. School books...now, this is a subject that gave me quivers every time a new school year came upon us. Too many times we didn't have the money to buy the most ragged of books, and they were extremely scarce, treated as gold, and passed down to younger brothers and sisters, or, if one was lucky, someone in town had one to sell. Herb was resourceful, and could always strike a bargain. Bettye Lou made friends quite easily, and wanted to learn, so could sometimes make a trade. It would be my fifth grade in school that I became disgusted that I had no books, and I would run myself crazy attempting to borrow books, and that didn't always work.

When new geography books in color were introduced by the county board of education, I knew absolutely that my goose was cooked. There wasn't that kind of money in my life, and I spent the balance of the year just yearning to have one in my hands for one night. I desperately looked over shoulders, across isles to the next desk, and tried to memorize the teacher's words on the blackboard, or study the maps of the world up there. It was agonizing.

I've asked myself why my mother did not feel education was important enough for her children, to attempt a visit to school teachers and make requests, at least, for consideration for us. For my children, I would have fought tigers, or sold my wedding ring, or thought of something, and the devil take the hind most, but she or dad simply did not care, or even seem to be aware. Granted, those days were times of great darkness, and poor people were a dime a dozen, and schools did not supply educational material, and nobody wanted to care for needy children. I did notice I was the only fifth grader who didn't have a geography book. I resent that terribly, even today.

Winter came on, and the bitter wind blew in through

cracks of the paper thin boards, long warped by time and weather, shook the shanty house, and flickered the flames of our lamps. Wood was used for the kitchen stove, but coal was used for the pot-bellied heating stove in the front room. With each gust of strong wind the house would shimmy, and another thin board would be dislodged, or moved. If we hovered too closely to the stove for warmth, our fronts would be too hot and our backsides froze. It was merciless; never ending.

    I tried never to hover too close. Dad always had his privileged place near the stove, sitting in his old, drawing chair, feet propped up, smoking hand rolled cigarettes and reading, or sketching, his mind seemingly at one with the world out somewhere floating in a dream cloud. I would watch him, and study the different changes that came on his face as he occupied himself. To me, it appeared he was entirely enjoying himself. How could he? I must have been mistaken.

> "Dear Jesus, you visit me at my
> lonely times, while I weep, and
> while I sleep, and you touch my
> soul with hope.

* * *

    As our food stuff reached bottom, mama's nervousness was quite apparent. She stood at the wood, cook stove frying potatoes while baking powder biscuits baked in the oven. She would sniff as the tears poured down her unusual pretty face, and she would wipe her nose on a piece of outing she kept in her apron pocket.

    Herb began to ride the school bus after school to grandpa Michael's with our Uncle Bud, then a high school student and great basketball player. Even though Bud was four years older than Herb, they were family, and struck a friendship that would last at least until the war broke out. Herb would not get off the bus at our stop, but continue on with Bud. Every chance he got he would go on to Grandpa's. He knew he could have food there, and a warm bed. But most of all, he could escape the poverty and hopelessness, the strictness of our father, and the constant stony, pouting of our mother, and to us girls he seemed unable to be too concerned with. It was too much for him, and I'm certain he was a bit ashamed of us and how we lived. Lord knows this latest house was something to be shunned, and wouldn't all the big kids on the bus see him go into that shanty, and make him feel more ashamed? Anyway, mama was also looking scrawny and peaked as time passed, but it wasn't her I worried about during that time; it was Bettye. She was becoming more skinny, and her hands shook, and the pasty face seemed swallowed completely by the large, blue eyes that appeared to want to cross at various times. She didn't laugh much anymore, and began to show more signs of lethargy, periods of depression and temper bouts, and during this whole time of her illness that lasted a good three years, she held passionate hatred for me. She had chosen me to take the brunt of her frustrations, her bewilderment, and I'm positive, her great fears.

Couldn't our parents see that something horrible was happening to their daughter, and if they did see it through their own selfish misery, why under the sun didn't they go plead--yes plead--for someone to help her?

We didn't hold each other in our arms in comfort, in loving care, to ease pain, even a small pat on the shoulder. Bettye Lou was still a little girl, only twelve, who desperately needed the best understanding from her parents and sisters and brother. But our family didn't show these things. The only understanding we knew was a striking of the hands, belts, and switches, the false shaming, the drilling into ourselves as inconsequential beings, and we were locked into a madness that if it did not cease this day, or this week, we would be lost forever, and Bettye could die.

Dad was too "proud" to ask for help. It made him look bad, and he couldn't feel like a man, but I feel that after knowing him for so long, all this family stuff couldn't be fitted into the closet of his mind and disturb his daydreams. He could sit with his feet up toward the stove, smoke his cigarettes, drink his cup of coffee, and fictionize great things he needed to be, but we, his seed, were such droll, smelly things. A burden.

The Michaels didn't like him, felt he was a type of nomad, hauling their daughter and sister around from place to place, along with us children, never staying in one place long enough to find out if he could make a living or not. He wasn't about to ask his in-laws for medical help for Bettye, and mother was warned, I know, not to bug them. Why couldn't our mother exercise that stomping, temper tantrum part of her to put him in his place, and seek needs for her children? I wonder if she ever tried standing up to her husband, and it didn't work? What if he had hit her while none of us kids were around, and that is why she was cowed down to him? I wonder: I never saw him hit her.

One cold, icy morning we got up, dressed, and all were complaining of sore throats, and coughs. Bettye was slow getting into the kitchen, and when she finally made her appearance, it was obvious she was barely able to stand. Dad was already sitting at the breakfast table, apparently in a low mood, and he started in on her, not making any physical advances, but began to rattle her with verbal complaints and orders. He had been on me until my sister showed, but now shifted his notice to her.

Her hands began to shake, and her eyes were large and darting about. Mama was busy at the stove stirring pan gravy- "thick' in' gravy"- to pour over the biscuits. Dad ordered Bettye to help her mother. She went hastily to the stove and took the spoon and began stirring the gravy. Suddenly mama let out a little scream, and quietly taking the spoon from Bettye's hand, tried to help her body to fall to the rough, wooden floor away from the hot stove, for Bettye had fainted dead away.

Bettye had a history of fainting, so like our migraines, our parents would shrug their shoulders and say, "She will come out of it. She will be alright." In a pig's eye, she would be alright! They never had migraines, deadly migraines. Dad and mama just couldn't understand why we were sickly.

It would be several more months before Bettye's illness would finally come to the attention of some of the relatives. It would become so bad she would be unable to attend school for almost two years.

As I write this, I almost can't believe Bettye went through such hell before the bitter cup was taken from her, for the most part. She never fully recovered emotionally, and I've seen her shed bitter tears in recent years as she herself tried to make sense of it.

It was just after the episode of Bettye's fainting that I noticed things becoming worse than ever, if that was possible. Oh yes it could be possible. Mama was beginning to have usual crying spells and depression. Herb was hardly ever around anymore in my memories, until the next year, dad grew less cheerful, and I--- well my shoes were wearing out, and I was stuffing cardboard paper inside them. Nights I'd lie awake and wonder what was to become of us all. And my belly gurgled in hunger pangs, but food wasn't uppermost in my mind. I didn't really know better, except that I was living in an unsatisfactory world. Where would it all end?

I'd ask Jesus if he had forgotten me. "Did you forget me Jesus?" He only answered me by letting me sleep. He was there all along. I just couldn't feel him.

Bettye and I got off the school bus, and tromped up the small distance in a slushy snow. The day was gray as I remembered, and to greet us was a frightened Peggy whose peaked face was just as gray. She was crying, and I wondered for how long. "Mama is sick," she said, and Bettye went to mama almost collapsed in a chair. She was gasping and crying, "What am I going to do?" Then she said, "my heart, my heart." She clutched her chest.

Bettye told me, "Go get Coy Anderson, hurry!"

I raced out of the house scared in a panic. In my haste I left a shoe in the snow, but I was unaware I'd lost it. I kept racing on, my skinny legs like pistons, and flew up the steps, and banged on the front door with my fist.

Mr. Anderson opened the door---I don't know how long it took, but it didn't take him long to get my drift that "mama's having a heart attack, come quick," and back I raced way ahead of him. He followed as quickly as he could carrying my shoe, and I didn't even know I'd stepped out of it in my frenzied haste. He went to mother, who was still limp in the chair. Bettye's eyes were still big and showed fear. She had put a damp cloth on mama's forehead.

Mama appeared relieved that Mr. Anderson was there, and with concern he asked her what was happening to her. She replied that her heart hurt, and she got dizzy and short of breath, and just knew she was having a heart attack. He stayed a short while until we all settled down, and he returned home. Mama was smiling by the time he left, but showed depression as soon as the door closed. Later, she told me to go get something that was under her bed in a flat box. It was dark and cold in that one bedroom, and I do remember I felt for the box, but upon my soul I cannot recall what the object was I was asked to get. I knew that my fear of mama's sickness made me unafraid almost, of the wildcats lurking under the bed. I do know I hurried back out.

Mother was thirty-six, and Bettye and I had birthdays without realizing it, again. Forget Christmas. We were lucky if we got some nuts and candy in our sacks. One Christmas was spent at the farm where all the aunts, uncles, and cousins congregated, but I'm not sure when that was. Back in those days only the parents were responsible for gifts for their children. It was not remotely expected that gifts were given outside of your own family, except perhaps the grandparents.

Somehow, we made it through that winter, then soon we were fortunate to move into another house with an extra small room for Herb's cot. The house was yellow and had 'bean' trees in front---the technical name escapes me---but, they had large, light green, lacy leaves, and the bark was much smoother than the oak. Oh how I missed my oak tree in Lavaca, but I'd been real busy after we left, and winter is no time to climb.

I stood out on the front porch in my high water overalls, surveying the bean trees, wondering if the limbs were situated where I could scurry up, and it would be ever so great if the tippy top had a comfortable place to sit. I stood, hands in pockets, looking from tree to tree, and I noticed a boy about my age come out of the house next to us, and shyly and slowly walk my way. He was thin, had his overalls on and was barefoot. I edged off the porch slowly continuing to examine the trees, while I darted looks at him.

On he came, until he was standing a few feet between us, put his hands in his pockets, too, and helped me look up at the trees. Almost a minute passed I'd say, when he said, "This un is the best climber," and pointed to the tree on the right. "How d'ya know?" I asked, still looking up. "Cause I clim' it." I'm interested. "Best huh?" "Yep," he replied. I said, "Okay! Les try it." Up he went as quickly as an Arkansas red squirrel, me following on his bare heels.

Soon he was slapping a smooth, sturdy limb with a great horizontal line to it where it connected to the tree. It was beautiful. We were high above the ground, and the green leaves afforded obscurity from all directions. It was exhilarating and I laughed.

"Do you walk the limb?" I queried.

"Sure do. Watch." He walked the length of the limb with no hands, turned and walked back.

I was impressed indeed, and said so. He grinned in pleasure and told me his name was Roy Dyer. I told him mine, and although we didn't slap our hands in a new act of friendship, we were tree climbing buddies, Crawdad catching buddies, and tin can hockey buddies. Even if he was a boy, I had a friend at last. We stayed friends while we were children, then went about our separate ways afterwards.

Jimmy Peters didn't feel well at all, but he was in school off and on. I didn't tell you about Jimmy earlier because I needed to introduce you to him, now we were in fifth grade. He was the son of our town's prosperous grocer, the only child. He always wore the best two-piece, cut off suits when we started first grade, and his best friend was Jackie Scott, who lived across the street from his home.

I was nervous all the time around the kids in my class, and in particular Jimmy, because he had unwittingly become the focus of my one and only crime, if you don't count the nickel incident and the Jenner twins as a crime. I certainly do, but actually Jimmy Peters came before Lavaca. We were in second grade at the time, and I was fascinated with Jimmy and Jackie, because they had plenty of the good things of life, were always spanking clean, and had loving parents. You might say I admired them. On the flip side, I didn't have those things, even the milk in little jars lined up on the window sill of the school house to keep the milk cold, was not for me. I can still see the little jars with names written on tags and tied with twine, and reading those names. I was lucky to have a biscuit with a slice of cold pan gravy inside it. At seven a child can be embarrassed about that, and I was always hungry the long day of school, for from 7 a.m. until 5 p.m. was simply too long to go on with a biscuit for lunch. I'd go out on the rock wall to eat my biscuit.

I didn't plan my crime, but my instant need was out of desperation. I looked over across the aisle at Jimmy's desk. Back then school desks were bolted to the floor, each desk connected to a small collapsible seat in front of it for the student ahead. Books were stored under the top of the desk with open sides of wrought iron, and my eyes were drawn to the color of bright, shiny red inside Jimmy's desk. An apple. The biggest, juiciest, red apple I'd ever seen. My mouth watered, and I quickly got my eyes in a sort of control mode by looking away and down at the work in front of me. I don't remember if we were studying, but Jimmy left his seat, or maybe there was recess, but somehow I got up and took the apple without any witnesses at all, and hastily put the apple in my desk, hidden alongside of my biscuit bag. Immediately, I was shocked at my sudden act of foolhardiness, and it went against my nature, and the rush of remorse forced me to reach into the desk and return the apple. It was too late. Jimmy was back in his seat, and so were the others, and class resumed. I was hungry. I didn't steal. What was wrong with me? I wanted to cry, but that was not good enough. I needed purging. I was wicked. Slowly I took out the apple, stood up, walked up the aisle and over to the teacher where I stopped, waiting for her to tell me to go back to my seat. She was a fairly young teacher, and stood for no foolishness. I knew I was in for it. I held the apple up to her, and told her I took it from Jimmy's desk and wanted to return it. What was I, masochistic, to confess this crime in front of my school mates, and the strict teacher? In front of a roomful of curious eyes that bored into me, and I felt myself blushing tremendously at my dilemma. I didn't confess because I wanted to be punished. I confessed because what I had done was a sin, and I did not want the apple. It wasn't mine.

Today, I could have pleaded temporary insanity. Then I stood there ready to receive my punishment...for I had stolen...thou shall not steal, God said. I did, and broke his commandment. The teacher took the apple, asked Jimmy if it was his. He searched his desk and said, yes.

The teacher forced me to stand in front of the class, face them, while she told the class what a very wicked person I was, and when she was finished, she got out her ruler, took her chair and brought it in front of the class, sat down and drew me face down across her knees, and proceeded to soundly spank me with the ruler. Through my tears, I still feel the pain, her checked dress just below my eyes, and my public flogging. Oh Jesus, were it only possible to run to you and hide.

Roughly, she stood me up, marched me to the back of the room to a corner, roughly sat me down upon a stool and commanded me to keep my face toward the wall. Tears continued to roll.

The door opened and I knew it was time for health lessons, for Miss 'Nelia Robinson had entered the room. She was a good friend of my grandparents, and knew my mother. I had met her at the farm. She always wore British skirts and matching jackets, English walking shoes, and held her tall frame as high as she could. She had class. "What is little Alma doing sitting in the corner? Miss 'Neila inquired. My teacher told her what I had done, and the needed punishment she was dispensing. I was a wicked child, she said. Miss 'Nelia asked something as, "She gave back the apple in front of all these children?"

The principal of the school came in by request of Miss 'Nelia whereupon she described what had taken place, and demanded the young teacher be reprimanded for her lack of knowledge in disciplinary measures of young elementary school children. Then Miss 'Nelia came to me, put her arms around my shoulder, and told me I was a brave little girl and no thief, for I had relented and had taken my medicine "like a true Michael." whatever that meant.

As I had told Jimmy and the entire class of pupils that I was sorry I had taken the apple, I felt no need to keep whipping myself, and I did not relish being reminded of it further. Very soon after that, dad moved us to Lavaca where I finished the second grade, and the third and the fourth.

So, here I was back again to meet these classmates, but now in the fifth grade. The second grade teacher was gone, and unfortunately for us Miss'Nelia was holding classes in a Ft. Smith school. I'll never forget her---never---coming to my rescue like that.

Sometimes I walked to school with Jimmy and Jackie, but not often. They didn't look like the same seven year olds I knew. I'd form up with a small group of girls on their way to school, chattering all the way, getting to know each other. But, Jimmy couldn't continue on to school. He was so sick he was in bed most of the time. He had what they termed back then as "leakage of the heart' that would not allow a future for Jimmy. I went by his home to visit with him in his room for a few minutes, then I'd leave and he would wave from his bedroom window. He was taken to a children's hospital somewhere where he spent most of the remainder of his life. I saw him a couple of years later, the friendliness and smile there, but he died when he was fifteen, never once saying any teasing remark about my stealing his apple. Rare, indeed.

That summer was hot and humid, and each morning I awoke to listlessness and some dizziness. I almost ceased to be very hungry, and I noticed Bettye Lou's eyes didn't look exactly right, and she moved about in slow, jerky movements. Peggy looked more thin, and her long thick curls appeared much too heavy for her head. However, her skin, tanned by the sun, gave her a more healthy glow. Like me, she ate little. One morning I could barely open my eyes, and very slowly I sat up on the side of the bed, and gave myself the every- morning test of shaking my head. This morning's test made my stomach churn in fear of the inevitable monster I'd fight until early evening. The migraine, as I would shake my head, if I was going into the headache, there produced a sensation of a ball rolling in my head that hurt. Try telling that to an adult, or doctor, for that matter. My eyes were extremely light sensitive, with jumping lights, and my hands felt tingly. As my neck muscles tightened, the pain accelerated, starting on one side of my head, and my stomach wanted to wretch. I would head for the cot out under the tree in the back yard to lie there sometimes writhing, then using a control method of lying quite still, for it hurt more if I twisted about or cried. At times my mother would put a cool rag on my forehead that sometimes helped. Noise, even the slightest sound, sent my nerves chattering with balls of fire, exploding inside my skull and behind my eyes. As the migraine progressed, I'd chill---in the awful heat I would chill. Similar to a hydrophobic dog, I thirsted for water, but couldn't drink it, because it came right back up, the spasms of vomiting causing more severe pain. At times I would sleep as one drugged, and during those periods of peace, I would wake with more strength to fight the remaining hours. I was so sure my Comforter would allow me the sleep, because it came to me immediately after a pain I felt I couldn't bear.

  Then, after my suffering had drained me of all strength, the blessed sun sank and I'd go throw up for the final time, and the pain began to leave. I would then drink a partial dipper of cool water. I wouldn't urinate during the day when I had the headache. If mother saved me something for supper, I'd eat some, then finally go to bed for the night. Tomorrow I would start out weak, but would gain strength as the day wore on.

The devilish heat must have been a trigger to migraines, for Bettye and I didn't have as many during the winter months. Winter gave us chest colds, croup, aching legs, and Bettye had bad tonsils that would become infected at the beginning of winter and continue on through spring.

Dad's answer to our ills was in administering laxatives. This would clean us right out. You bet. So, one morning soon after mother complained to dad that we girls were looking puny, dad lined us up at the water bucket in the kitchen. Peggy took her half a pill, bitter as gall, large as an aspirin, brown and scratchy, with a little gagging, and Bettye came next. Her nervousness was quite apparent, but to do a good job for her daddy, she forced the bitter pill down. Next it was my turn----the rebel----the one who got those NR pills stuck in my throat every time. I was nervous, and this made my throat constrict. I did so want to swallow it down with my glass of water. I didn't use a dipper this time. Dad handed me the glass of water, then put the pill in the palm of my left hand. I didn't look up at him----couldn't make my eyes meet his. He told me to take it. I made my first try and failed miserably. I coughed it back up into my hand. He told me in a louder voice to take it again, I stuffed it into my mouth and gulped water that strangled me. Up came the mushy pill. Dad slapped me across the wet mouth, saying if I didn't swallow that one, there were others in the tin box, and we would stand there all day if it came to that.

I noticed more dead silence in the house as this continued. Who knew how it may end? I had a feeling I was back fighting the same old war, and there was no time at all. Time stood still, and dad and I were moving in some slow motion that didn't exist. Where was mama? Did Bettye Lou run off and plug her ears to shut out the noise that provoked her own demons to rise up.

Dad took another NR tablet and roughly stuffed it between my teeth, then poured water down my throat. Again, I strangled and up came the pill, and water that gushed out of my mouth, down my chin, and over the front of my dress. Again, dad, real angry now, slapped me harder across the face, and I fell to my knees on the floor that was wet, and he roughly jerked me to my feet by my left arm, and said for me to stand there.

Calmly now, dad took out another tablet from the tin box, almost slowly in his movements. I'd had some time to recover enough that a bit of resentment was crawling inside me. Anger was rearing up, but those two feelings I was beginning to be acquainted with, also chased away the nervousness and bungling. Calmly, I took the tablet, set it on my tongue, and drank a slow gulp of water and the unfriendly object went down my throat and into my stomach. "See what happens when you obey me?" my father said before he strode out.

I swore I'd construct my thinking on the bitter pill taking. No more silly dramas at the water bucket. I would practice swallowing beans, peas, whatever, holding my throat open, forcing my throat open. Let dad think he trained me right, I could care less. I would be cool about the whole thing and calmly accept the bitter pill, drink a sip of water, and stiffly walk away, never looking at him.

My father never cursed, but his words stripped me of all my brave character, and left me bereft of all confidence. I often felt I became a ferret, and survival was uppermost on my mind. He hadn't whipped me with that belt since that beating in Lavaca, but the thumps on the head with his knuckles, and hair pulling continued on to Midland, and a quick slap to the head was still his style.

Sometimes, instead of dosing us girls with NR tablets, He would give us another kind of laxative I could handle more easily. Black Draught, a mixture of powered Cascara bark stirred into a glass of water was a formidable, potent drink. If you didn't have whatever should ail you, it would give it to you, and what a price! I feel the harsh laxatives we children were given especially with very little food in the stomach, could cause dangerous reactions, such as bloody flux, and even death. All three of us girls have suffered the bloody flux.

Chapter Six

"we are the wandering ones,
we are here, then we are gone-
no home for our weary bones,
no deep roots to call our own."

    My father got a job in Van Buren, not far from Midland for the last three weeks of our school year, and decided to take us with him. The job was offered by an old friend of Aunt Vesta's from Wichita, who built bridges and overpasses. This job would be short, but the pay was good. After all, dad had a good head on him for mathematics and blue print reading, plus he had worked at other bridge sites in Missouri. He wasn't going in cold.
    We left on a cloudy day, after closing our house, there in Midland, and dad, who had gone on ahead, had rented a one room apartment, large and airy, with drapes closing off beds for privacy. Herb was not with us again. We would be back soon---back in Midland---too soon.
    Bettye Lou, despite her slowly creeping sickness, decided to enroll in Van Buren school. We had a choice you see. I, on the other hand, opted not to even attempt to make up grades for such a short time. I always discovered if I did, I found myself thrown into more progressive systems that were virtually impossible to make passing grades. Bettye needed

peer friendships. I needed to learn to roller skate.

Mother puttered about the apartment, singing and making friends with other tenants there. Actually, it was a hotel, but did accommodate some people looking to stay put for a while, and to have cooking privileges. She was deliriously ecstatic about foods we could now afford to buy. In a few weeks we girls had put on some much needed weight, even though we continued to be thin.

I loved the comfortable beds, the blessed food, the relief from stress, the movie theater just a block to Main Street that showed all of Bob Burns' funny movies with Martha Raye, Shirley Temple, Popeye, and Betty Boop cartoons, and I was learning to tap dance from a girl at the hotel. Roller skating was a passion, and I seemed to have very few scraped knees.

We were back in Midland too soon, but we were very glad to see our friends again.

My exact sequences are not awfully clear in my mind of the happenings that came fast and furious that time we lived in Midland, but I will attempt to keep the continuity smooth for clarity. I am actually dubious concerning four episodes of memory worth relating here. The margin will be comparatively slender, none the less.

Dad decided to build Herb a car for the Soap Box Derby coming up real soon. Dad had help from a friend of his there in Midland, and they used a closed shed to construct the thing to be locked up tightly when no one was working it. Rules specified strictly that the young man racing the car should be the designer and builder. Here things broke down. Who was going to sign an affidavit to that? The town mayor? We had no mayor.

Well, dad and his buddy got busy. First the schematic of the design dad wanted was drawn to specifications. Secondly, dad's buddy who was backing Herb in the Derby momentarily speaking, brought in all the supplies, and with dad's tools were ready to start constuction. Thirdly, Herb was ready to get started on the car, but to his chagrin and great disappointment, he soon got the whole picture. Dad and his friend would build while he sat and watched. Great, he didn't hammer a nail, put on a wheel, even paint the finished car, so he wanted no part of the excitement of the whole business.

The day came soon enough before Derby Day, when the car came off the line, rolled out for all to see. It was a thing of beauty, graceful lines, weight to spec---a gorgeous black, shiny thing with a great yellow-jacket painted on the bobbed tail. It's title: Sugarloaf Yellow Jacket. We were all agog. The whole town cheered. Even Herb grinned in complete surprised pride. The car had the look of a professional, especially the art work. Dad, his buddy, Herb, Uncle Bud----the whole family, turned out for a practice run for speed and accuracy---- certainly couldn't have the steering pull to the side, or have the rudimentary braking system break or fail. No, sir-ee! Of course, dad had his book on speed required to beat to win the race.

Race day came. The Sugarloaf Yellow Jacket was tied onto a trailer being pulled by the buddy's car, and somehow the whole family and other interested people, headed out for Ft. Smith, thirty miles north, to the greatest sloping street chosen for the race.

I can remember the pretty day, the lovely tree-lined wide street of cement, cordoned off to traffic, and a starting line at the very apex of the hill. The street at the bottom where the race ended was superbly selected for the little, shooting cars to have length coasting before braking.

Other entries came in, and we were all curious about the designs, and a shaky feeling came in my stomach, because the competition really looked formidable. They came from all over, and the winner would be going on to compete in another state for the top prize.---the final race off.

The cars were being situated at the top, each one taken to his place within his lines; while the assistant held the car, the drivers entered their seats. The assistants held long poles with a hook loosely held behind the seat, and when the flag was to be snapped, they were to lift the end of the sticks up, and off would go the cars down the beginning slope, picking up speed as they went along.

Dad was nervous, Everybody cheered. Herb and Uncle Bud looked calm. But, one hitch! The cars had been weighed but the boys were not who rode in them. The Silver Streak, built like a huge bullet, next to Herb, intimidated him some, but when the boy walked up and eased his tremendous weight inside the bullet, Herb and Bud felt really uneasy. The heavier the load, the faster the speed picked up down hill.

Well, you know what happened, already. No amount of argument would persuade a judge to alter their final decisions, and we all drove the thirty miles back home as if the wind were knocked out of us. Of course, Herb had won a couple of small prizes which he split with his assistant, but dad and his buddy brooded. Herb wasn't awfully disappointed, and if he had been, I would have lost some respect for him for forgetting he hadn't built the Yellow Jacket at all. The game belonged to dad.

> *"Remembering my affliction and my misery,*
> *the worm wood and the gall*
> *my soul has them still in remembrance,*
> *and is humbled in me."*
> *Lamentations 3:19-20*

It was the middle of summer, and I was very unhappy. Embarrassed too, for I had received notice that I would have to be held over for another full school year of fifth grade. I had passed every subject except arithmetic, but in the thirties, we had no two semesters, no make up lessons, no summer school, and if a student does failing work in one subject he was automatically failed in the full grades' work.

Bettye Lou failed her grade, also, and she was feeling as low as I was, but there was very little we could do about it.

Mother, caught up in her own world of disappointment, apparently didn't care. Why should she start crying now? Like Scarlett, tomorrow was another day, and her interest lay in her own world of needing desperately to hope for something better for herself. The constant needs of us children were a draw back to her in some way we didn't comprehend. Therefore she kept ignoring, or missing, the now obviously acceleration of Bettye's sickness.

One real warm day Bettye got out of bed almost in a dream like state. She went into the breakfast table with an unsteady gait, her hands moving aimlessly in all directions, the nervousness frightening. She sat down at the table and reached out for the sugar bowl, but missed it altogether, her hand seemingly uncontrolled sent a cup flying half way across the table. A startled outcry from mother made her look up exposing a pale face, but it was the eyes that put us into complete shock. "I declare Bettye Lou, what is the matter with you?" Mother said before she saw the eyes. The rest of us, or I was, and I'm quite certain the others must be crazy to miss the behavior, were appalled at the wide open stare, and the eyes crossed. The beautiful blue eyes were crossed! Bettye Lou tried to speak, and the words were toneless and a bit slurred. Peggy as young as she was, remembered some of the horrible times we would all spend trying to get through Bettye's sickness. We would be in for a long siege of it, and the awful ignorance of doctors, and the bewildering scope of the deadly malady, all rolled into an attitude of almost indifference, were against any speedy treatment if proper diagnosis were correctly rendered.

Oh, I'm positive my parents felt trapped further by this untimely 'thing' that was invading their lives, adding to the troubles that constantly hounded us, making their hopes and dreams for a better future almost hopeless. Bettye's symptoms didn't simply appear one morning. Oh, no. They culminated that morning, screaming that there was something dreadful to be faced as quickly now as possible. I watched the symptoms for years becoming more prevalent as stress upon stress invaded the inner world of a sensitive, nervous child; Bettye Lou was desperately ill. Hadn't our parents seen this, or did they feel it was something she would "grow out of", or did they just plain not care if she died, or lived? My sister went through her days in extreme mood swings, and we didn't know what each day would bring. The entire house became a combat zone, a virtual cuckoo nest. Her temper tantrums were awesome, where pots and pans, knives and forks, and stove wood were hurled as deadly missiles against foes seen and unseen. But strangely, she had days of calmness, and she and I would sing our songs together, my harmonizing with her soprano. She learned to pick out cords on the piano in her times of calm; we would sing and be happy for a while. It would be singing that would allow Bettye and I to be sisters, even though we didn't actually bond, as it were. Regardless, she needed medical help and no one was there to help her. That is, until Grandpa Michael and Uncle Justin observed Bettye's nervous behavior, and informed mother to take her to see a doctor in Hackett. They drove mother and Bettye, and made sure the doctor gave it his best shot before returning home.

The old doctor gave Bettye a shot of something, probably to pacify everyone, but I'll wager he didn't have a clue to her problem, except she had started her periods, and they were not 'normal'. Feed her well, he instructed sagely, lots of milk and vegetables. Mother was in tears when she got home with a worn out Bettye. Where would she get milk-of-all-things?

Herb went to Bud and told him Bettye needed fresh cow's milk, to ask Grandma Michael if she would let us have food stuff from the farm. [Dear Lord, I often wondered why my grandparents who had the large farm and all that food, allowed their own grandchildren to almost starve to death.] That summer we did receive some food from them, but not on a regular basis. Of course dad wasn't on good speaking terms with the Michaels, would never have asked for an apple at any price, and mother was reluctant to go to them, too.

Later on, dad wanted to go to Nowata and see his parents and sisters. The car he had gotten somewhere, I believe was a four door, Ford A-model. Or perhaps he borrowed it, so we paid Nowata a visit. The visit turned out to be valuable in a way for Bettye, at least, even though she wasn't aware of it. My parents were lectured profusely by Grandpa May and a couple of my Aunts on the order of not properly taking care of us children. Bettye was taken to an opthalmologist.

He came up with nothing.

Bettye was constantly scrutinized by the Mays and Grandpa calling her "Becky" and talked to her. Her erratic movements caused them alarm. Grandpa told mom and dad something I'm sure they didn't want to hear as we were leaving."The best thing you can do is put her away for treatment."

Was this good advice? Shouldn't my parents have taken Bettye to a hospital where there would be needed treatment, and a more serene setting? I have pondered this over the years, and I came up with the answer, NO! There were no nice serene places back then, and we were very poor; we could never pay the likes of one of these. I thoroughly believe Grandpa May meant Bettye was mentally ill and should be put in a state mental institution when he made his remark to my parents.

Subsequently, we returned home and hoped we could deal with Bettye's problem. Someone else suggested another old doctor in Ft. Smith as perhaps a likely candidate for a diagnosis and treatment. His final diagnosis was that Bettye's thyroid wasn't functioning properly. He prescribed sunshine, fresh air, proper diet, rest, a big dose of "winacordia" per day. What ever "winacordia" was. He also cautioned us to stay out of Bettye's way when she had tantrums, and certainly do not provoke her anger. Heavy advice indeed.

She would go into depression and cry, and the temper tantrums continued along with the migraines. Her cup runnith over. She chewed her wrists and walked until she was exhausted when she had migraines. I felt so sorry watching her struggle to reach a decent plateau of conquering her pain. She reacted to her migraines differently than I did.

I've remembered since that mother seldom drew Bettye into some of the things she liked to do, but I suppose mother just didn't think of it. Bettye liked to cook and sew, needle work, but it didn't happen.

I was the number one focus of Bettye's attention when

her mood swing rose into a high gear of action. She would punch me with the inside of her doubled fist, swinging from the right side and up into my face or side of my head, or back of my head. She screamed to the top of her lungs. "I hate you! You can't do anything! You are ugly! I hate you!" I would carefully skulk out and shimmy up the bean tree and wait out her anger.

Waiting out her anger was a wasted effort on my part. After I would feel it safe enough to descend the safety of the tree, I would walk around the side of the house, looking before me and behind me, open the screen door, peek inside cautiously before proceeding further when there would be the sudden bellow of rage and the closed fist would crash against the side of my head. I would look up, and she would be standing her ground ready to strike again, then I would beat a hasty retreat.

Later on at nights when I would be sleeping, there would be a surprise kick of Betty's foot into my back, and before I could recover, both her feet would be in play and I'd end up on the cold, rough, board floor. Every time I tried to crawl back into bed, she started her attack again. Again, I'd try with the same results. I learned to just sit on the floor shivering in the cold blackness until Bettye fell asleep, and I'd ease back onto the bed to discover she had rolled herself up completely in the covers.

Why didn't I tell mother? Bettye warned me she would kill me if I got her into trouble. I believed her. Besides. mother wouldn't have done anything about it, anyway.

I was taken back to Nowata a few years in thought, whenever Bettye would show a streak of anything resembling madness, which was the first time I could correlate her behavior, not actually realizing how to crate it in my mind so young, but I knew enough to believe it wasn't right for her to act in this manner. We found ourselves between crisises, having to live off dad's elderly parents, so poor themselves living on pensions only as I recall, and the tempers must have been short along with the food supply.

I was looking out the bedroom window watching the

pale shadows of a street light filter through the trees, the winter cold making my breath steam the glass pane in front of me. Suddenly there was Bettye Lou standing next to me. Her hand went out to smear the glass, and said something such as "I know a game we will play," and she spat against the pane. "Now," she continued,"you lick my spit. Go on lick my spit." she waited.

I watched the frothy liquid slowly begin to make a rivet down the glass. I was disgusted, and taken by surprise at her command.

"No," I said.

"Yes," said Bettye Lou, becoming very angry.

"No."

"Yes, you will do it," and then she grabbed the back of my head pushing it, forcing my mouth and nose against the glass.

"You---will---lick---my---spit!" she said between her teeth, jamming my face forward, and from side to side to make sure her spit was all over me.

She jerked my head back, peered at my face, was apparently satisfied, then let go of me, smiling.

"There," she said pleased, "you have licked my spit."

With that, she left the room. I did not tell mother. I was ashamed.

With dad's punishments, mother's slapping hands and screeching voice, and now this elder sister so cruel, it seemed I had no place to hide, no safe home anywhere. I felt trapped, but there was one puzzling hitch to all this that didn't make sense at all. I was miserable away from some of my family-----my mother and little sister Peggy.

My brother didn't enter my life often, oh, he was there, as I've explained, but not in all the scenes, and didn't become frequently involved. He was looking out for himself. He didn't care. He was trying to survive too.

There were times, very rare times anymore, that dad would focus his attention upon Bettye and my singing. Our voices were maturing somewhat, and we spent more time practicing. We began realizing our voices were becoming more compatible as time went on, and we were singing more in church and school functions.

Dad had an idea that he would like to put on an act at the next function. As he was an artist, he felt he wanted to do something different. Bettye's health was always a touchy subject, but she had days that were, to us, almost perfect. Her eyes still crossed and uncrossed themselves, but singing was something she loved to do---if only dad didn't make her nervous, and I would be on my best behavior. We practiced in the front room, and even if the piano was in there, dad wanted us to sing acappella, because Bettye's voice was high and pure, and my harmony blended in perfectly. The song dad selected was "The Old Rugged Cross." He put his props up, a tri-pod he had made that held a large square of white paper tacked to a thin board backing, tall enough for him to stand as he worked with colored chalk. He was going to "Chalk Talk" as Bettye and I sang.

Amazingly dad was gentle with us, and we responded with this in pleased excitement. We did everything right. Timing was a factor to this act succeeding. By the time we had sung two stanzas and two choruses of the song, he was to finish on the very last note of the very last chorus.

Bettye and I were in our best dresses and shoes, and dad was dressed in a dark suit, as we waited back of the small, school auditorium out of sight. Dad carried his tri-pod and chalk, and we were ready to be introduced. We were a little nervous. Finally our act was introduced as "Tom May and Daughters," and on stage we went, Bettye and I first, and we stood almost center stage, and waited, our hands folded down in front of us. Dad didn't take long to set up, and nodded as some woman softly touched a key on the piano.

Bettye softly hummed the note in her throat, so I could pick up my harmony on her first word of the beginning stanza. Dad looked at us and gave a slight nod, and we began our "Rock of Ages." The audience was perfectly silent, and I recall seeing white upturned faces wanting to be entertained.

As we sang dad worked magic with his colored chalk, standing to the left of his tri-pod to give the audience full view of his progress. We continued our song softly, and sometimes so low it was almost a whisper, and we could hear and intake of breath and an 'ah' as the form of dad's picture with the amazing light took on more clarity. Some people were standing to get a better view.

Bettye and I reached the middle of the last stanza, and we lifted our voices stronger as we sang, "When I rise to worlds unknown," then we softly finished with, "Rock of ages, Cleft for me, Let me hide myself in Thee." Dad stepped aside and the applause was big for a small town.

I turned to look at dad's drawing, and almost gasped at the beauty of it. The cross appeared as if it had been carved out of stone, tones of purple, blues, red, with a heavenly light shining forth drenching the cross in not only gorgeous light, but darker hues at the bottom where it stood upon a hill of rocks and stones. It was magnificent! We pulled it off, and we were elated.

We didn't perform the act anymore, and it was a shame, but dad had decided to continue following bridge building with his construction friend, and we were going to be left behind to mother's unhappiness.

We decided to go and stay the weekend at the farm. The days were warm, and we needed some nutritious food. Bettye was doing fair, and we all hoped she would soon recover completely, and I was eager to have eggs for breakfast, desserts, and good vegetables. The whole milk was a big treat. The late summer crickets and other insects were busily making their insect noises, and butterflies, especially the monarchs, were in transition.

We never greeted our grandparents with hugs and kisses. We just said "hi," and Grandma Michael would say, "come on in." It seemed to go that way time after time. Grandpa accepted dad, because of us kids and mother, so he always tried to be friendly while we were there. The grown ups talked at the supper table, and Uncle Bud and Herb usually talked across to each other, and at times laughed at their own private jokes. Later, just before the sun set, Uncle Leon another of mother's brothers, came by wanting to use Bud's mare, Bess, to go to the Richardson's on a chore he said was urgent. Grandpa told him to be back before dark, because the road across Riddle Creek and past the old, almost forgotten cemetery, was pitch black after dark with the over hang of the trees. He left in a hurry. It was almost dark when Uncle Leon came dashing in on a very nervous Bess. He was having a time controlling his voice when he told the story. As he and Bess passed by the cemetery and under a large tree limb over the road, the horse became skittish and reared up making shrieking noises, and while Uncle Leon fought strongly to stay in the saddle and calm Bess down, a loud panther scream rent the air. He looked up in time to see a "black" blur leap off the tree limb, and Bess swiveled about in fear, as the blur, made a rake at her left rear flank, and she took off up the road almost to the Walker's place, before Uncle Leon got her stopped, turned about to return back to the farm. Coming back, both he and Bess were reluctant to approach the cemetery, but he patted the mare to soothe her, and any moment he felt the panther would be waiting to pounce, or perhaps stalk them in a round-about way before they got to the farm. Nothing happened.

Bud, anxious for his horse, and feeling good that his older brother was alright even though quaking still, he examined Bess's left flank. There was a scratch mark, indeed, with a little oozing of blood. The horse continued to shiver as if chilled. He led Bess to the barn to attend to her wound, and rub her down.

Talk of the incident continued as we all sat out on the front porch in the dark. Uncle Leon was convinced that it was a panther, but just perhaps it looked black in the dark. There had been some rumors that black panthers had been spotted in the Sugar Loaf area, and had been chased away from the winter pastures where cows calved, by farmers checking on the new calves.

I was becoming a little tired and we all needed to go to

bed, and everyone else felt the same. Uncle Leon went to his house: He lived in the Peanut house with his small family at this time, and he was eager to be off. I couldn't sleep. Bettye, Peggy, and I were put on pallets on the dining room floor. There were no lights of any kind. My open eyes felt as if they would drown in the darkness, and my poor, worthless soul would be forcibly drawn out through the sockets and whisked away to Netherlands of stalking black panthers with yellow eyes. Everybody was asleep, except me. I could hear snoring, loud breathing, snorts, teeth grinding-----everybody was unconscious. Except me. The next thing I knew, I was reaching for more cover and it was morning.

The black panther would stalk me in my dreams until I was sixty-years old. That was an extremely stressful time for me, and I had decided it was about time to call in the Big Gun- My Protector, report to Him I'd had all I could take and wanted that panther gone forever.

Later on that winter in Midland I lay in a cold bed, my feet drawn up trying to feel some heat, I slept restlessly. And I dreamed.

My mother was crying and calling me, saying "Alma, I need your help. Help me. Help me." "Where are you?" "Under the bed," she cried. "There is a panther under the bed here, and he is clawing me. Help me." I raised up from the cold bed. The window pane was broken, and cold wind poured in, making a dreadful mourning sound. The curtains were shredded. Again I called, "Mama, give me your hand."

She gave me her cold hand, and I could hear the panther growling in warning as I pulled her out from under the bed.

Suddenly, my bare feet slipped and the panther was dragging me under the bed, his claws tearing at my legs and feet. I screamed, and woke myself. My legs were asleep, and pins and needles were assaulting them, so I frantically began rubbing them to promote circulation.

It was going to be a long haul for me growing up with the new bothersome thing to handle, along with all the rest.

I finally found a friend. A girl friend, eight months

younger than I, a little taller than I, with blond hair and blue eyes, very fair skin, and a great gift for making a lonely girl laugh. All the time we spent together it was happy time.

Querita. Yes, Q-U-E-R-I-T-A was her name.

She was a couple of grades behind me in school, but as we lived close together, it was natural we clicked.

Her mother and dad were older, and when their two oldest children were near grown, Querita came along. So Querita always seemed to be an only child. They were poor people, too, but more stable, and more love being shown.

We romped about like young cub lions, at her house mostly, but we could often be seen walking along the streets of Midland, chattering constantly, amazed at what really good friends we were.

We actually played Tarzan, attached ropes to the bean tree limb to swing to and fro, and dad's saw horses with boards lying across them for us to jump upon as we made our landing. We tried the Tarzan yells until we ran the neighbors crazy. Then we would become tired of that game and go on to her house where we would occupy ourselves with her piano. She had learned to play some, and as I was the one who could "cord" only, she taught me to play a duet with her of the song, "Under the Double Eagle." We spent hours perfecting that song, and it certainly filled in our time out of school. Querita's dry humor was something else, too. She could master that. One day she told me that a friend of ours lost his mother. I was upset, and it was true, and I asked my friend, "Why did she die?" Querita mulled that over, looked at me, shrugged her shoulders, and said, "Well, the breath all leaked out of her." I was a little stunned. Then she burst out laughing, and I laughed, and we went off toward her house, me hoping her mother had something for us to eat.

* * *

I truly wonder what, if anything, my panther fears could have begun a couple of years before at Lavaca when my father and his buddies went deer hunting in the Ouchita Mountains, when he proudly brought home a gray-striped bob cat. [I doubt it.] He didn't get a deer for food, but he surely got his bob cat to show off.

After showing the poor creature all over the small town, he finally brought it home and dumped it on papers onto our kitchen floor to stay there throughout the night, keeping it from hungry dogs until he could skin it the following day.

There it lay, motionless, through a lone night for me, it was for sure. The full moon shone through the kitchen window, and from my bed in the next room I had a clear view of the cat. I watched to see if it moved until my eyes were tired of looking. At times I was certain it moved, or, at least, jerked a leg. It was a big bob-cat, the likes I had never seen before, and I did not once want to pet it, and once the skin was carefully removed and salted down, then stretched to dry, I would look at it curiously. One bullet hole marred the pelt where dad made a perfect shot into the chest. For years mother had a cute, throw rug set, out of the way of traffic until we left for California in 1943. I truly feel the bob-cat didn't determine my later panther fears, because I saw the dead cat, understood the pelt would be used, watched the process of drying, and the pelt became a house hold ornament. It was similar to a friend.

Dad told us from his deer perch blind in the mountains, he watched a doe and her fawn enter the clearing he was watching. Then he saw the large bob-cat cautiously pad forward in a crouching position, ready to take the fawn. He fired, killing the predator, and saved the little fawn. His buddies backed him up on this.

I was under conviction, and my head spun with dizzy elation of something I couldn't describe. I thought people only told inaccurate accounts of their being "saved" to go along with the masses of people who were Christians, but what was wrong with me? Could I be wrongfully injected with a dose of the Holy Spirit along with these masses, or was I actually experiencing the working of the grace of God? I was like a love sick calf, never knowing if I was coming or going, but it was all different from what one human had for another human. I was being pursued by something bigger than my puny life.

I knew Jesus. I knew my comforter, my Protector, without being totally infused with the Spirit that counted; the Holy Spirit of God. I had plagued the Lord, and asked so many questions, and he always kept me from being run over by trains, or burned alive, and he always came to me to gently rock me to sleep and dry my tears.

We were visiting my father's parents in Nowata, and I began to hang about my Uncle Jim's and Aunt Nannie's, my cousins, Stella, Ralph, and Ray. Ralph was my age, and teased me horribly about how skinny I was and how silly I talked. But it was Uncle Jim I needed to talk to. He was a renowned Baptist minister, and he certainly could help me with my problem, I thought, so I approached him in an almost hesitant manner. He was reading, but laid aside his book, and slipped the glasses off to peer at me.

"I think I need your help," I began.

"I'll be happy to if I can," he said, his blue eyes piercing, but I think he already knew my need. "Now tell Me." "I can only think about the Lord Jesus," I murmured softly. A big smile broke his serious look, and he took my small hands in his. "Ah," he said, just like the wise man he was.

"And you need him in your life, is that it?" he continued.

"I've had him all along, and I know he is there, but now I don't know what to do next," I answered.

"Alma, God loves you and, now, He wants to send the Holy Spirit to dwell within you, to be your guide in all matters. His son, Jesus Christ, is to be present in your life, and you are to have a special, personal relationship with him." He hesitated, looked at me closely and asked, "Do you understand?"

"Yes, I said, "but, I am under----uh,under---"

"Conviction?" He filled in for me.

"Yes, What do I do next? What does God want me to do now?" He was all big smiles now.

"You, young lady, are being saved as we speak," he said,

so happy I thought he would split.

"Now you will go forward Sunday night and confess your sins and be embraced by the angels in heaven."

Uncle Jim prayed a prayer of thanks to God, and asked Him to guide me and protect me, his special child, Christ's child.

I left feeling much better, and while my petition was being put in to God, I went in search of Cousin Ralph. I had to bust him in the mouth.

Sunday night, I went forward, and told the people present that I wanted to give my life to Jesus, I was happy, but tears spilled over anyway.

The moon was bright as I got to Grandpa's house on Sycamore Street, but the lights were all out. Everyone was in bed. I needed to tell someone, but who? Grandpa was a Methodist and didn't care for uncle Jim, his son-in-law, so that was out. Grannie?--Naw. Certainly not dad, also a Methodist... of sorts. I know, I said to myself. I'll tell mother.

The front door was unlocked for me, and I quietly went inside, careful not to slam the door, or kick over something. My eyes adjusted, and I could see the moonlight shining through the bedroom windows, and cautiously approached the side of the bed where mother was lying. Her head raised up off the pillow, and I knew she was awake, so I knelt down and whispered, "Mama, I was saved tonight."

"Go to bed," she said back to me, and I took off my clothes and laid down by Bettye on the floor pallet.

That was it. It was never discussed.

It was 1937, and I was twelve years old.

* * *

I don't really know why I felt I must dig deeper into my mind and perhaps come up with something that will make a monster out of my father. As I've said many times before to my sisters, I did not particularly like him. Actually, I stayed out of his way, went about my childhood business as much as possible, and felt free when he left for a job that would keep him away for some time, I could tolerate mother's switchings, but I could do without my father's more harsh physical abuse. When I left, if mother wasn't distraut over what she accepted as abandonment, never knowing if he would return or not, I, on the other hand, was euphoric, running about like a woods deer, crazy wild as a desert burro.

Two incidents come to mind, because they make me feel uncomfortable every time I think of them. It is true I was never sexually molested, but were the other times I barely escaped simply because I was a rascal of a child and young adult, and I feel strongly that God watched over me? It is also true I seemed to have a built in radar warning system that told me to flee a situation that just didn't feel right. If I had been sexually molested, it would have had to be when I was so young I couldn't remember.

One of these incidents involved dad, and even though there was a sexual overtone, one was done in presence of my family and I think my Grandmother Michael, and was considered a scolding that turned into a tease. This is difficult to describe, and I must be very careful not to distort the happening, or make it appear more humiliating than it was.

But it surely happened.

We were living at my grandparents for lack of a home. Of course, dad was between jobs, and he was stressed, I'm sure, because of the dislike for Grandpa and my Uncle had for him. They ridiculed him, because he couldn't seem to have a permanent, or stable job.

None the less, I was thirteen, wearing a flour sack dress of questionable design-sort of little, flitty flowers on a white background mother made that was too tight across my chest. I was a late bloomer in the breast department, very skinny, but I did have the beginnings of little marbles, two of the most painful, sensitive little nubbins that poked out against the harsh cotton fabric. They were raw.

I was called in on the screened back porch for a talking to. I don't recall what I had done. Maybe I hadn't answered a call to perform a chore. Who knows now? While the others looked on, I went up and stood as close to dad as I dared.

I didn't cry until the scolding ended and a teasing grin came on dad's face. He reached out, while saying to me, "here you are growing titties and you act like this," and grabbed my right marble of a breast between the knuckles of his two first fingers and gave a twist. I remember the pain and humiliation. I yelled and fast as a rabbit, ran out the screen door. I can still feel the tremendous anger I felt for him. Maybe, this anger along with other personality feelings, kept me wary, and safe. I didn't like anyone to touch me, or hug me too closely. Man or woman. I do remember this now. I was a laughing, singing, dancing little thing, but I also had a wild streak.

The second incident was a scary one for me, because it was the first indication of my built in alarm system. I was only eight or nine, went home after school with a chum who needed to change her clothes before we could play out. Her mother was not home, but a drunken man was there drinking from a bottle.

My friend went to her room to change. The man started talking to me. I stood waiting for my friend. Suddenly, the man reached out and pulled me over onto his lap. I sat on an erection which startled me, the first bad feeling emerging, and I got up off his lap and raced outside to wait for my friend. I asked her if that was her daddy. She said he was not, but was her mother's boyfriend.

I still wonder if my friend had been sexually abused by him. Chances point that way. Poor children are so innocent. Why aren't mothers more aware.

It was only several years ago I asked a psychiatrist who knew me well why I'd never been sexually molested? He laughed, and explained it, "Look at you, your personality. If you were to be raped, the rapist would have had to kill you, and the sexual molesters just happened to not be murderers. You are one of the lucky ones."

Thanks for my divine Protector. Thanks for the alarm system. Thanks for the wild streak. Thanks to God.

Chapter Seven

As Betty's health worsened, I appeared at a standstill except for occasional migraines. At times I experienced weakness and a swimmy head. Mother said I was too active, that racing about and standing on my head did a lot to cause the headaches. I knew of no other child who suffered migraines. Jimmy Peters was the only other child I knew who was sick, and I knew he didn't have headaches. My legs ached, too, and I was told that I was growing tall too fast. I wanted to be tall. That was neat, but I didn't like the leg cramps. When we visited Uncle Leon in Slatonville, I borrowed one of the Waters kid's bicycle, a spindly looking thing, but sturdy enough to ride the smooth ruts in an otherwise graveled road.

I tested myself on it, deciding I was going to give the very slightly inclined hill a go leading up to uncle's house. I started out great, then coasted back down the hill, caught my breath, and began my second ascent, pedaling like crazy to gain more speed before I hit the half way mark to the top of the hill.

Before I reached the half-way mark, I suddenly ran out of steam, my legs began to ache and were so weak I had to break before I leaned the bike over to literally fall off it onto the road. My head was dizzy and a screen of black was beginning to close over my eyes. My breathing was too labored to simply be a simple case of working up steam. My chest hurt, and I could barely lift my hands. I couldn't even holler for help. The road was deserted, and nobody could spot me where I lay, I gasped, and coughed, rasping coughs.

It seemed to me I had lain there forever, basically unable to stand, and my extreme exhaustion kept me there until I slowly dragged myself up to a standing position. I began to breath easier, my head cleared, but my legs still felt weak, and they trembled ever so lightly. I breathed deeper now, but I felt ill, like when I would come down with a cold.

I brushed gravel out of my bloody knees, and palms of my hands, picked up the bike and walked it up to uncle Leon's. I told mother I fell to explain my condition, but I didn't even try to explain why. I didn't feel up to par for a few days.

It is exceedingly frightening when a child does not trust her father, especially when he is only giving a warning, that what he says to protect that child is not accepted, and danger is imminent---perhaps death.

While still at Uncle Leon's, I must have been wandering about searching for something and decided to look inside the barn. Uncle Leon and dad were close by talking as I entered the big open doors, the floor strewn with straw. I had reached the back of the barn where halters, straps, and other leather accouterments were hanging, and I had my eyes on these and my mind elsewhere when I heard dad call out.

"Alma! Stay in the barn. Don't come out. You hear?"

Alarm systems went off in my brain, and I was almost paralyzed with dread that I had done something and dad was going to hem me in the barn and use some of the leather stuff on me. Of course, this premise wasn't truly valid, but I was reacting to my father's past behavior which had always shown to me punishment without love, and usually expedited sporadically and without compunction, I was tensed to the max as I turned about, expecting him to be right at my back.

"Stay in the barn! Do not come out!" dad yelled out, outside the barn.

In a split second I raced toward the open door, throwing all caution to the winds, my feet barely stirring up the straw. I was making high jumps as fast as my feet hit ground that would spring me higher, and I sailed out the doors, and there was dad, his face looking frightened, a look that quickly turned to anger.

He grabbed my spindly arm and jerked me about in time for me to see Uncle Leon laying with deadly force into the neck and head of a large mountain rattler with a hoe. The snake had been coiled in the middle of the double doors, probably was there when I entered, and I never saw it.

Uncle Leon said that as I ran out, I leaped over the snake that struck at my foot and missed by only a few inches. Dad, furious because I did not obey his warning, jerked me about and soundly swatted my rear with his bare hands.

All this was awful for me. Was I not level headed enough to handle a warning from my father to stay put? Why didn't I stay put?

Not only was lack of trust a factor here, but I truly feel that if dad had called me in a more gentle way and explained that there was a snake coiled up in the middle of the door, and after they killed it I could come out. And, I know now, too, that if Uncle Leon had been the one calling out to me, I would not have reacted as I did.

I feel bad about this; that I went into an aimless panic. What about dad? What must he have thought of me, or did he ever think on the real reason I did not trust him?

Bettye was becoming worse in her behavior. Her tantrums were more frequent and more intense as the school year approached. We stopped singing completely, and I always managed to cause her distress. She bellowed at me, swung her fists at me, and cried incessantly. The mere sight of me ticked her off, so I started attempting to stay away from her as conveniently as I could. We all started into school with some trepidation, for the older we got, the more we became closer to realizing our poverty and the unhappy situation that appeared unending. Even Bettye gave classes her best shot, but her worsening equilibrium imbalance soon became a focus for taunting by some of her old school chums.

One day when Bettye and the girls in her class were

playing basketball in the school yard after regular school hours, the girls started teasing her. I was off to the side watching the game when the teasing began, and one larger girl approached Bettye menacingly, yelled at her and gave her a rough push, sending Bettye sprawling onto the rough, dirt court.

I picked up a stick and raced out toward the court, screaming in fury at the top of my lungs, brandishing the stick. Bettye was sobbing and nervously shaking. I could instantly tell she was having trouble, breathing too harshly, almost asthmatic, and I tore toward the big girl, who broke away running, laughing at first, but when I kept coming after her she stopped the laughter and picked up speed. I chased her almost to her house, before I stopped. Unhappily, I trudged back and walked home with my sister. She was heartbroken, and conveyed to me an unbelievable hopelessness. Her shining spirit had been almost brought to its knees, and was at its lowest form, I believe, at that particular time. She needed help, someone to care about her, and for her. Was everybody going to stand back and watch her die?

At this time, she pushed me away, farther and farther. I was younger, and a pain in the butt, and certainly not to be counted on to help her in her fight of a private hell none of us knew about. Only her behavior and nervousness told us of her pain. She was pretty, and the shape her slim body was already showing could shame other girls, and her smile, when she could smile, was dazzling.

It was during this time that my sister would be out of school a lot, and as it turned out, mother stopped sending her altogether. What were my parents thinking of? Wait until Bettye lived, or died, or whatever? Recently, I asked my mother why she and dad didn't pursue medical help for Bettye? Her answer was so simple---they didn't know what to do. My problem in not being able to understand this reason probably is due to the way I acted later on about my own children----get help for my children even if I must sacrifice my own life; yell, beg, whatever it took. But, perhaps I am being too harsh. As I've said, those times were extremely hard on the poor. Maybe mother really didn't know what to do, but I'll bet dad would have known, if he had cared enough.

Meanwhile, we were not progressing at all, life-wise, and the cruel days passed. Each day was simply another crack in our psychical being, more fuel added to the relentless fires of bad experiences emotionally, and the lack of expectations of physical needs to maintain our survival. Sooner or later there would be a weaker one of us to fall, never to pick up the torch of tenacity and keep going.

Bettye was angry and chasing me. It had been raining all day, and we were thrown together in the house where reading, drawing, and other activities weren't working, so we became somewhat bored. Finally, the rain stopped, and Roy Dyer came over. Up the bean tree he climbed, and I was enough ahead of Bettye to get a proper run at the tree, and up I went. When Roy and I got up as high as we could, I turned and looked below to see what Bettye was doing, never thinking she would climb the wet barked tree with dripping limbs. But, by gosh, there she was making progress out of sheer determination, in her overalls, and stupid-looking brown, high topped tennis shoes we had back then---her out-door court, basketball clothes. She kept coming up and put a foot out on the foremost big limb. I wasn't aware of how she was hanging on, when to my horror, her slick shoe sole did not provide her with good footing, and she fell heavily onto the sopping wet ground upon her back. The back of her head took the same power blow as did her body, and she was out like a light.

Roy and I descended the tree in amazing speed, he going off yelling for his folks, and I was screaming after seeing Bettye lying there upon that ground like a poor rag doll. I knew she was dead, and dad not being home, I raced still screaming up the back road to Mr. McFaddin's house. Mr. McFaddin ran out after hearing all the screaming, caught me racing toward him, grabbed me and led me back by the hand, me sobbing my head off. We got there when Mr. Dyer and others were carrying the unconscious Bettye into the house, and laid her upon the bed.

She was breathing, they noted, but barely. Her eyes were closed, and her face, bereft of all color, looked like a death mask.

I was in a fit of shaking. Couldn't seem to stop, and I remembered the uncontrollable chattering of my teeth. Roy came as far as the front porch, his eyes big as saucers, himself pale from fright. We both blamed ourselves. At least, I blamed myself. Would dad whip me? Would he banish me forever to the farm? The worry was a double whammer. The time was about four p.m. By dinner time Bettye still hadn't regained consciousness. A couple more hours passed. Mother lit the coal oil lamp, and the neighbors sat with her at the bedside. Waiting. For Bettye to die.

Midland had a doctor, but nobody sent for him. I remember the doctor well, for he had set Jackie Scott's broken leg after we kids were jumping ditches. There was a doctor. Maybe he was out of town; somewhere else.

I don't remember dad, or Herb being there. I'm sure dad was there and my memory didn't record him.

Bettye stayed in the unconsciousness state until midnight, so mother said. I do not remember sleeping that night before Bettye woke, but even though I was one to stay awake nights, I don't really know if the vigil was until the morning, or what happened. I do know Bettye's fall was serious, and I would guess she had received a severe concussion. She didn't come out of the accident feeling well at all. By all indications, her health deteriorated. She was set back. Once again, she got up on her two legs like a determined kitten that had been wounded, and tried so hard to keep up.

Two years later, Bettye was so sick that all school for her was suspended, and everyone stood back with almost indifferent attitudes, and watched as she fought to gain a new hold on life. She still threw temper tantrums, and cried bitter tears of depression, and the rest of us hung on. Her eyes went back to normal, her equilibrium returned almost to the way it was before the sickness struck, but she would always be Bettye, sweet one minute and throwing things the next. She was Bettye.

The school was presenting another night of entertainment, mostly musical, and I was asked to sing, not only in our choir in the alto section, but in a special duet with another classmate. We practiced daily until time arrived.

The music teacher requested all boys wear white shirts and dark pants, and the girls were to be in white dresses. I went to my mother and told her what we were to do, and that I needed a white dress. I also asked her and the family to attend. She told me it couldn't be done, and the days passed.

I didn't know what to do about the whole situation, and felt another set back from my family. Even though I wasn't surprised, I was disappointed.

I finally decided to go talk to a young woman near us, and across the woods, who had befriended Bettye and me in the past, whose last name was Duffle. I told her my problem, and to my excited surprise, she not only fashioned a white dress for me, but washed my blond hair and put soft waves in it. I was beside myself with joy. I could go to the musical and feel so very good about my appearance.

I really didn't know what my parents thought about it, but my excitement had to have made them aware of what was taking place, because dad approached Herb, and told him to make sure he escorted me back home afterwards. It was a long walk to school, and near our place was a dark wooded area extending almost a city block. There were no street lights, except one faint yellow one on Main Street, but that was the extent of it. On top of that, people in Midland in the late thirties didn't have porch lights, unless it was Mr. Peters, so on the moonless night I felt safe with my brother to see that I was to get home.

The musical was a big hit. We kids sang our hearts out for the friendly audience on the same stage where dad gave his chalk talk while Bettye and I sang. Later, families stood about talking and congratulating their children, and praising the teacher of the almost perfect presentation.

I stood about as parents left with their children, and a small bus left with its rural students. My brother wasn't anywhere to be seen, so I waited some more. Soon the man who locked up, saw me and asked how long I would be. I told him Herb should be here shortly, so he asked me to stay outside and wait. He shut off lights, locked the door and left.

I will say this much. I thought I had never seen this much darkness, but I was familiar with it in my nights. This was such a suffocating blackness I was as a blind person, but I eased down the concern I felt by telling myself Herb would be along any second. I waited some more, then some more. I was getting cold, and soon began to try to force the terror back as I came to the conclusion Herb wasn't coming at all. He had forgotten all about me.

I tried to visualize the walkway from the school, across the yard, and into the street. There were no sidewalks, so I had to use my head, tried not to panic, and slowly move along step by step. It was a long way home, and it was getting late. If there had only been a moon that night, I would have been much braver.

Lights were mostly off in the houses, but as I moved along, hoping I was in the middle of the road, a small lighted window here and there would tell me where I was. When I got to Main Street, the pale light on the pole there seemed like a welcomed, old friend. But, soon I was out of the light, and began the long approach past dark, silent houses and the dense copse of woods. We lived in the very last house up past the dark woods.

I tried to think of other things more pleasant as I stumbled along, praying I was staying on the straight line. It was slow going, and soon the "pleasant thought" plan disappeared with a great 'pop' as the black panther with yellow eyes invaded my terrified mind. In my panic I still knew enough not to even attempt to start running. That would be unwise of me. I'd fall in the little branch of water where Roy and I caught crawdads, and ruin Miss Duffle's dress, and I'd be a mess.

Of course, the panther padded silently stalking me every stop of the way, and if I ran, he would run after me, and tear me to shreds. For all it was worth, I couldn't stop that scenario at all, hard as I tried. My strength lay in how calmly I could be about all this. Finally, I reached our house, and amazingly, my eyes had adapted, however late, and I saw faint outlines---the house, the front porch. I was here in one piece, but began to worry about Herb. If I go into the dark house and dad hears me, and he does not hear Herb come in also, I'd get Herb into trouble. So I sat on the front porch, up against the house close to the bedroom Bettye and I slept in, raised up my knees and pulled my dress over them, and waited. I was really getting cold now, and my head was drooping. I could almost imagine dad knew I was there, but I tried not to make a sound. But, as it got very late, I had to go in, ease in the door ever so quietly, not to wake anyone, took off my shoes in the dark and the dress, and climbed easily into bed beside Bettye. I never heard Herb come in. I was dead tired.

The following day, dad called Herb into the front room, but I did not hear the few accusing words dad said, nor did I hear Herb's replies. But, I closed my ears with my hands, and ran out the back door when dad took his belt, and, as I was told by Bettye later, forced my brother to take off his shirt, and proceeded to whip him across his back. Herb never made a sound.

Herb came out the back door, his shirt in his hands, his eyes blazing, and he said to me, "This is all your fault---- all your fault." He walked down the road to town.

Herb was out with a girl that night, and he had other things on his mind; something much better than taking his little sister home from a school musical. He never got over blaming me and I carried guilt until I got big enough to understand.

*   *   *   *   *

Mama stood looking out the kitchen window, watching the new fallen leaves scuttle across the dirt yard. She watched for a while, her hand holding the curtain back, then began a poem:

"come, little leaves said the wind one day.
come over to the meadow with me and play.
Put on your dresses of red and gold;
For summer has flown, and the wind grows cold."

There were two more verses, but I can't remember them. She had an almost forlorn expression on her face, and I was sure she was beginning to dread the winter closely ahead.

It was a beautiful poem, and today I still do not know the name of the poem, or the title of it, but I catch myself voicing the words over, my mind dancing with the perfect rhythm of the lines.

The sound of mama's voice was indeed a lament of foreboding, for the coming winter would be a nightmare of extreme proportions. Had she only known at the time she was reciting the poem! I feared for her sanity and her very life.

I wondered when in the world had dad built that skeleton like structure, painted orange with two seats up front, all open to the winter, wide--long flat bed for transporting a large amount of ---something. It was his latest hair-brained idea, and this one certainly wasn't going to get off the ground, I was wagering. I'd always heard that fools only dreamed and a genius acted on their dreams. Well, dad was doing it alright, but what? The sedan car was gone. Dad must have sold it, because I don't remember it after our latest trip to Nowata when mother acquired Old Shag, a Persian cat, and the way I remember having the car was that Shag, short for Shag Nasty, slept up under the rear window all the way back to Midland. I wasn't usually consulted in matters of sudden moves, or dream schemes, so can't say what the plans were, but I'll just bet I figured out it was of such enthusiastic certainly that it would make us rich---again. The orange "thing" was carelessly termed a "truck", and he no doubt built it where the Yellow Jacket was born a thousand years back.

Dad took Herb out of school, at sixteen, a high school football hero for the Hartford Hustlers, and I'm positive it was against his will. I really don't remember his mood at the time. All high school students were bussed to Hartford, nine miles away, from the Midland area, and missing school for him was against his grain. It was about the last of November, 1937. With big plans of going off and making it rich in the big yonder, as sugar plums cerebrally floating in dad's brain, we all bedded down to get some sleep. I couldn't help but wonder how mother was taking all this. The morning came dark and cold as we all hustled out of bed for the big departure. I looked out the window and watched a quiet, healthy snowfall coming down with wind blowing, and drifts beginning to pile high. It must have been snowing all night.

Soon, mother had a pan of biscuits and pan gravy on the table. She wore a strained look on her face and something else---anger. I couldn't say as I blamed her.

By mid-morning the snow let up, but left roads seemingly impassible. That, of course, didn't stop dad. He and Herb bundled up like a couple of Russians, and darned if they didn't wave good bye to us and got onto their seats after brushing snow off the "thing", prime and start it. Great billows of white smoke filled the air from the scrounged-up tail pipe, and we watched at the kitchen window as they went carefully up the road by Mr. McFaddin's house, turned and was soon out of sight.

All the control drained out of mother, and she sat down at the kitchen table amidst all the breakfast leavings, put her head down, and sobbed. We girls were quiet, but felt a premonition that it was going to be a very long winter, and we were so right.

It wasn't too long before I discovered mother had very little knowledge where dad was heading. There was very little food stuffs in the cupboards, water was almost gone, which had to be carried from under the hill down toward Mr. Bailey's place, and our woodpile was low, and only a few chunks of coal were left under the deep snow. It was a dismal atmosphere, indeed.

Bettye was still sick, and winter was one of her worst

enemies. She had chest colds, infected tonsils, and generally ran fevers. Peggy almost seven now, was susceptible to chest colds, and we all suffered croup. How long mother could stretch the food was anybody's guess, but from her marriage to dad, she must have learned good. We had flour, corn meal, some lard, coffee, sugar, split beans, a few small, frozen potatoes, popcorn from grandpa Michael, and a couple of cans of Pet Milk. I remember clearly the picture of the Jersey cow on the milk labels.

School was closed indefinitely, for the gray clouds saw fit to hang around and greet us with more snow. Everything was at a standstill, and all of Midland lay under the white, fluffy stuff. The only sounds we heard were the wind as it whipped around the corner of our thin house and rattled our thin panel windows, and limbs of snow laden trees crackling to fall into deep drifts. The whole landscape was sterile, and our fires were puny at times as we four beings huddled around the kitchen stove. Mother closed off the two bedrooms, and we didn't bother to keep the pot belly stove going. We had to save the wood. By Christmas we were almost out of food, and precious little wood was left. Mother was becoming completely useless, as she sat by the stove crying, rocking back and forth, her expressive hands moving constantly, as she droned on and on, "What am I to do? What am I to do?" Peggy tried to stay close to mother, while Bettye and I put on our thin coats and worn shoes, took an old Red Flyer wagon, and set out to gather in wood. It was getting colder, had stopped snowing, but the days remained somber as the stubborn clouds refused to leave. We trudged out toward the railroad tracks, where some dead trees had shed their broken limbs, and we filled up the wagon, and as much wood as we could also carry.

Then a miracle began to unfold for us, we saw the possibilities available to us as the Midland train started passing through, a shorter train provided by the coal mine industry in our area, so it always ran much slower than the bigger and longer trains.

The engineers saw us three, little urchins gathering

wood and sticks along the track, and threw kisses and waves, and something else very precious--lumps of coal, longer lasting than dead wood! We laughed to thank them, waved our pleasure at them with black, grimy hands, and felt such a burning spark of rebirth at someone's caring for three strange, small specters in the snow. We took the loaded wagon, heavier now, back home to show mama, and she could be happy again.

Throughout the trial winter, we girls stood out by the tracks waiting for the Midland train. Sometimes it didn't come, but when it did, we knew the lumps of coal would be thrown down to us by hearts that cared. We knew those engineers had children of their own, and we always went through our dances of thanks to them, jumping for joy, waving and cheering.

Mother fed us popcorn with diluted Pet milk poured over it, and small portions of it that one morning, but we girls didn't mind too much. We hadn't come down with any bad cases of pneumonia despite being out gathering wood and carrying water. The days were still without the sun, adding to our misery that much more. We tried to walk to the post office often just in case dad sent us a letter with money to buy food, but there never was a letter. This added to mother's suffering. Why didn't he send us some word that would end our dread of each coming morning.? Even mother's parents and brothers couldn't bother to check on us to find out if we were alright. Of course mother seldom bothered them unless she had been compelled out of desperation, and she usually had to endure recriminations, and as she termed it, tongue lashings, if she asked for help. On this particular day , mother wanted to wash some of our clothes and we needed water. The hill was icy and extremely precarious to unsteady feet as we reached the rock-walled well with a pulley unit, and galvanized bucket to be let down and drawn back up again. It was a miserable task, the frozen bucket sticking to already frozen fingers, but we had to get water---we couldn't do without.

Going back up the hill was the hard part, but we always managed to make it to the house without too much spilled. It was to much for mother in her fragile state, and she slipped and fell at the back steps, her bucket skidding about, spilling all its precious contents. She screamed out, then in complete abjection, beat the hard ice with her fists, yelling out her extreme objection of her hopeless condition.

I was terrified that she had reached the end of her courage that may allow her poor spirit to flounder and, perhaps die. Her hair was in disarray, her face whiter than the snow she lay upon, and I felt by the look in her eyes that she cared neither for her life, or ours.

I squatted down beside her, and helped her up as Bettye held the door open for us.

"The water. The water," she kept saying. I told her I'd go after it, not to worry. We got her inside, and all three of us took off her wet shoes, her thin coat, and settled her in the rocker next to the stove. Peggy hovered about her, soothing her as I grabbed up the bucket where it had fallen, and made off down the hill to the well. As I neared the well the sun broke through the clouds in the West and turned them to ribbons of red and gold. Momentarily, there was an uplifting of my heart, but just for a brief moment. I felt guilty of the fleeting feeling of hope inside my heaving, skinny ribs, but couldn't take my eyes off the brave sun until it faded, then I scurried up the hill.

Mother had collapsed into a pitiful heap in the rocking chair, her strength drained from her slim body. Her eyes darted about the room as she rocked, clasping her hands and wailing, "What am I to do? Oh mercy, what is to become of me?"

The next day mother told us we would just have to starve and die together. This was the end. We couldn't make it. We could all just go to bed and stay there. We would die of starvation and freeze.

Bettye said, "No we will not." Her blue eyes snapped, not in fright, but in disgust.

"I can go to Mr. Peters," I said

"Yes," said Bettye. "Go and ask for what we need."

"But Virgil Peters told us he would not give us more credit until we paid up for the bill we already owe," mother whimpered.

I was already in my coat, and Bettye and mother were making out a list of necessary food stuff for me to get. I'd go to the post office, too, and maybe, just maybe, there would be a letter from dad and Herb.

I entered the blessed warmth of Mr. Peter's grocery store, and waited until the store was empty of customers. I gave Mr. Peters the list, and told him we needed food.

He shook his head and said, "I can't give you anymore groceries on credit. The last bill hasn't been paid, and I can't continue carrying you."

"But we have to have it. We have to Mr. Peters." I refused to take the list he was handing back to me.

The door opened and a man came in cheerful, talking about the weather and Christmas coming up. I backed up to get out of his way, and stood there. The man left with his purchase. I stood there. Other customers came and went, some who knew me and smiled briefly. I would not leave until I got the badly needed food. I kept my eyes on Mr. Peters as he moved about.

Finally, Mr. Peters began putting groceries in a bag from my list. Without moving or saying a word---without a grin on my face, my scared heart just soared. If a little girl can thank her Jesus, this little girl did. Mr. Peters shook his head a couple of times, wrote up the new credit bill, and handed me the bag saying, "Give the bill to your daddy now. Tell him I need to be paid." I nodded my head, said "thanks", and left.

My heart hurts now as I think back then, and I look inside my modest home, the electricity, bathroom, proper heating, microwave, electric blanket--oh the electric blanket is a dream come true.---all the conveniences fifty years can make, and I weep for my mother, sisters and brother of the actual suffering endured back in the awful thirties. It seems as if I cannot fully appreciate the comfort I enjoy now, because of the memories of our suffering then.

School had opened again by the time Christmas came. Dad and Herb had not returned, and I believe we three girls stayed home until the weather became better, and the snow finally melted. None-the-less, it was still icy cold, and the water in our bucket in the kitchen had ice on top when we arose from bed in the mornings. We girls continued to collect wood, and lumps of coal, and mother didn't go draw water anymore; we girls did.

We knew there would be no Christmas for us again. Mother's relations didn't make an appearance at all in our need, and I, like mother harbored some newly found opinions of grandpa & grandma, especially; they, with so much food that I actually dreamed of milk, butter, eggs, hot breads, fried chicken, cuts of beef and pork, sugar-cured hams,---the list is endless. They appeared indifferent, or just couldn't be bothered with a daughter who married against their will, and the children produced by that marriage.

It was Christmas eve when mother told us quite bluntly there would be no presents for us. We knew that, but what I can't understand is why didn't mother try a little more, be more resourceful, and, at least, make little Peggy a rag doll out of scraps, buttons for eyes, embroidered lips and eyebrows? Bettye and I were older. We expected it. But Peggy would have been delighted with something mother could make on her sewing machine, and stitched by hand, to put in a child's stocking who still needed to count on Santa. That little girl suffered all through her life with us, loved us unconditionally, and would have been miserable without us. She depended upon mother and dad. Why couldn't they have pinched out a little love for her, at least, and stopped thinking only of their problems, and their feelings.

I can't remember when dad and Herb returned home. I do know that they did not bring money, and I never heard explanations of where they went and what they did. Herb had very little to say. He seemed to have grown up quietly, began smoking cigarettes, rolling his own, got back into school without a hitch , and gave the pretty girls a chase they would never forget. He was extremely good looking, and had charming ways. Or so all the girls thought. Bettye, I, and Peggy couldn't see any of the charm; the gals shrieked about. After all, he was only our big brother who basically ignored us. And mother was beginning to look at dad differently, I suspected. She felt he was not faithful to her when he went off alone on "jobs".

One day, I found dad's wallet lying on the floor in "their" room, and picked it up. I carelessly flipped it open, and there looking out at me was a somewhat attractive woman wearing a full, fur collar, in a picture signed by love. I sucked in my breath as I stared at the face. Mother called me from the kitchen.

I held the wallet out to her, and asked her who the woman was. Normally, she would have scolded, or slapped my face for snooping, but when I saw her face whiten and her lips draw up, maybe I did something more wrong than would have drawn a scolding.

"Where did you get this?" she asked me with tight lips.

"On the floor'" I answered.

"That's your dad's old girlfriend who lives in Nowata."

I had heard later on when dad went off on jobs without us, he had this girlfriend meet him, and dad had a good, old time of it. I didn't want to speculate too much, but I felt I could probably believe it.

There were three times I can remember mother asking me to write dad when he was off working, to remind him to send money for food, and rent, and fuel. She told me what to write. I couldn't understand why she didn't write the letters herself, or why she chose me to write them for her. I asked myself back then why dad chose to completely ignore us, and wouldn't supply us with our needs when he worked and made good money on the bridge construction.

Today, I have the same opinion as I did back then. He cared little for us, and he didn't provide for us properly. I think he loved mother, and needed her sexually. That is when he would come back home after a job. I also feel that when we moved to his jobs with him, it was at mother's insistence, to be in his bed instead of the other woman, and we were fed when we were with him. That is my opinion.

Shortly, we locked up our house in Midland and moved

to Prairie Grove, Arkansas, where Bettye, Peggy, and I entered school. Herb chose to stay at Grandpa and Grandma Michael's, riding the school bus into Hartford to continue school there. Bettye and I continued our duet-singing in church and in school functions. After that we were back in Midland again to stay only long enough to wait for dad's next construction job.

Bettye's health was improving, and she had gained weight and height, for she was fifteen at this time. I never hit out at her, or slapped at her, although she continued her physical abuse of me, and her harsh tongue could cut steel. With her two years upon me, she loomed over me, her fists battering rams. Actually, we never got out of our treatment of her from her sick years when the doctors warned us never to irritate her to start her on her rampages, but I thoroughly believe those years had spoiled her, and it was simply too late to make any alterations, or adjustments on our part to rectify the obstreperous behavior. I, for one, was awfully weary of having to walk on egg shells to keep her in a harmonious mood. Bettye continued to resist me, and told me in so many words that she was older and smarter than I, prettier than I, could do anything so much better than I, and, always the clincher, that mama and daddy loved her best.

Of course, I was beginning to spot a bundle of holes in her redundant and incessant tyrannical verbage, its total purpose to crush my own self-esteem and keep me in a state of humiliation. To be quite honest, she was bombarding my mind with degrading remarks that began to disgust me. I didn't want to fight back physically, a crude act I felt was unseemly for rational people to behave. But, then, I never considered Bettye rational.

I ran from the house, hitting the screen door, down the steps, Bettye in hot pursuit. I'd done something to cause her to seek angry revenge, and I was in trouble if I couldn't escape. She caught me by the hair of the head, slammed me down on the ground onto my back jumped upon my chest with her knees, and proceeded to bang my head onto the hard dirt. Then, she clamped both hands across my neck in a choke hold and demanded, "Say calf's rope! You say calf's rope, you hear?" ["Calf's rope was a euphemism of "I surrender" in our part of the country then.] She was hot and sweaty---she always seemed to me all our growing up years, to have a higher degree of body heat than anyone else I knew. I wanted her up, off me. I tried not to show my panic of being held down, which I tried never to get into, and I didn't want her to know of the phobia of mine, so I said "calf's rope". She pushed harder on my chest with her knees, and told me to repeat it, and louder. I did, and she got off me, looked at me as if I was a snake, and told me never to cross her, or she would hurt me bad.

All through our lives together she always managed to make subtle statements, or remarks to me, of how she could hurt people, her laughable threats were so obviously made up to attempt to gain control of me in the very beginning, and has continued all through life to remind me of her hold over me. I was really surprised that she didn't actually know I was simply allowing her to be the bully as always to keep peace. By the time I was fifteen I could have overcome her so easily but, as I said, I wanted peace. Once, I'd had all I could take of Bettye and her bullying ways, so, once again I allowed her to chase me out of the house. Out on the road, I could run like the wind, so as I was ahead of her, I stopped, turned about, stuck my thumbs in my ears, flapped my fingers, and stuck out my tongue. She went bananas, and pursued me with added fervor, and up a tree I went. You think that was smart of me? Oh, no, I was up a tree. She sauntered back to the house. I would eventually have to come down, and I knew she would be ready, but with what kind of weapon?

Suppertime, I decided I would give it a try. Perhaps Bettye had other things to do, but I knew better. Bettye was like dad in that they could be patient. Mother was not patient. Mother could slap me over and over again, and it would be over. Bettye had a devious mind.

I left the safety of the tree, because I certainly couldn't perch up there all night. I'd have to face the music, but carefully

I went around the back side of the house, when from behind a nearby tree there was a sudden movement, and with her fists doubled together for maximum force, she swung catching me smack on the forehead and over the ear. I was knocked completely down, shocked at my own surprise and stupidity. She quietly went into the house.

I washed my face, the tears were streaming at this point, and I was so glad the wash pan and water were out on the back porch. That would give me time to recover.

When I sat down at my place, my face was clean, the bangs covered the blow to the forehead very well. I tried to act natural. The blessing was said, and I looked up at Bettye who was looking at me with a one-sided grin [like dad's], the look saying, "You licked my spit, you licked my spit." I gave her a matching grin, dislike for her pouring out of me.

When dad took us to Eureka, Kansas, it was the very first time I went to an out-of-state school. We arrived in the dead of winter, a thick snow covering everything. I was sick with a severe chest cold, and bronchitis, croupy coughs that wouldn't subside, especially nights.

We were checked into a boarding house upon arrival, and I will never forget the wonderful breakfast of eggs and milk we had around a long table with a tablecloth, and the warmth from the heating system an amazement to me. The beds had great thicknesses of quilts, and the mattresses were also thick and extremely comfortable.

In about a week dad found an apartment that was temporary, and later moved us into a larger apartment close to schools for us girls. I had never been in a junior high school, or middle school, before, and soon found out how very far behind the Arkansas school system was than in Kansas. Books were supplied by the schools, and we were so beside ourselves with joy.

It was in Eureka that I discovered an amazing curriculum of special studies such as music appreciation, and bookkeeping. I also discovered that I was so behind in mathematics, I received an incomplete, for I could not begin to catch up in time to understand math, before I was to move on again. In all other studies I progressed very well. I especially loved the music class where Peter and the Wolf, and a Mid Summer's Night Dream, came alive to me under the tutelage of a very nice teacher that guided us through the stories as the music was played. I can still hear her soft voice going along with the music, and I felt almost swept off to far away places, soaring high, then low; dreamy, then thunderous, hearing separately every piece of the orchestra, every instrument, distinguishing peace, action, movements, anxiety---the complete excitement scale that I was so hungry for.

There also was gym period where I learned I liked basketball, and when I ran track I did very well---well enough to be on the track team, and spring training began in earnest. I was going to be number one track runner for meets and final tournaments. I was elated.

Misfortune struck. I had turned fourteen on my last birthday and wasn't prepared for what happened, how naive I was. How very ignorant I was. I'd had slight cramps for a day or so, only knowing I had never before experienced that feeling before. Oh, good, I thought, all I need is another pain to put up with.

On May first, I awoke to a stronger cramp, and discovered the blood. I told Bettye something was really wrong with me, and she laughed and told me to go to mother, and she would fix me up. When I told mother, she sort of smiled and said I was "slow" about it, and fixed me the usual feminine contraption, told me to stay away from water, and don't bounce around so much. I was truly sick, I decided, and I hated this situation. Nothing else was explained, and I took mother at her word.

I started off to school on this hot day, a thick pad wedged between my legs, trying ever so hard to walk my usual self, needing a drink of water so badly as I passed drinking fountains in the halls, and ---well--- when I got to gym class, I told my teachers I would have to withdraw from track, because

I wasn't suppose to "bounce" around. Everything was completely ruined.

My happiness was snatched away from me, and I went around with a sulky face. Dejectedly, I walked home for lunch. I was awfully thirsty and dry mouthed by this time, and asked mother if I could please have some water, please. She laughed and told me, "of course, you have to drink water," and laughed some more. At fourteen I should have known better. But, why didn't someone sit me down and explain the normal monthly function of a woman's body?

I was never told about Bettye's difficult menstruation. It was such a horrible thing, a dirty thing, to grandma Michael, and my mother, and was so with Bettye too, for she kept it from me. Why? I needed to know these things. I was upset with mother and Bettye about this, and wished I had someone to talk to about it. Someone else would have perhaps told me it was not "dirty", and made me feel more comfortable with myself when it happened. The "don'ts" for women on their periods were unnecessary in those days, and I soon realized I could bathe in warm water, and the more I bounced around, playing basketball, the less I cramped, or had problems.

Poor mother didn't know how to talk to us. As for the water, she meant that I shouldn't get wet and chill myself. Basically, she could not communicate with us.

Dear, Aunt Vesta came down from Wichita and inquired of dad and mother if I could visit her for a week after school was out. Dad had another month until his job finished, and she thought I'd be company for my cousin. Patsy Jane, who was my age, and whose clothes Bettye and I wore over the cold winters. I wasn't there one full day before Aunt Vesta took me into her beauty salon, which conviently was an extra room in her home. She ran her long fingers through my straight, blond hair, grown longer since dad's time was taken up, and mother could care less. She batted her dark, brown eyes, and announced "Today, I am going to give you your first permanent." I was so surprised I could hardly speak, but only clamped a hand tightly over my open mouth.

"You really are, Aunt Vesta?" I asked when I got my voice back.

"Yes, and it will change your whole appearance." She studied me in the mirror, then continued. "It will be soft curls, and when it has grown out some, will look very pretty."

I was so thrilled I could barely sit still for her to roll and clamp on the long cords that hung like spaghetti hanging out on the dome-like contraption over head. The solution was beginning to make my eyes water, but my dear little heart was singing, I'll never ever be ugly again, I thought, as I stared at myself in the mirror while Aunt Vesta worked away. Her face, too, looked elated at her profound idea, and I knew I was in the hands of an expert.

It took forever and a day, and I thought I would fry under wires the electricity charged through, but in the end, after carefully testing a couple of rollers, it was pronounced "done", and the endless unclamping, unrolling, more solution applied, then shampoo and rinse, were completed, and towel drying began. As my blond hair dried, it was lighter and shinier. My Aunt clapped her hands together in delight of the miracle she had wrought, and I could not, for the very life of me, keep a silly grin off my face.

"Is this really me?" I asked, feeling so much joy.

"This is really you," she replied, then proceeded to give me a lesson on beauty in all other forms.

After the exciting week was over, and Aunt Vesta had given me a couple more dresses, she returned me to Eureka, where my family and I began packing up to leave once again. I do not know what they thought of the new me. I don't remember if they noticed. They must have.

We would never return to Midland to live. Dad rented a house in Hartford, nine miles south of Midland, where I began eighth grade, a new gymnasium was being finished, and it boasted of a football team....Herb was a star football player....a band of sorts, and good musical section. I was so hoping things could settle down with dad job-wise, and we could put some roots there. I preferred Eureka, but I'd take anything that looked promising, if only.....

The house in Hartford, the first house we lived in in Hartford, is what I mean to say, was in some sturdier condition than I'd experienced in my life, but the 'shanty house' was just a room bigger, and I peeked in behind the kitchen, and sure enough, there was Herb's cot set up in the same extra little room. I wondered what it was about those designers of those houses back in that part of the world that begged to have that one little extra room, but now I feel it was actually meant for a bathing room if someone cared enough to put in a little wood stove, or a kerosene stove.

Poor Herb. Good grief, he was eighteen years old, finishing his last year of high school, and I was betting he would be so glad to leave home at last, and try to make a difference in his life. At this time in his life I felt he would not allow our father to pull him in on any useless schemes and try to point him in a direction as unrewarding as his own.

Bettye was sixteen, so much healthier, appeared less stressed, was immediately popular in school, and our singing picked up both in school and church. Bettye was selected as soprano in our high school girls' trio, being in the ninth grade now, and Herb also was providing a good baritone to the boys quartet. Things looked good. Even Peggy felt some restraints were off, and made friends with girls in her grade school class.

I had one thing on my mind. Basketball. I was on the junior girls' team, then Geneva Hobbs, a girl in my grade, and I had a great honor to be chosen not only on the junior girls' team, but "sit the bench" on the senior girls' team, wearing the big girls suits. Oh, it was so fantastic I walked upon soft, silvery clouds.

The best thing of all was that I watched one of the best girl players I'd ever seen. She was a forward that could move with more grace while applying it with speed, and she could out-maneuver and out-jump anyone I had ever seen. She was professional material, her name was La Rue Glidwell, and my role model. I wanted to be just like her.

Dad was beginning to sluff off again, spent most of his money on shoe repairing equipment, and sat down to decide where he wanted to go to put in a shop. Satan's horns! Here we go again! Things were getting tight again, and mother was back on her treadmill of anxiety. At that point I felt mother had about all she could take of the poverty-level of living, but I guess he talked her into his latest venture.

But, first mother laid down some demands herself. We were out of food, and needed clothing again, and she told him that "commodities" were given out in Ft. Smith, and some of the people in Hartford were receiving them, and there was no shame in accepting the government's offering.

"I will not take charity! No way will I take charity and make a fool of myself", he told her.

I didn't think mother would stand up to dad, but she was showing some sense. "Make a fool of you? It is not you I'm worried about, Thomas May, it is the family. We need it, and you and I are going to Ft. Smith tomorrow." Mothers eyes blazed.

When my parents came home late afternoon the next day, they brought boxes of food stuffs, blankets, and clothing for us girls, even shoes. But dad was in a black mood, talking about his humiliation, his embarrassment having to sign up, and line up in front of so many people and receive charity. It was almost too much for him to bear.

It was no shame for me. I don't know if Bettye wore her dress, but Peggy and I wore ours, and held our heads high. Other children in school wore the "commodity clothes" too.

The fun of summer was over, and the winter started a-fresh, and I was feeling dubious about the whole matter of dad's taking off to Barling with his shoe repair equipment. It didn't startle me that I had no faith in anything he did.. no surprises left for me about anything he felt he suddenly must do. My lawzy me, he would fairly be whistling as he packed the car, seemingly no cares at all in the world, and anyone with good sense could tell he was happy to be gone from us and the tremendous responsibility we were to him.

It was God's plan to make man with urgent sex drives, to take females and impregnate them, and dad simply could not be held accountable, so he appeared to think, and therefore when he felt trapped with the pleading of his family, he would go off to hibernate somewhere, but why Barling, for Pete's sake? There was nothing there at all; not enough people to make a living repairing worn out shoes back then. Was he really in Barling?

I was pondering on all these things as I trudged up to the Barker's little store with the gallon, galvanized, kerosene can that had a small potato clamped over the spout to keep from spilling a drop of precious liquid. Snow was coming down, and the gray clouds enveloped the late afternoon sky. My feet slipped on the new layer of snow, but oddly enough I was not cold, and not too depressed over something else. It always passed, whatever it was, even though it left an indelible, additional dent in my memory. I must hurry, because mother needed the oil for the two lamps before darkness set fully in. I held eleven cents in the palm of my left hand, a dime and a penny, and felt quite at home doing what I set out to do; just out of my duties. Seems like I was always on my way to a store somewhere. We were down to scratch again, and mother put on her worry face once more. I knew that as the days passed with no word from dad, or money, she would become irritable and cranky.

Herb was no help what-so-ever, his days being spent on school, football, and girls. He returned home late at night, slept on his cold cot, then was gone again the next morning. I'm sure he was doing odd jobs for the towns' people and grandpa Michael for spending money. He did become active in the First Baptist Church, and had become a BYPU leader, a youth leader, and was well thought of there in Hartford. But, his almost complete indifference toward mother and us girls remained, I'd say, throughout his life. We must have been a disappointment to him.

I always thought too much about everything and

decided to put that out of my mind as I reached home with the kerosene. I knew I could expect more experiences to nearly overload my brain. Just count the hours, and sure enough, there would be another Stella Dallas drama unfolding. My shoes and socks were soaked, and my feet cold. It would certainly get colder tonight.

Days passed, Christmas came and went without much splendor--I can't remember any gifts, again, but who cares about that?---and, January was terribly cold. No word from dad came that I recall. I vaguely wondered if he had his Nowata woman with him, wherever he was, his stocking feet up to a pot belly stove, sipping coffee, and sketching.

Bettye and I got out and dug up bricks to heat on the stove for us to wrap in newspaper, or rags, and to put at the foot of our beds for warmth. Sometimes mother used old regular clothing irons, of which we had two, but my sister and I needed to do some thinking on our own now we were older, therefore helping our situation and not relying upon mother, who couldn't seem to think beyond her own misery.

Our coal pile was down to scraping the top of the hard earth for the loose, fine grained coal, some resembling the fineness of sugar grains and we could not be caught in another awful mess as we were in Midland. Poor mother sat and sniffed.

It was about bed time, and mother wanted us to get to bed so we could save some of the scuttled coal grains for the morning. I was planning on seeking help the following day somewhere as I prepared for bed. I noticed Bettye peeking out the side window, ignoring the bed call. Mother told us to blow out the light, and went to her bedroom. Peggy slept with her while dad was gone for warmth, and Bettye said she had to go outside and pee. I waited.

Soon, Bettye came back in carrying two large chunks of coal, her hands black from the residue. She grinned from ear to ear as she showed me, holding them high, saying, "Shhh", and she carefully put them inside the coal scuttle next to the stove.

"Where did you get the coal?" I asked, grinning myself,

too, with her.

"From Jimmy Walker's big pile of coal," she quietly answered. "Bettye, that is stealing!" I giggled.

"I don't care if it is stealing. We are freezing, and he has a new ton. He won't miss it."

For obvious reasons I had to go along with her excuse. There was mother almost useless, and Peggy was only nine, and Herb couldn't be counted on, so Bettye had saved the day, as it were, and if I had been asked if Bettye would do it again, I'd have to say, "By golly, yes. And so would I." Our ferret beings screamed survival.

I think it was early in February, 1940, dad returned home late, no warning, no announcement, just came back into our lives for what? That night we girls were hustled off to bed and the door closed. And the sounds began, not in their bedroom, but on the floor near the warm stove. I knew exactly what they were doing, and so hoped it would be over without mother getting pregnant. I had felt dad was always sexually driven, but I learned that night that my mother was no frigid woman.

Somehow, we made it through the winter. Herb graduated, and wore a borrowed suit from Uncle Bud, a black suit, and even though I did not attend the commencement, I remember how handsome he looked dressed up like that. I wondered what his plans were for the future. I hoped success and good health for him.

When we couldn't pay our monthly rent at the Fourth Street house in Hartford, we moved into a house over in the "gap" on grandpa Michael's farm. We were lucky school was out, so we were off again hauling the worn out furniture yet another time. Grandpa was good enough to loan us a Jersey cow for milk and butter.

Trouble began to brew between my father and mother's brothers, but I never heard the details. I felt it was a serious matter this time, but no one would talk around me.

I went over to my grandparents home by their request, and I thought nothing about helping Grandma about the farm. Not much was expected of me, I suppose, but why was I there in the first place, and not over with my family?

One day, Grandma had one of my uncles drive us to Mason's Dry Goods in Midland where clothes were bought for me, a complete outfit...green dress of soft material, shoes, socks, underwear...the whole works. But, I wondered why nothing was being bought for Bettye, Peggy, or mother. Something was definitely not right here.

Soon after that, I heard snatches of angry remarks coming from the kitchen about not only my dad, but my mother. I wondered about it, yet still kept quiet.

I was summoned into the kitchen by grandma calling me. After I reached the kitchen, I saw grim faces, and I was asked to sit down at the table.

"We have something to tell you, Alma," grandma said. I waited and finally grandpa cleared his throat and said to me, "How would you like to live here with us?" I asked "Why?" Grandpa stood up, came and stood near me.

"We, your grandma and me, are drawing up papers to adopt you." I stared at him in disbelief.

"We are taking it to court in Ft. Smith," grandma said. She was nervous. Again I asked "Why?"

"Because your daddy and mother don't want you," grandpa said.

Sudden fear was like a knife in my heart as I tried to take it in. It couldn't be true, could it?...but, I kept having flash backs to the other earlier trip over here, when I felt abandoned.

"No!" I screamed, and stood. "You are lying to me. They do want me! You are lying!"

Sobbing, I ran out the front, through the same gate I ran out when I was eight, up the same road I ran then, the same old hurts, flooding back with much more force than I could almost bear, finally cutting across a field of wet early, summer hay, my legs scratched, my shoes and socks sodden and muddy.

It had stopped raining and clouds were almost clearing,

but a somber mist still hovered around the mountains, and I could feel the moist cold wind soaking my face and hair. I continued to run, great choking gasps of air almost bursting my lungs. I slowed as I got within sight of the house. Wispy smoke rising from the kitchen stove-pipe flue caught my eye, and I thought it serene enough. I approached from the back, past the well, the lonely cow in the barn lot, and upon the porch. I stood for a moment to take in the atmosphere, the quiet occupants. I saw Bettye first. She looked depressed.

I asked, "Where is mother?" She nodded to the kitchen.

"Is she okay?" I said.

"She has been crying again," Bettye replied, and shrugged her shoulder.

I was glad dad wasn't there, and naturally, I didn't see Herb. I knew Peggy was in the front room occupying herself with dolls, or something.

I went into mother, and told her what had happened, then asked her what was going on. She put her apron over her face and sobbed more.

"They are real mad at us, and they all want to cause trouble." All this didn't enlighten me at all.

Soon, the bigger depression pall lifted to settle into a lessor depression pall. I was doing my part, handing mother kitchen things and helping Bettye set the table for the mid-day meal.

Nothing else was ever said about the 'adoption' and I decided to keep a low profile with mother's folks, because the rumors drifting in and other talk, led me to believe, regardless of my father's weak points, that they were not to be trusted too far. They had treated dad shabbily in the past, using his expertise in many of his talents to further their greed, then not hesitate to dismiss him without paying him for the services he rendered for them.

I pulled away from my grandparents and most of my uncles, except Uncle Leon, who was much sweeter than the others, I thought, and tried to help and cheer me when I was little and hurting.

But, with all this and the fact I was fourteen, I couldn't help but think back upon the many times my mother and we children were almost without food and fuel, and then observe the "slopping" of grandpa's hogs and the food he threw out to them would have made a feast for us. The farm wasn't so far away either when I stood my ground in Mr. Peter's grocery to beg for food.

As I grew, I was able to fill in some gaps of the mysteries taking place around me, and I became more skeptical of this world; what it had to offer. Life wasn't through with us by a long shot...yet.

The race we were soon to face would be far more than we could bear as our hearts were torn into shreds, the petals pulled out of our "Fragile Flower" to be thrust under the dust of an uncaring world.

*   *   *

Chapter Eight

It was shortly after I had returned from my grandparents, and as we were all around the dinner table, all six of us, that dad informed us that mama wanted to say something to us four children. All four heads turned toward mother who, regardless of her feelings of sickness lately, managed a little smile, and a blush spread over her face and neck.

It was so quiet we could hear birds chirping and the soft lowing of the cow. Mother's hands nervously picked up her silverwear and put them back down only to reach and repeat the process. Silently, we waited.

Finally she spoke, stuttering a little, apparently embarrassed with herself. "I want to tell you now...I know you are all a little older now, and I don't know how you will feel about it...but...but, I am going to have a baby, and.... and, I don't feel too well, but you kids need to know."

She dropped her head, a sign that she would wait for us to speak, to show our approval or disapproval. Herb ducked his head, and was silent. I glanced at Bettye, then Peggy. I had a strong feeling that Bettye already knew, and I, well, I had been a bit worried that it could happen. Peggy laughed and said, "A baby?"

Then, there was chattering, as much chattering as was allowed, never confusion, but excited chattering. Dad remained silent. "A little baby," someone said.

"What will it be?" someone else asked.

"We don't know," mother said, "but I feel it is a boy." Her head was up off her chest, and she was watching us. What did she expect? Disapproval?

"What will we name him?" someone asked.

"I think Tommy," said mother, now unabashed, and picking up on our excitement.

I noticed that dad had that funny, one-sided grin that never showed his teeth. What was it? I know, and my heart sank a little, that he was not a happy camper, that more so, he was a little angry about it.

"We have more news," dad said, "we are moving into Hartford again, into the Patty house close to town. We will be nearer to school, and mama will be near a doctor."

Well, of course it had to happen. We couldn't stay in grandpa's house, especially with mother's condition. Will dad take care of her properly? What sort of doctor could there be in a little town of less than a thousand people? Bettye and I were worried about mother, and although we knew she had been under a lot of stress because of her family's extreme dislike for dad and whatever happened recently, I blamed myself for some of the worry she suffered, even though now I fully believed I was only a useful tool of proliferating a hate battle that went on and on--that had nothing whatsoever to do with me.

Mother was having some pre-menopausal symptoms, was forty, and with her severe bouts with depression and anxiety, she might be in for a rough pregnancy, not only harmful to her, but to the baby, too. Apparently, only Bettye and I were deeply concerned. I didn't ask Peggy, because she was still so young, but she stayed close by mother as much as she could. Later she would be very concerned.

The Jersey cow was returned to grandpa with heartfelt thanks, and I suspect Herb did the honor, and we packed up our furniture and moved to the Patty house in Hartford.

Back home! We were back to the place I wanted to call home. If I couldn't have Eureka, Kansas, or Van Buren, I'd surely take Hartford. I liked the kids, I liked school, I liked Mr.

Roberts, and Miss Mabel Bright, nice, dedicated teachers, and kindly.

One thing, I couldn't believe that town had three doctors and an attorney. Of course, Dr. Alexander was retired, and I wasn't positive he counted, and Dr. James was older than Dr. Greer, and I might add, grumpier than a doctor had a right to be. Mr. Goodwin, the attorney, was semi-retired, a very nice person, and there were fine grocery stores, a drugstore, a Green's Cafe, that had a great beautifully lighted nickelodeon, a bank, two garages, a beer parlor...yes, a real one...only beer though, a dry goods, filling stations, an undertaking establishment, McConnels, a music publishing place, shoe repair shop, bank, theater [Saturday's only], a couple of bootleggers, and a cemetery that was filling up fast. We were in hog heaven. I never ever wanted to leave. Please. I prayed, let this be home.

Mother suffered a lot, I fear, that long hot summer, carrying the little baby we wanted so badly, and even though she was under Dr. Greer's expert care, she began to show the dreaded signs of "uremic poisoning" that threatened both lives. We girls tried to ease her household chore-load, and help with cooking and laundry. Mother began to sew the baby's layette, and purchase as she could, his blankets, shoes and stockings, sweaters and caps.

Where dad was working at this time, I simply can't remember, and even though Herb was still about, I feel he was working for grandpa Michael on the farm. I'm not clear on this, but in my memories of this particular time, they vaguely entered a memory, then, poof, were gone again. I really can't recall how useful they were, to mother, at least.

I listened to a heartbroken remark my elderly mother told me just the other day. After she said it, I had to suppress my tears until I got into my car to return home. She was staring out of the nursing home at the lovely fall color of leaves on the trees in the boxed-in garden. In a little sing-song way, she said, "Your dad told me that Little Tommy wasn't his baby." Tears rolled down her cheeks. My hate boiled once again inside me, but all I said in a quiet reply was, "He must have been mad when he said it. I wouldn't worry now about it."

She looked at me with the faded eyes, and said, "I try not to think about it, but I don't sleep anymore, and I sometimes stay all night in the chair and think. I can't shut the bad stuff off."

It has been at least ten years since I used my rifle for silhouette shooting and bull's eye targets for my hand gun; I'm too old now, but I can't pretend I am something that I am not. When I see my old mother's hurt, and my hurt too, I so want to go out into a secluded place, set up the targets and shoot, shoot, shoot, until I've spent a thousand or so rounds ...to blow away the anger...to blow away the hurt...to blow away a hate, that at the bottom of it's deep well lies a broken love that I called dad. But, then, some sanity returns, and I finish my visit to Pinewood, and hurt is back as I honk my horn and wave to her through the front window as I'm leaving.

By September 1940, mother was still hanging in, big stomach, and her poor legs were so swollen, it was a miracle she could walk, and walk she did, or waddle would be the correct word. She should have been banished to her bed, but she had new neighbors she became acquainted with who clucked over her like mother hens, and she always had time for them, and the minister of the Baptist church, and his sweet wife, never ceased to pamper her somewhat, so she tried to get about after rest periods. Everyone was so worried about the uremia, and dread was in our hearts.

We girls started school that to us was one continuous, exciting, and fun-filled time of books, friends, great teachers, sports, laughing...ah, laughing was so much fun. Life was fun today. Bettye and I became movie crazy, trying to attend every Saturday matinee, or night, and Bettye was popular, and dating boys.

Bettye and I were always together in most of our activities; singing, school, church, but I learned to "walk on eggshells" around her at all times. She could change from a smiling angel into a crazed demon in the wink of an eye, and she was always vindictive...seeking revenge in any matter, real or imagined. I always felt I should watch my back.

Peggy, what a lovely surprise Peggy was when we discovered her singing. We heard her, no doubt by accident, but she had it. The high clear tones were right on key. It wasn't long before we had incorporated her in with us, and instead of the duet, we had a trio of May sisters. She had heard Bettye and me sawing away on our songs for so long, it was quite easy for her to glide smoothly in with her sweet tenor. With practice we were good; with proper training, we could have been great, but that wasn't possible with the way we lived. We wouldn't make our careers in singing, but we pleased our audiences, and we had something special that cut a break in our otherwise worrisome existence. It was therapy for us, and it gave us a feeling of hope...a sense that we did matter, and so we had more spark to go on. It helped us heal, I feel, and Bettye; what about Bettye? Did our singing contribute something for her to grasp onto, and pull up out of a seemingly hopeless sickness and surge on in a more normal way? I think it was beneficial.

By the time Bettye and I had reached our teens, our competitive and combative forces were headed for courses of collision that would last until this day.

Instead of taking the initiative by being the older and more experienced one by two years separating us, Bettye chose to instrumentalize her more aggressive feelings by using force and control; she chose me as her enemy. And rather than grooming me as her closest ally, she had allowed resentment and jealousy to alienate me, and thereby weakening both of us in our struggle against the same environment of existence. We could never be friends.

That summer was a bad one on everyone. We had no electricity and, so didn't have fans. Air conditioning was unheard of for people like us. All of us suffered, especially Tommy. He was put in diapers only, and mother fanned him, and gave him plenty of water.

Mother needed help with the house work and laundry,

and a lot did fall on Bettye's and my shoulders. I really didn't mind much, except Bettye had begun to be irritable, picky, and nagged at me constantly. She also seemed to feel that she was in command, because she was the eldest, so when her temper flared, she did not hesitate to swing her fists. She was dating, and house chores cut into the time she needed for herself, and she needed that time. I was somewhat interested in boys, but my hormone system was a bit slower kicking in.

Dad had brought in bottled pop for us to put in the old ice box, and we were allowed one each per day. The pop included a variety of flavors of Nehi, Grapette, and Coca Cola. Bettye warned me not to drink "her" Nehi orange, she said dad bought it especially for her . So one day while she was looking, I opened one of her oranges, which sent her into a screaming rage. She lunged at me, knocking me down under the dining table, and as I tried to get up, she would kick me back down. Somewhat stunned, about all I could do was deflect her blows.

By the time I came out of the surprise attack, my own temper flared, and I wanted so desperately to hurt her--to stomp her---to--yes!--to kill her! I could hurt her, and I got out from under the table , my right mind completely gone. I wanted my hands around her throat, and I wanted to squeeze until I made her call "calf's rope"; but she had gone, and, as I saw the pop bottle spilled out on the floor, I felt nauseous. My own uncontrollable temper was making me ill, and I felt ashamed that I would allow that to happen to me. I did not want to ever he like her, never in a million years.

Bettye boasted about her temper and her pugilistic prowess, especially over me. She told all my friends what a "fraidy cat" I was and how she could control me by beating up on me. No one was around to witness the ridiculous altercation, and as it would serve no purpose, except for more discord, I didn't talk to mother about it. But, years later when I mentioned this to her, she asked me why I didn't fight back. I told her I was afraid I would kill her. She told me if I had fought back, Bettye would not have bothered me so much. Actually, it wasn't my nature to fist fight, nor did I find it a pleasant feeling to lose my temper. Both, to me, were low-life behavior tactics to force control upon another who appears stronger, and presents a threat. Verbal intimidation was a basic tool Bettye used on me, and if that didn't produce the needed results for her, she put her uncontrollable temper in gear that physically could be dangerous, especially if she used a weapon, such as a stick of stove wood, a hoe, or a kitchen butcher knife. Herb and I were familiar with these tools.

After the orange soda incident, I felt depressed, and out of socket again. I felt I could not handle Bettye, and it would be impossible to help unimpeded around the house, and while nobody cared, I put a few clothes in a paper bag, counted out my change, and caught the bus to Midland, and Querita's.

I stayed at Querita's for a couple of weeks, and felt able to laugh. Her mom was sick, and the two of us cleaned the house, cooked meals for her dad, mom, and us, played the piano---under the Double Eagle must have forced her mom out of bed, for she finally got up and weakly moved about--and we went to church evenings, sitting in the back pew while the 'Postolics [Assembly of God] held a week long revival.

When the revival ended on the last night, all the converts were taken to a pond, the water oily looking by lantern light, and water moccasin snakes had to be beaten off with clubs as the believing converts were "dunked". Querita and I shivered with excitement, and felt the preacher was so very brave to stand in the dark water up to his hips to baptize quite a few people. I was unabashedly having fun those two weeks, and did feel some tiny spark of remorse, because I wasn't home helping. And I missed the baby terribly.

Uncle Leon was in downtown Midland when Querita and I walked past Mr. Peters grocery, and he yelled, "Hey, Cotton Top, want to go home with me?" I got my change of clothes, and went home with him. After a week I was back at Querita's and wondering if my family wanted me home. Silly question huh?

I'd been gone a month when my sister Bettye appeared at Querita's door. "Alma you have to come home now," she said. She looked hot, tired, and angry. Oh boy. "You have to help me work around the house, I can't do it all!"

"Okay", I said, and grabbed my change of clothes, told the Dugans bye and left.

"Who brought you?" I asked, for I didn't see dad's car out front.

"Dad." She pointed up to the main street. "He parked up there, and told me to walk down." She was beginning to cry. "I don't think I can make it if you don't help,"

When we reached the car, dad didn't say a word to me; not a greeting. He started the car and we went home. There was no talk almost the nine miles to Hartford. Dad was still silent after we got home. Things appeared strained between mother and him. But, you know what? I was glad to see the baby, to hold him and talk to him, and Peggy, could Peggy have shot up so fast in only the month that I had been gone? Mother looked ragged about the edges, and I swore I'd try to get along with Bettye if I had to continually smooth her feathers.

>Precious one, why did you choose us?
>we are not deserving.

Tonight I carefully took the baby shoes out of the little white box that my mother had written on the lid, "my baby's first shoes" along with a single, tiny white sock with a supporter still attached and I felt them come alive in my hands as I caressed them. Yes they came alive in my hands, even after these fifty-two years, and I could hear the far away whistle of the approaching train, the wind howling about the eves of the house, and I could feel a precious little baby's hands as I had touched them then. Something else I felt as then was my broken heart, and the sobs came along with the tears, and I wondered if I would be able to write about my little brother.

For the past three days I cannot write about Tommy. I've bustled about, writing around him, looking through materials, making all sorts of excuses to circumvent that subject. I'm hoping I will be able to get through it after I start.

October 8th, 1940 we were hustled out of our beds early while it was dark, and we said "bye" and "see ya" to mother before Herb accompanied us up to Mrs. Bean's house to finish our sleep there. It was time. The morning air had a biting chill to it as we trudged along the hill. Soon I'd be fifteen and Bettye seventeen, and we must leave the house while mother went through the labor and birth of the baby. We were frightened, because of mother's bad health, and I wondered why she couldn't be taken to the hospital in Ft. Smith where she and the baby would have better care. I was so angry with dad for not providing for them. I wanted to pound something I was so frustrated.

The sun was coming up when we were allowed to return home. We were greeted by mother's cousin, Irene, at the door and she let us come in. We were nervous, and as we went to the stove all we could see was what looked like pillows, or blankets on a kitchen chair. We looked in on mother, who was resting, her face so pale surrounded in all the wondrous dark hair, so we went back to the stove.

Irene, who was an R.N., was on guard, and cautioned us as we slowly approached the chair. Our eyes had to have been round as saucers as we visited the tiniest little human we ever saw. He could have fitted inside a shoe box. There was dark hair, almost black, or so I thought, and he was sleeping. But the biggest surprise was the baby's color. He looked bronze, and Irene said he weighted "about" four pounds, but she was guessing. She told us the uremia mother suffered was a cause of his color. Later on when he opened his eyes, they too were discolored---his iris's were brown and the whites as bronze as his skin.

"Will he be okay?" we asked Irene. She looked exhausted. "We hope so," was her answer.

"Are you going to stay?" we asked her. She nodded her red head, and smiled at all three of us.

That certainly was a relief to us, but I wondered why someone didn't suggest the hospital, and if I wondered why, then, even in 1940 hospitals were urging the women to come in for their deliveries, and proper care of both mothers and babies. But, rural Arkansas---well----.

Later, Irene told the story of the doctor in charge of mother, who upon seeing the unmoving baby and his condition, stayed only long enough to cut the cord, and see to the last details for mother. He said the baby was dead, then clamping his hat on his head, and picking up his bag, he unceremoniously left.

Mother told us about how Irene, her dear cousin, who murmured something about "bull----," took the little still form to the warm stove, and after warming baby oil, began to rub and massage the bronze skin. She worked with him, gently turning him over on his stomach on her lap, rubbing and working with him. It paid off. The baby suddenly began to move a little; he then let out a plaintive cry. When mother heard the cry, her tears turned to laughter and Irene began to talk to the baby and mother all the while assuring both that it would be alright. She was there for them both, bless her big heart and determination to help heal. She also was extremely put out with the uncaring doctor who had abandoned them.

Irene put boric acid into the baby's eyes, swabbed out his mouth, got that little, child heart working smoothly as a Swiss clock, then boiled a little water containing sugar for his first food.

Between Irene and Mrs. Bean, Mrs. Moore, and other of mother's friends, the care of the baby and mother magically got done, and with time mother was up, and the baby had a few weeks of struggling to do before he began to lose the color and gain strength. Then one day we looked upon the little miracle baby, and saw blond hair, blue eyes with normal whites, and a fair, peach skin.. His hands, satiny, moved all the time, and he was not too happy away from mother who talked to him constantly, and rocked him, always touching him, helping him feel secure. I liked what I saw, all of us fell madly in love.

Herb had made Tommy a square clothes box from ply-board, painted it light blue, and Peggy cut pictures of the Dionne quintuplets from a magazine and pasted them on the lid. The little baby now had his own clothes box. He was fed from the bottle, a formula of canned, condensed milk and Karo syrup, and began to thrive. He was a pretty baby, who at times appeared frustrated, and explored his surroundings with his small hands.

One afternoon when I was sitting in the west window rocking the baby and singing to him, the late, bright sun suddenly shone through the pane and into his face. His body recoiled as if he had been jabbed by a finger, shut his eyes tightly, then cautiously opened them, and stared into the sunlight in a mesmerized way. He became still as stone, reached his small hand up and waved it back and forth in front of his eyes, and take the hand away to continue staring. I looked into the blue eyes, and swimming within the irises was a milky-white substance that moved in circles. I was stricken with horror.

"Mom, Mom", I yelled out. "Come here. Look at his eyes. Oh, mom, look at our baby's eyes! He's blind."

Mother was quickly at my side, and looked into Tommy's eyes that were still gazing into the sun. She saw and gave a terrible moan, as she took him from me, I quickly got up, and sat down for a more through look before the sun sank behind the houses and trees. She allowed him to watch the sun drop down out of sight, then she rocked him, hugging him to her chest, and the tears streamed down her cheeks.

"That is why he touches so much and waves his hand back and forth in front of his face---to see his hand." She cuddled him in her grief. "At least he can see something."

I went out on the porch even though it was cold, and cried more while mother quietly talked to her baby until the others started coming home.

The other day at Pinewood Nursing Home, my elderly mother told me she remembers the incident so clearly, as if it was yesterday--when I called out to her, and we discovered the baby's blindness. The tears came to her eyes, and she didn't want to remember too much pain at that time, but she is plagued by the heart breaking ghosts of so long ago. Mother seldom sleeps, and there are times she sleeps in her comfortable lounger, rather than go to bed. I look at her and wonder what pain is locked up inside her memory that she cannot escape until her time comes.

When she is in a nostalgic mood, I will casually ask her about times, people, places. This I compare to what I write here, to clarify, too, if I'm lucky, and she knows, a happening where my memory is cut off and she can fill in important things I do forget.

Herb, and dad too, I think, went up to Wichita, Kansas, Herb to land a promising job with an aircraft company, Cessna, but I'm sure dad didn't stay for long. It seems dad was back home soon enough and I don't recollect any lucrative job. At this time, even my being older and I should remember more clearly than when I was seven or eight, it seems dad was another vapor; sometimes there, sometimes not.

However dad didn't appear when mother asked about eye doctors, specialists she could take Tommy to for an examination, diagnosis and possible surgery. God love her, she was getting some spunk, and from people in Hartford who gave her an education about the changing times, and the possibilities of a better way of life. But she loved this little, frail, baby boy, and so much that she would fight for him, even though she was still restricted by past difficult years, and perhaps by dad.

Mother added to the earlier statement she had made to me at Pinewood, and I wasn't surprised; heart breaking, because my mother had been a dutiful wife to my father. Now, old, she tells more than ever. It seems dad rejected Little Tommy and said to her the baby did not belong to him based upon the simple fact the baby was defective. Oh, I felt so sorry for her, and if only I could meet him face to face right now I would like to ask a few pointed questions. Do you think I shouldn't feel that way? This abused, scared, child, grew up, and while I always wanted to honor my mother and my father, I should have confronted him years ago, and told him the one honest statement--that abusive fathers and husbands are cowards to the core.

When the appointments were being set up for mother

and Tommy, some of the good friends, Irene, or another of mother's cousins, Hazel, who lived in Ft. Smith, would turn out to be guardian angels in the situation. A Dr. Moulton was selected to be the ophthalmologist; that is, Dr. C. Moulton, the first, already renowned as the pioneer of cataract surgery. His clinic was located in Ft. Smith about thirty miles from Hartford.

The diagnosis was that the baby had liquid cataracts, and the procedure Dr. Moulton wanted to perform was first, go in behind the eyes with a needle and gently stir the milky cataract; keep it moving until the second procedure--to carefully extract some of the liquid substance, and the third would withdraw the balance of the cataract, and with the help of glasses, Tommy would be able to lead a decent life of sight.

Mother had stayed overnight with Hazel, her cousin. Later, after one of the surgeries on Tommy's eyes, she rode the bus, a rattle trap thirty miles of stops and starts, bumps and grinds, people swaying up and down the aisle, jostling about, she arrived in Hartford about 4 p.m., so tired, and the baby was cranky, because of his ordeal. I'll never forget it, but soon things were getting back to some normalcy.

Dad had taken a bridge job along the Rio Grande River between Canutillo, Texas, and Las Cruces, New Mexico. So, we closed up our house, in Hartford, and had a driver take mother, us girls, and the baby down there.

We girls began school in September 1941, in Las Cruces-- -me the tenth grade, Bettye, the eleventh, and Peggy was still in elementary. The high school was promising. Bettye and I joined the girls' glee club, and I was chosen to be on the cheerleading team, colors of powder blue and white pom pom's, little pleated skirts, a dandy school band and things were looking up. There was one flaw eating away at our hearts. Our baby wasn't feeling well. He didn't seem to be able to come out of his lethargic period and he had crying spells. He was also losing weight. Mother and we girls were frightened.

Las Cruces was another lovely small city, but by now we were programed to definitely not get attached, for breaking away from people, friends and certainly a better way of life, were there only to briefly experience---I suppose to give us a recess; a break. But some of our despair was following us and we did indeed, receive a lucky break by being here, for Las Cruces not only had a great school system, but good doctors in the small hospital, and the wonderful A & M State University nearby. Like Eureka, Kansas, this place was at least twenty years ahead in living conditions and progressive city administrative actions. I felt a lot safer here.

Little Tommy continued to deteriorate health-wise, and one evening the whole family took him to the hospital in an emergency. Mother put him into the arms of a nurse to be properly examined while we sat nervously in the waiting room. Mother gave all the necessary history on the baby and finally a doctor approached her and dad to gain permission of his admission for further testing the following day.

How we missed our baby. Every time I looked at mother's strained face, I knew she was suffering most of all. She and dad returned to the hospital the following day after testing and the news was not good. The lab had run tests on Tommy's blood cells and the doctors had determined he needed whole red blood immediately. The doctor had a great plan how to get it.

The doctor whose name I do not know---just another White Knight in shining armor who always manages to come up on the anonymity lists all over the world----called the Las Cruces radio station and asked them to put out an emergency announcement: Little baby boy needs blood, the type-urgent- and to report to the hospital.

I remember Bettye, Peggy, and I sitting in the hospital hallway that night, our eyes taking in the sight of bodies, big bodies; big, big, bodies of young men walking past, and was told by a nurse that all these enormous guys were the New Mexico A & M football team here to be tested for blood matching for our little brother. They heard the emergency announcement and quickly responded. They were line backers, full backs, quarter backs, running backs, tail backs, split ends---if a good football team had them, they were all there.

Our eyes were going goofy.

Suddenly we felt safer again somehow about the baby. If the football team was for him, and the doctors were in there pitching, maybe Tommy would be well again. Just maybe.

Down the lighted hall a door opened, and one of the giants emerged, sleeve up and holding a bandage on the inside of his arm. He was blond with the typical crew cut and grinning proudly from ear to ear. He was euphoric and his steps indicated his immense pleasure. He was almost dancing with excitement.

Mother was leaning against the wall, ready to move on the crook of a finger, when the young man approached her announcing proudly, "I...I just gave my blood to a little, sick baby...to a little baby."

Mother smiled up at him , and told him," Yes, that is my baby."

"I..I'm so glad I could do it...so glad my blood matched."

"You have my deepest thanks," mother touched him gently." "We thank you so much." Then the tears came. He put a large hand on her shoulder.

"Oh I am so happy it was me," the blond giant beamed down at mother. "Just think...he has my blood in his body helping him to become well."

Mother talked a while to the happiest of fellows, exchanged names, and he told mother the doctor advised him to be on call, even though he had other blood matches. He waved "bye" to us and left with some of his buddies, jabbering away.

I wondered why Tommy needed so much blood when he had no injuries and pointedly asked mother. She didn't know. Where was dad tonight, was he just there and I just didn't store him in my mind? I'm afraid to push mother's memories too far, for her sake. If she appears agitated, I do not ask anything of her, except perhaps what was her favorite rose bush in her California yard. That is bad enough for it starts bouts of nostalgic weeping as she realizes the ending of her life, and how much she has lost and can never regain, ever again.

The doctor came to see us after the blood transfusion, or should I say, the first blood transfusion?--and he was explaining the baby's condition. I did catch enough to wonder about it and store it. It went something similar to this; "The baby is small for his age, and due to his blindness is developmentally sub-normal, although not retarded. He has a blood condition that will require transfusions."

Again we left without our precious little boy and I caught mother crying in the bathroom a couple of times. Later she carried a look of fear in her eyes and I know her arms were so empty nights.

Before we finally brought Tommy home, the doctor had run more tests and found the need for another transfusion. He had mentioned something such as this: "poring the blood in...and...where is it going?"

What do I think today, after all things are done and said? I fully believe my little brother had leukemia, and it was acute. He was going to die because that was 1941 and leukemia was a pure and simple death sentence. The white blood cells [leukocytes] were gobbling up the red blood cells, which I could have understood even then, if it had been explained to me.

Another niggling thing that continues to prod my memory off and on since was, if mother had been told by the doctor in Las Cruces the seriousness of Tommy's illness, would she have understood what he was saying to her, especially if he used the term leukemia? Did my father take the time to sit down with the doctor and ask important questions? I don't think so. We were not aware of that at all, which isn't proof, but I don't think so. I don't feel, in my heart, he cared about the baby, our angel.

Well, my pom poms got a good work out at a practice football game in Las Cruces High, and a Main Street parade all the way down the full length, under banners, and the football players marched in full regalia. And that was it, and we had just begun again. Dad's job was over, and we had to pack up. Our destination: Nowata, to visit Grandpa and Grandma May. Tears rolled for us three girls. Tommy had his first birthday on October 8.

Bettye, Stella, our cousin, and I were roller skating

December 7, 1941, Sunday, when we heard Pearl Harbor had been bombed. We were still in Nowata, and would be leaving for Hartford soon to get back into school. It had been at least a month and a half that we girls had missed school. And our little Tommy became weaker with each cold day, and the worst of it was, while her heart was breaking, mother was succumbing to another confusing time of inevitability of the powers she could not battle. Poor broken swan. Her grief would become unbearable soon.

        *   *   *

Chapter Nine

Precious one, why did you choose to leave us?
were we not deserving?

It was five a.m. in the morning when the sweet baby voice whispered "issen, issen," and I was already awake, wondering if he would be all right. "Issen, issen," he continued to mother. He lay in bed between mother and dad, his little ears more kean than ours.

I heard mother stirring in the darkness, and soon I heard the faint, forlorn whistle of the fast freight train that moved through the sleeping towns making its snake body of box cars, and flats of heavy equipment on toward the west into Oklahoma.

"Isen, isen," he repeated, and mother said, "yes, honey, listen, listen. The train is coming."

We were back in the Patty House where our furniture was stored, the rent dutifully sent every month from Las Cruses to secure a place to come back to.

Herb had bought Tommy a crib, and it was great in warm weather, but the cold is when mother would put him in bed with her. I lay listening to the baby and mother, and the approaching train. It was an event for him and as the trains came through, he heard each squeak of wheels on steel rails, I'm sure.

After the train whistle could no longer be heard, Mother would attend to her baby, and make a lunch for dad to take to work with him. She now had a kerosene kitchen stove complete with an oven for the biscuits and muffins dad liked so much but we continued to use coal for the heating stove in the middle room.

I do not remember Christmas in 1941---just can't bring it to mind--but, I do know Tommy wasn't getting well, and I could see the heartbreak in mother's eyes. She knew she wouldn't be able to keep him, but I think she would treasure him for as long as he was with us.

Dad had a job that took him to Camp Chaffee near Barling, and so drove the long distance to and from work. A neighbor woman who also worked in Ft. Smith would ride along with him to and from work and this upset mother. She certainly didn't like that arrangement at all and voiced her opinion to us about it. She could confide more in us now that we were growing up.

The baby's condition worsened. The Hartford doctors did nothing.....especially when they could not diagnose Tommy's malady. Every time one of us girls ran to get a doctor, they would grumble about "getting out in the cold, when there was nothing to be done, anyway...so useless...waste of time." etc.

Mother sat rocking the baby trying to coax him to drink his warm milk, or make him comfortable. She would tenderly change his clothes, taking him close to the fire to make sure he wouldn't become chilled. His little hands would reach for her face, to feel it, to make sure he "saw" her as clearly as he possible could.

Neighbor ladies came by and sometimes "spelled" mother, and Bettye and I took turns holding him while she took needed breaks; but, she wanted to hold him as long as she could. Her rocking chair had been padded with pillows to make her comfortable during the care of her baby.

To our horror one night, Tommy started coughing, racking coughs that began to weaken his small body. Mother used chest rubs with warm clothes, and it eased up some, but a neighbor brought a stick of peppermint candy for the baby to suck on. Mother gently offered it to him, and he accepted it. He had teeth, but he was too weak to bite, so he sucked the candy. After a few minutes the mucous from his chest came up into his throat and mother racked it out with cloths. It eased his coughing, and he slept.

Early the next morning when the baby was unresponsive, and even his whimpering stopped, mother asked dad to take her and the baby to the hospital. He had to pick up neighbor Lily Louise and go to work, he remimded her, and told her to have one of the girls go to get a doctor. He would go by Uncle Bud's house and have him come take her. Then he left.

There was thin ice crust on the wet puddles in the roads, and frost hung on everything as I raced up to the old doctor's house. I was gasping for breath when I pounded on his front door and waited. Finally he opened the door.

"What is it now?" his face was as grumpy as his voice. "You need to come see about Tommy," I said, the words quivering for the fear as much as the cold.

"There is nothing I can do for that baby. He is going to die, and it would be useless for me to go." He began to shut the door, hesitated, then said, "Tell your mother I'm sorry."

"You're not a doctor! You're not a doctor." I screamed as he slammed the door.

I whirled and raced back at break neck speed, crying tears that got in the way of my vision. I was so frustrated, my fists were in knots, and my teeth clenched as I wished death on that old doctor. But it wasn't the doctor I was aiming my frustration against, and it wasn't frustration.... It was anger and hate for my father. He should have taken mother and Tommy to the hospital. They could have been halfway there by now.

We were in fearful agony as we waited for Uncle Bud to arrive, and my poor mother sitting with her coat on, the baby wrapped tightly against the cold weather, made me even more wild. I went back on the front porch to look for Bud, and I was saying, "The dirty son-of-a-gun! The dirty son-of-a-gun," over and over, while the cold started my body to shake uncontrollably, and I couldn't stop my teeth from chattering. What kind of father would do such a thing, even if he didn't want to admit Tommy was his, or if he felt only death for his son? I despised this backward place called rural Arkansas where people played on the breaking hearts of others, and I despised my father for never really living up to something decent once in his life, and turned his back on his own dying baby, his suffering wife, and we girls; to go do what? instead of staying and helping? The dirty son-of-a-gun.

Bud made the corner up from our house, hardly, screeching the tires on his little A-Model coupe. He stopped and hastened into the house, and took a look at the baby, took him from her after we girls kissed the beautiful, little face, and guided her quickly to the car. Then, the little car took off very fast, heading toward Sparks Hospital in Ft. Smith.

Bettye, Peggy and I went around the house looking at the rocking chair with the pillows, baby articles and clothes thrown about in haste with tears streaming down our faces.

The following day had to have been on a Saturday because dad was home all day off and on, never going to hunt up a telephone to call the hospital. Was he receiving information from some source we girls weren't told about? However you cut it, he did not go up to lend support to poor mother.

I don't know where Peggy was staying, but that evening, dad gave Bettye and me money to go to the movie, the Saturday night movie. We were surprised, but accepted it, even with our anxiety over the sickness of Tommy. When we reached the house we fumbled with matches in the dark to light the lamp, and that was when we saw the note in dad's handwriting. "Girls I've gone with McConnell's [funeral home] to bring mama and Tommy back, He passed away tonight." I'm afraid we weren't too quiet about our grief, and soon the neighbor ladies were in to calm us down, and to wait for the family Limo that would bring mother and our little brother back.

Little baby boy, precious, fragile flower, what was your purpose? Why did God send you, only to suffer, and die so quickly? Did you unknowingly give something to us...to the world...other than your beauty and our heart break? You were shunned by your father. You were shunned by two town doctors, but you were so loved by your mother and your sisters.

And, so we buried you during a downpour of rain, into a grave filled with water, and the wailing of your mother was a sore thing indeed, and so your sisters wept regretfully that your beauty would never grace our lives again. The angels poured down tears of sorrow for us, but shouted in their angelic happiness to take you up in their arms...once again, after all, you were one of them.

There was a break in the weather, and mother looked up, her eyes swollen in her grief, and there flew a blue bird over the tent covering the grave to rest on a bush close by. It appeared to her to be surveying the knot of mourners gathered there.

"Oh look," mother said pointing to the blue bird. "There is a blue bird come to say good-bye."

We looked and the bird looked back, never wary, but sat quite still. Then it lifted up and flew back near the tent, and was gone. In the cold sleet and rain of January, a blue bird made a timely visit.

That night quiet sobs could be heard from mother as she awoke from a restless sleep only to discover her empty arms, arms that would never hold her baby.

And, in our room, we three girls choked back our sobs, but when the 5 a.m. freight train made its first audible whistle coming from the east, mother's sobs turned into heart broken moans, and we could not hold back our silent crying.

Two weeks later, mother's parents paid us a visit, to present us with a notice to vacate the Patty House, for they had purchased it to be moved immediately over on a place above their farm. We hadn't even known there were negotiations to sell our rental, but we had been quite busy recently, to say the least.

It was brutal on mother, who still had not regained much strength these past two weeks after Tommy was buried. It was an ugly slap in the face for all of us, standing around, seeing but difficult to believe, that grandpa and grandma Michael could be this harsh. There were other houses to be sold for removal, and as I stood watching the loveless faces of my grandparents, I thought of them as vindictive, mean people.

Today, that lot where the Patty House stood is still empty. It just lies there, the corner rectangle green and lush, no eye sore that, and trees have grown up shading the grounds about it. It looks sort of lonely, and I wonder why it has never had a house rebuilt there in these fifty-one years, for it is now located in a wonderful location. It's a lovely lot.

After we vacated, sobbing about, because this was Tommy's house...the house of his birth, and nearly of his death....we moved down across the railroad tracks, closer to the trains. Some of our school chums lived in that area, and it probably was good for us to start again in another house. We tried, believe me, we tried to move forward regardless of our grief. Mother was trying to pull out of her shell, and we continued on to church. Mother and us girls that is. Dad did not attend except on important occasions such as funerals. He didn't bother to attend his Methodist Church anywhere we moved.

Let the trains come and go. We began to adjust in a blue fashion, trying to disregard the depth we could allow ourselves to fall into, unless we attempted to be strong. We would mention occasionally to one another how thrilled Tommy would be if he could be this close to the trains. And we would smile, however a bit wobbly.

That summer Herb came down from Wichita with the lovely, sweet girl he was in love with. Her name was Sylvina Munoz, with dark eyes and beautiful black hair, and her bubbly personality endeared her to all of us. He had chosen her to be his wife, and she was wild about him. Their happiness would soon be interrupted by the war, as he joined the U.S. Marine

Corps, and would see many battles in the South Pacific campaigns, and be wounded several times the two years before the dreadful war ended.

Also that summer I met Aubrey, a tall, lanky kid that looked like Charles Lindberg, walked like him, and I thought he was so cute. Six feet tall he was, wearing city clothes; nice slacks, Florsheim shoes, sports shirt, and expensive jacket.

He came up to me while we were attending a school function at the gym, and asked me if I was Alma May. I told him yes.

"Do you remember me?" he asked. I studied him up close briefly. Dark slicked down hair, parted on the side, green eyes with very long lashes, a nice smile, and nice, clear complexion.

"Why no I don't." I replied, but I felt myself blushing under his gaze.

"I'm Aubrey Pickle." Hartford had families of Pickles, and I was trying to put the name with the face.

"I saw you on the school stairs for the first time when you were in eighth grade." I felt his eyes pleading with me to remember, and I did barely.

"Why yes, I do," I smiled, then. "You were in Miss Mabel's grade."

He smiled wider then, his teeth white and even. He lightly touched my elbow and guided me over to the side. The noise was almost deafening, He absolutely towered above me, and his cologne was almost subtle, yet masculine.

We talked a bit more, and I turned to see Bettye and Bill Wilburn go out the door, so I'd be walking home alone. More people left, and I began to ease toward the door. Someone called his name, and I saw friends of mine, guys. He waved a hand to them, and asked if he could walk me home. No warning bells were going off, so I nodded my head, and we walked leisurely out on the walk.

There was a full moon absolutely flooding everything with a silver light, almost white-like, and we could see people some way ahead almost clearly as day. I always loved the moonlight. There were no boogies while the moon shone.

I walked along, my hands clasped behind me, trying to gear my stride with his long one. We sort of soldered, or ambled, as we lightly talked and asked about each other.

"Do you mind if I smoke?" he asked as his hand went inside his jacket.

"No I don't mind." This was 1942, and cigarette smoking was an "in" thing to do.

He unhurriedly spoke, taking drags off the cigarette and blowing the smoke away from me, saying his parents went to California where shipyard work was frantically in full swung, and he had gone to school in San Pedro, then dropped out to take a job as an assistant to a sea diver, who welded damaged ships hulls underwater. I thought that was magnificent, and told him so. "I'm here on a short trip." He dropped the cigarette and ground it under the nice leather sole of his shoe. "I'll be going back in a few days."

We walked down the train tracks and up to the porch of our house.

"Thanks for letting me walk you home," he said softly, not to wake mother or dad.

"Thanks for walking me."

He touched my arm, and said, "would you like to go somewhere, do something before I leave?"

"Yeah, I'd like to."

"Okay, good night then."

"Bye," I said, as his tall figure went back up the road to the tracks.

I went into the house wondering about Aubrey Pickle. He looked so grown up. He can't be very old if he was in Miss Mabel's class of sixth graders when I was in eighth grade. Could he? Maybe he was slow. No, he wasn't slow. He was more mature than the boys in my class, or older. I vowed I'd ask his age next time.

I got up the following morning wondering if I'd actually met this nice, well mannered, good looking guy. Decided I had and went and washed my face, had a quick breakfast after dressing, and thought, "Hum...okay so I'm dating. I'm suppose to date. I'm as old as the hills--sixteen, had a slim shape almost like a boy's....32" bust..21" waist, 33" hips...good grief!...all skinny legs...112 pounds, and 5 feet 4 inches tall. Oh well, maybe I'd fill out more like Bettye, who had 36" bust, 20" waist, 36" hips; yeah, sure Alma, you will fill out like Bettye. It will never happen. So what? Gimme another year.

    I went to the mirror to take another look. My hair was nice, medium topaz blond with lighter sun streaks, a little tanned, and blue-green eyes. The lips pouted. Great teeth. Only one pimple. Not too bad Alma, not too bad. Actually I liked my looks, and decided I'd better sharpen up on clothes, maybe work at Grandpa Michael's on ever changing crops, as Bettye and I had been doing when we could get over there, for money to buy things we needed.

    Today was today, and I had things to do.

    My father sat another winter by the stove in a closed off room in the Bartlett place drawing murals on the wall, and drinking coffee. The walls had been papered with a thick tan color, butcher type product lacking designs so he took his charcoal pencils, and fashioned creatures of the forests....a large grizzly bear, rearing upon its hind legs in a frighting stance, the eyes fierce, a menacing attitude, and my old nemesis my nightmares, an almost life- like black panther in a leaping crouch upon a rocky cliff. Both creatures loomed out, the wild eyes following everyone about the room who entered there, never at rest, always the dangerous predators.

    I admired his talent, but despised him for not putting it to better use, what was he thinking as he busily created the animals that certainly wouldn't benefit anyone? Why did he hide his talent from the world? Why had he quit his previous jobs as newspaper artist for advertising clothing?...or, quit his comic strip back while we were in Nowata?...or stopped painting murals on hotel lobby walls? Indeed, he was a puzzle.

    One day he decided to go to the west coast to work in the shipyards. Mother asked Uncle Leon for enough money for train fare, and enough for room and board until his salary began rolling in. And I think all of us, including mother, were extremely glad to see him off. I don't remember his actual leaving, but it was quite a simple process of his short walk with his suitcase up the road parallel the train tracks to the depot, and board a passenger train. He left the car with mother, who did not drive, but Bettye did, so we named the '37 Chevrolet sedan the Green Sparrow, and took it to school, to church, visiting, and into town on rainy days, and sometimes it was taken on dates. Even Aubrey drove the Green Sparrow with mother's permission, and we would go over to Mansfield to uncle Leon's cafe for Cokes.

Dad, out of lives, was like a breath of fresh air. Mother began taking interest in our basketball games. I was one of the three starting line-up forwards, and it was a sure bet I'd stay the whole game, if I didn't foul out. I was co-captain, and as the captain would graduate in June, the following year when I would be a senior, I would become captain. I was happy, the happiest I had ever been in my entire life. The only flaw was our broken hearts over the loss of our baby. We had his picture up on the piano, and we talked to him always as we passed, and some days, our tears ran.

Some nicer days after school, or on Sundays, I would walk to the cemetery, and to his small grave. I'd sit and pull at the grass, feeling the nearest I could be to him.

I'd look up over the top of the trees and into the sky, as if I might see a miracle there that would explain my <u>why?</u> The birds sang in their various songs, and rabbits would browse close by. But, I never received an answer in the clouds, or the sky, and God never spoke, never explained. I would drain my tears out, and when there were none left, I would pat the little mound that grass hadn't grown there yet, and tell him good-bye.

I knew about how things were. I didn't know why they happened, but I would have a dream-desire, to rake all the dirt off the grave, reach into the tiny casket and lift up my baby brother, and he would open his eyes and see me, and he would smile, his little white teeth showing, and I would carry him out of that place. But, that was silly. It was only a strong desire brought on by my never being able to see him again. I'd grow old, and decrepit, but I'd never stop loving my little brother.

Later in life I felt I had never brought about any closure concerning his death, and that was possibly caused by my feeling that he shouldn't have died as he did, or died without being able to see, at least. If he suffered the dreadful blood disease, he could not have survived. If, however, he didn't have leukemia, there was no reason under the sun that he should have died. I blame dad for his lack of concern, false pride, and lack of loyalty. I blame mother for being so naive, or for her lack of strength in serious cases as this one, to fight with all her strength to save Tommy, at least. And I blame myself for succumbing to all the adult reasoning, if reasoning is identified as adults sitting about on their back sides and simply waiting. Poosh!

We moved again with help from mother's brothers to another, sturdy house we called Ada Smith's house, to secure our furnishings, for we would follow dad to California as soon as Bettye graduated from high school and Peggy and I completed our year. The plan was to pay the regular rent in storage until we could return as soon as possible for our household goods.

Mother and one of my uncle's went to Ft. Smith to trade in the Green Sparrow for a '39 Mercury sedan we girls immediately named the Black something-or-other, an extra gas ration stamps were issued by the government because we were re-locating to Southern California while dad helped build ships for the war effort. I did not want to leave my last year of high school at Hartford. I also wanted to play basketball one more year, but it wasn't to be. We paid our last visit to Tommy's grave to say farewell and it was so hard on us, especially mother. We managed to get through it, and with a competent driver, we left June, 1943, for the west coast.

The furnishings in the house were not as secure as we had planned. Almost immediately the house was broken into, some things taken, and our private papers scattered or destroyed, correspondence touted by bruiser mentalities as something to be made fun of, and, so, mother's brothers moved all furniture and goods to their various homes. I especially missed the little orchestra piano and the lovely library table, and never had a chance to see them again. The balance of the furniture was of no consequence. I lost my childhood scrapbook of movie stars, and my 8 x 10 glossy, black and white picture of the boxing champion, Max Baer.

Mother's cat, old Shag who had traveled from place to place with us, was taken to grandma Michael's to live out her years there.

I had no idea that I would stay away forty-seven years, and that the circumstances of my return would be determined by someone else's wishes, who would not be around to witness yet another mess I'd be getting myself into. But that is in the now.

Grandpa and Grandma Michael

Mother and brood at Lavaca

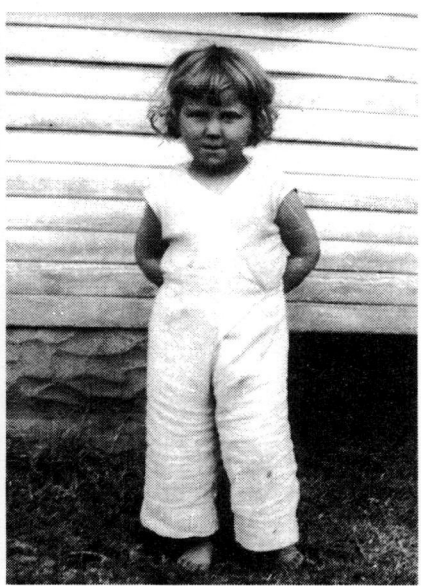

Herb, Alma (center front) Bettye (Rt. with cat) and neighbor girl, Lt.

Peggy

Tom May, 22

J.D. May and family
(Dad, far left)

Grandpa and Grandma May

The beginning

Showing off my baby girl

Pa and Ma Pickle

Querita and Me

Bruce

Bettye with Tommy

Vicki, 12

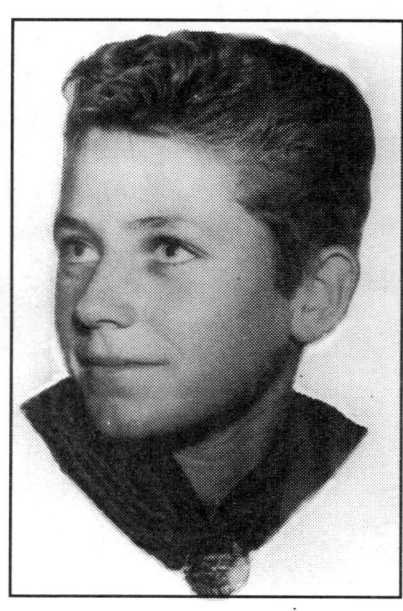
Tom, Eagle Scout

Chip holding Vicki's son Robert

Scott, and bride Patricia Navarro

Vicki and her Prince Charming, Thomas Lloyd

Part Three

I'm Tired and I Want To Go To Bed

"Oh Lord, correct me, but with judgement; not in your anger, lest you bring me to nothing."
Jeremiah 10:24

Chapter Ten

We departed Arkansas on a bright warm day, taking Route 66, in the black Merc, laughing for the sheer thrill of a brand new adventure, great hopes; a far, far better world for us despite the hideous war. Mother's face grew sad at times, but she managed to perk up and join the rest of us in our exuberance, a state of mind where all things had to be better, and hope springs blessed at times. We did need a change. We deserved a change.

At this time, brother Herb was a United States Marine, fighting now somewhere in the South Pacific, and this added to mother's periods of quiet, and I'm certain she was constantly worrying about him . We had made arrangements for trunks and boxes of needed household items, and clothing, to be shipped by rail from Hartford depot, and it would probably arrive in San Pedro about the time we did.

It was extremely hot in the desert states, and as we came to a rise in the highway, a long silvery, two-lane road shot up into our view, snaking off in shimmering heat waves for as long as we could see, then abruptly disappeared up to another rise, or rounding the base of a small butte. We had no air conditioning, and all windows were rolled down where blasts of hot air stung our faces and reddened our eyes, and our long hair blew in tangles about our heads.

Bettye usually sat in the front seat with Jim, our driver, a very nice, young man who graduated with Bettye's high school class. When he became tired, we would pull over, and Bettye would help drive the long, boring strips of road while he rested, or we would stop for a cold pop, and some food. There were no rest stops back then, but we managed to stop at service stations to wash ourselves and brush our teeth. Mobil stations were the cleanest, we decided.

    We traveled as long as we could nights, usually stopping after midnight to pull over to the side of the road, open the doors and windows, and sleep a few hours. All along the highway could be seen cars and trucks pulled off to the side, doing the same as we were doing, and strangely enough we never were frightened, or felt threatened by other travelers. It was as if we were all in this game even if we were complete strangers, but we were Arkies, Okies, hoards of southern and mid-western states people going for the same reason...to the west coast to finally work in the ship yards and have a better future.....and all because the "dirty Japs" bombed Pearl Harbor and forced us into a bloody war that horrified us, even if it was providing us with something better than pan gravy and pinto beans. Such a diversity; the terrible war, and hope. We were all aware of how we felt, and in a sense we felt guilty, but something happened we hadn't seen before in our lives, anyway, inevitable progress racing ahead, leaving behind the squalid, hungry, back house existence of the despondent thirties. I could feel it. So could the others.

    Out of the war would come the good, too, not only would we count our dead and wounded; but, our strides toward scientific medical discoveries, research of every walk of life, not simply military war weapons of ghastly proportions that could kill millions with a single "wonder" bomb. Suddenly like a shot in the arm, our country rose up out of the stifling dust of complete bankruptcy to become almost overnight a roaring lion of plenty. Yesterday quickly became obsolete. We awoke from a long sleep.

    We finally left the dust devils of the wide and lengthy expanse of the deserts behind to arrive in the Los Angeles area where we felt we had discarded blinders to suddenly enter into a world of unbelievable magic. We had never seen so many people, or so much traffic, and to me, it appeared time raced ahead; everything was bustle, busy, and hurry. The noise was startling, also, and the stench of oil refineries overpowering.

The sunshine was a blinding whiteness, unlike Arkansas where everything was bathed in a golden brightness, and I looked up to discover a thin layer of fog as yet to dissipate that served as a filter causing what I thought of as "white sunshine".

Traffic became worse as we approached San Pedro. Street cars that connected the area to Los Angeles , to Wilmington, and Long Beach, added to the clamor of a busy industry giving its all to the war effort. Harbors were choked with all sorts of ships, tugs, and barges, and high way up on a scaffold a welder's arc flared as repairs were made to the perpendicular bow of an extremely large ship. Some ships were in dry docks awaiting repairs, and the pa-pa-pa-pa of tugs lugging large vessels up the harbor were echoing above other noises at intervals. The screeching and horns of all types of vehicles were vying for leadership of noise volume.

I looked ahead as we traveled among the traffic up Gaffey Street, and covering the area overlooking the break water leading out onto the open sea were dozens of silver- hued balloons, floating gently above strategic areas and objects on the ground secured to the ground to prevent drifting away. Their function was to obscure important and possible targets for enemy planes from the air. Fort McArthur was just beyond this line of balloons.

"Big Bertha" was, indeed one of the biggest anti-aircraft guns anybody had ever seen. To us she was quite visible as she sat serenely on a long, flat rail car, carefully covered with camouflage netting. Even in the inactive position, she was formidable. She was docked off 22nd street down toward the west coast ship builders where dad worked as a machinist. I always had a desire to go see "Big Bertha" up close, but that was forbidden.

We were soon settled in a new, modern housing unit located up on Western Avenue north of Peck Park that was still in progress, and as soon as one unit for four families was completed, four families moved in almost before the paint was dry. We had a living room, a dining room, and kitchen downstairs, two bedrooms with bath...an honest-to-gosh bathroom, a lock-the-door-and-bathe-in-hot-suds-water every night bathroom. What a dream to pee and flush.

This sudden change of living as if we had been so long in a nightmare and transported to another planet, did wonders for mother. The haunted expression she had worn for so long began to fade, and the novelty of dad bringing in a regular check each week, plus over-time pay, began to be a continuous thing of happy amazement, and I, for one, could barely allow myself to believe it would last. It was too good...to wonderful to last, I told myself.

We continued to run into people we had known in Arkansas, for it seemed we were all clumped together in the two largest wartime housing projects. All of us hungry ones swarmed like locusts down upon this lovely harbor, so it was no surprise when Ann Wilson from my Hartford class and I got together to storm the San Pedro High School halls to finish our senior year. We needed to cling to the familiar, not only for support, but for friendship. We had no idea what the students would be like, how they dressed. Both of us did so want to finish school in Hartford, but as it wasn't to happen, we gritted our teeth to make the plunge.

Our mothers had gotten together, and without our blessing, must have hit the cheapest stores in Pedro to purchase our school clothes, and to our dismay came back home with their purchases. I do not know how Ann felt the moment she saw her new things, but I was so bitterly disappointed that when I went upstairs with my new things, I broke down in tears. I could not wear what mother had purchased for me. They were cheap, cotton blouse, non-descript ill fitting dress and skirt, and a pair of Mexican-type, leather strapped shoes with high wedgie heels. She informed me the shoes were so cheap [money value] she couldn't pass them by. What was I to do?

Peggy was twelve, starting junior high, and when I

caught a glimpse of her face after mother's shopping spree I knew she was unhappy, too. We couldn't do anything. Mother was adamant about the finality of the purchases, and we best be satisfied.

As Peggy and I prepared to enter school in the fall, Bettye was planning her future. She wanted to find a job that would pay her good money, and that was to head out to a ship yard, join the other young women, who were fast becoming "Rosie the Riveters", and apply. She was nineteen, and her needs were clothes, and hopefully, a car. She was aggressive and enthusiastic, so signed up as an apprenticed welder.

In the meantime, though, we wanted to have some fun. The beach was a good place to start. Herb's wife had given me a neat, two piece bathing suit, and Bettye had one, so we enjoyed Cabrillo Beach, Redondo and Venice, along with new friends we had fortunately made in the short span we had been in California.

Long Beach Pike was another great hang out for teenagers....all sorts of rides and things to see and eat....and boys...mostly very young sailors who were anxious about their futures, and it showed in their eyes. We talked, but didn't touch. This was brand new ground for us, and we had to be cautious. We were green.

There was a teen hangout at the five roads on Gaffey Street where no alcoholic beverages were served, lots of juke box music featuring the big bands...Tommy Dorsey...,Glen MIller, Benny Goodman, all the other greats with Sinatra and Crosby, Ella, Dinah, O'Connell, lending their voices as never heard before...dance music to jitterbug gyrations we soon picked up on. Our eyes were open wide with innocent awe, and we couldn't believe what we saw. We both, Bettye and I, grasped onto this life-line thrown out to us after years of deprivation, so grabbed that line in an effort to forget that time, and threw ourselves into the happy frenzy with all we had. We knew adulthood was upon us, and we had but a short time to dance and fling ourselves about with "In the mood," and slow dancing to "Moonlight Serenade."

One fairly, happy night, two tall guys walked through the door, stood looking over the heads through cigarette smoke, then gave each other a little nod of success, and made their way through the crowd toward us.

Bettye looked up, eyes wide. "My gosh, its Weldon and Aubrey."

"Where?" I turned around and the two were headed towards us, where we were seated around a table drinking cherry cokes.

Weldon was dark, good looking, about twenty-five, and hailed from the Hartford-Mansfield area. He had also dated Bettye a couple of times sometime back. Seemed that county in Arkansas had sent most of its citizens to the west coast, I thought.

I really didn't know what to say to Aubrey, and have forgotten most of it, so it couldn't have been anything other than simple conversation, but as it turned out, we four became double daters, and our spare time was filled suddenly with the two of them. Everywhere we went both of them stood out like sore thumbs, because in observing a crowd anywhere, there were uniforms of every branch of the service, and Aubrey and Weldon were civilians in street clothes. Unknown to me, Aubrey was a great fourteen and a half months younger than I. I looked about fourteen, and he looked at least twenty. I did not know this then, and I probably wouldn't have become upset about it at a time when I wasn't looking for any serious relationship. Later on was entirely different. Weldon was 4-F status, a physical disability I knew nothing about. Both of them worked and had money.

Bettye had worked about three weeks when I found her crying up in our bedroom.

"What is the matter?" I asked her.

"Close the door." She whispered, and I did.

She wiped her eyes and nose, and said, very seriously,

"I've made up my mind about something, and I feel I have to do this."

"Do what?" I persisted.

"Listen," she sat up, legs crossed. "I've worked, and brought in my pay checks, and dad is there waiting for my check, signed over to him, and he gives me barely enough to have bus fare and my gear."

"He takes your money?"

"Yes! and he told me this is the way it will be. I work, and he takes the whole check." Her eyes blazed, suddenly. "I can't live indefinitely like this, never being able to buy anything, or get a car, or get out into my own apartment." She was a picture of despair.

I was becoming nervous now. I wanted college after I graduated, and this didn't sound to good to me. "So what are you going to do?"

"I'm going to marry Weldon." She announced this as if she was choosing the lesser of two evils. It was obvious she didn't really want to get married. But, she had another announcement, or should I say, advice?...for me.

"And as soon as you graduate, dad and mother are going to want the same from you, so you better get married to get out." She rubbed her reddened eyes.

These were ominous words to me, and while I felt pity for my sister, I couldn't discount her warning as untrue, or as scare tactics. Upon the fringe of my being in the house, hearing words and seeing things, I remembered fragments of dad's and mother's talk concerning what was being done with Betty's paycheck. They were putting it in the bank to help build up an account that would afford them a home some day. But what was so unfair was they were taking the money from Bettye, who wanted to be financially secure in her own life. If they took it, she would have nothing. She was correct.

On July 28, 1943, Bettye and Weldon were married at a neighbor's house...mother and dad certainly didn't have the wedding and cake in our apartment. Aubrey was best man, and I was maid of honor. After the wedding, we four went cruising; to a portrait studio there in San Pedro, and had pictures made, then went out to dinner. I suppose it was as festive as we could make it. Weldon had shown he had ideas for a good future, so perhaps Bettye would be free to help build a home with the enterprising young man.

Bettye was ensconced in her honeymoon apartment in Lomita, and Peggy and I took the twin beds in the bedroom, and we had a few weeks to go until school started.

I could hear my parents talking in their bedroom, near muffled voices drifting through the walls, as they made great plans for the future...their future...save for a new home ... save for furniture...save all they could...for this, for that...a new car, and on and on until that seemed to be all they had on their minds. After bills, everything left went into the bank. A fever took hold of them.

Mother began buying herself new clothes, and wanted new wedding rings. All the other wives about were buying the same things. She talked of a new car, but production lines of the automobile makers in Detroit had stopped making cars in 1941, right after Pearl Harbor was bombed, and were churning out weapons and equipment instead, so all new cars were on hold for the duration. She accepted that. If everyone else was waiting, so could she. But, where she was frugal also dad, was with Peggy and myself. They refused so often, that we were doing without items necessary for school, such as gym clothes, lunch money, and sometimes bus fare, or fees for various classes requiring supplemental books, or miscellaneous items.

Aubrey began to teach me to drive, using his 36' Ford sedan, and soon I was going about without a hitch. Once in a while, he would offer the car to me for the day while he rode to his work with a friend. He was generous.

I got my very first driver's license in Long Beach, failing the first written test, for I hadn't studied their hand book on proper California laws of the road. So before leaving, I asked for the book, and studied quickly. I asked for an alternate test, passed it, and took my driving test around the block, finally depositing my exasperated and sweating instructor. I had my driver's license, without the silly photograph they didn't have fifty-two years ago. In Arkansas everyone in our area went to Waldron, and requested a license, which was promptly issued, not many questions asked. This state of California surely was a horse of a different color.

A week before school started, Aubrey surprised me with gifts, so many gifts, I couldn't take it all in.

"What is this?" I asked him as he stood smiling at what he had done.

"Just things you need to start school," he answered, calmly. "Open them." He lit a cigarette with a Zippo lighter, and watched me over the flame.

I began to open boxes and sacks. What I began pulling out stunned me with surprise. "What...What...?" I sputtered. He grinned.

There were Sloppy Joe sweaters, red, yellow and brown... the most wonderful looking, and the new feel was breathtaking. Next, came black and brown skirts, light weight, the fabric the best I had ever seen on any woman, and two, small, clutch purses, the ideal design for a teenage school girl to carry along with her books.

I hesitated while my heart settled and a new dread filled me, and I dropped the beautiful items. "I can't accept these." I said this tonelessly, the better part of protocol taking over, while I did so want them. Oh how I wanted them, and felt I needed them, but I couldn't.

"Come on, Alma, I got these for you because you need clothes, and you have to look good," He urged the things toward me, this time bringing out saddle oxfords, all white, size just right. I was puzzled.

"How did you know my size?"

"I found out," he replied secretive, but more in a cajoling tone. "Who, Bettye? Surely not my mother! She doesn't even know what color my eyes are." I looked up at him suspiciously. Oh, lawzy me. It was my mother. How could she?

"But,...But, they...mom and dad won't allow me to keep these." I spoke with a feeling of doom.

"Yeah they will. I already know."

"Aubrey, do you make a lot of money...to pay for all this?"

"I pay by payment plan. Each month." He pulled me close to him. "Come on. It will be okay."

One thing I learned about Aubrey early on was that he was completely generous with me. It was too hard to resist his fantastic gifts, especially when my folks chose to close their eyes, because they were no where close to supplying these kinds of wardrobe items. Anyway, I was really sick at heart over my parents lack of concern with all of us children from way back. The total absence of parental protection was one of the qualities I was all too familiar with. They just didn't care.

And before me stood this tall, good looking guy...well, kid...who wanted to buy me things I could never afford to get for myself, and his taste was impeccable, his selections perfect, whether for himself, or for me.

By the time I was beginning my senior year at Pedro High, I had a start on good clothes. My pride and joy was a pair of denim Levi's boy's jeans, size 12, mind you. I couldn't fit too well in lady's hippy, wide-bottomed jeans, but I did love my Levi's I wore horseback riding through Peck Park with a group on Saturdays. Pants on girls were not allowed in school back then.

Soon, I was being overwhelmed with Aubrey's presents, though. Added to all the other things were a nice wrist watch, a necklace, dresses, blouses and tailored slacks, and a light-weight, lovely coat, just right for California winter mornings and nights.

I, and Ann, my girlfriend, were doing well in school, adapting to the difference in education, and a variety of cultures, and we soon were popular, excelling in most of our studies, but partially in our athletic abilities. GAA, girls after-school activity, and in choir. We dropped the sad faces, put on our best smiles, laughed and talked with all groups of students.

I was beginning to be asked out on dates by boys, but I couldn't accept. Aubrey would never hear of it. Besides, I guess you might say I was "his girl". I owed him so much. Guys became puzzled as I continued to turn them down, until I told them I was going steady.

Our bunch of teenagers were stressed to the max, because we were wartime teens, and the war was taking its toll on our 17 to 18-year-old friends and relatives. We were constantly in a state of panic, dreading the casualty counts daily, and poor parents waiting for that horrible messenger of death and the abominable telegrams. A small percentage of girls in the high school had married their sweethearts on their last leaves spent together, and a few were in their first and second trimesters of pregnancy. It was allowed, but the last trimester was forbidden for them in the last stages of pregnancy to be exposed to other young students.

I remember one day, a weak-kneed, pregnant girl was led out of her classroom, crying bitter tears, relatives supporting her, leading her down the hall. The rest of us stood wondering, but not for long. We knew she had been told her unborn baby's father had been killed. It set a dark mood over us all. I wondered about my brother, and Ann wondered about hers. It was day to day, hour to hour, that the pall rested with us all. So, later on we tried not to feel especially gloomy. We could do nothing about it, so must take up the long days in trying to have fun, and be normal. But we were stressed, and it did show in some of us.

Back home in Hartford, our little town was being decimated of its prime young men as the months went by, and not only was the Pacific Campaign getting bloodier, but the European front as well. And it seemed that each letter mother received from there, someone was dead, or missing in action. She was having her problems, too, and her reactions were irascibility and impatience, and at times we didn't attempt to approach her at those times if we needed to talk to her about something. More than once we refused to bring up subjects at all, for we wanted to keep her as calm as possible. She was exhibiting signs of pre-menopause, and as she always suffered PMS terribly, all of us were in for a worse than ever bumpy road.

The good-looking guy was asking me a question, and his thick lashed, green eyes narrowed a bit. He touched my arm, and moved closer to me. Lately, it seemed to me his usually clean breath smelled of something more than Sen-Sen, the tiny chocolate-colored pill we termed a breath freshner back then. I had smelled that kind of breath once before when I was very young, and now identified it as alcohol, or liquor of some sort. I didn't expect this from him, because I still lived in a semi-child's world, or I was a silly little fool to believe the sex act didn't include me....yet.

We were parked up at the usual teen parking place above Palos Verdes, where steamed car windows meant guys were scoring with their dates, and frequent shrills of laughter came from girls having the time of their lives. There was a panorama of twinkling lights, most of them somewhat muted due to the blackout codes, but there nonetheless, all below us from ships coming through the channel to dock near Terminal Island, mostly merchant marine vessels, to Redondo Beach to the left of us. I could make out the Long Beach ship yard where today the Queen Mary sits in all her aged splendor for all to see and visit, and Signal Hill with its wooden derricks shooting up like skeletal ghosts who looked down upon the pumping horse-head shapes of dozens of active oil drawing robot mechanisms, and I marveled at this world. It was unreal.

I turned to look at Aubrey, so close now. We had been close before, nuzzling, holding each other, and kissing, but this was much different. He was making a demand in a sense, that I didn't want to hear.

Again, he asked, "Do you love me enough to prove it to me?"

"I don't know," I mumbled, feeling somewhat threatened, but I didn't want to make him angry.

He slapped the steering wheel angrily, and said, "Okay, Okay," and started the car. We rode in silence, and he was driving a little too fast for the dangerous curves, so I asked him to please slow down. Finally, he slowed, reached over and pulled me close to him. We listened while "It Had to be You" was being sung on the radio.

"Now that is our song," he announced. "Our song

forever. Just yours and mine...always."

I had to be home early, especially on a school night. Gullible as I was, I believed that after he dropped me off, he went home and went to bed.

Aubrey took me to meet his family. I had never met them, except his elder brother Cotton, who graduated ahead of me in Hartford, and not only was a basketball star as well, but, at this time Cotton was an Army Air Force bomber navigator somewhere flying critical missions over Europe. To me, he was an All-American hero, just as I felt about Herb.

I liked Aubrey's parents, who were much older than my own parents, but they had produced eight children, Aubrey being the youngest, and had raised them in Hartford while Pa Pickle labored in the coal mines to support them all. Ma Pickle was kindly and sweet; a slim woman who wore her long hair braided and circled tightly about her fine head. They were people who were the backbone of the country...the salt of the earth. They were God-fearing and gentle, and obeyed the laws of God and man.

They had known grief, a grief that crushes parent's heart's; that of losing three small children on separate occasions to the diseases prevalent back in the twenties when imminuzations were unheard of in that area of the world and doctors almost non-existant. I thought of our little Tommy, and the grief we felt; but, to feel this awful pain three times made my heart go out to them, even if it was so long ago.

Stel, Aubrey's only sister, was ten years older than I, married with one little girl, and lived next door to her parents. Apparently, she was the family spokesperson, small and attractive, and her blue-gray eyes could blaze in sudden anger. Those eyes looked me up and down, left and right, surveying every small pimple I had on my face, and I immediately became intimidated. Her very presence bespoke chairperson-of-the-board, and had she barked out an order to stand to attention, I would have clicked my heels, and given her a very fine salute.

She could rip up one side of her youngest brother and

down the other, and have him standing mute before her; but as he turned away there was always the tiniest of smiles on his lips. He adored her, and she him. She would have killed for him, I decided.

There I stood in all their presence; Pa, good looking, with a kindly air about him, but a strength shining through...ma smiling, with her hands locked across her apron in front...Stel. Did she like me? I couldn't tell. Later, after the years, I suspected she didn't.

The days passed, and I was hard pressed to focus most of my attention upon Aubrey. I would walk out of the school, Ann and I, and there would be Aubrey waiting for me. Sometimes we gave Ann a ride home, then we would ride around until I'd have to go home, and after dinner he would be back, and we would ride around...cruise...or take in a movie, or head for the Pike. The only words mother would say to me were to be in early. I usually attempted to be in by ten, and Aubrey would respect that. It would be sometime later on I'd learn he would head for a bar down in Pedro and wouldn't be back to his house until three or four in the morning. But it was becoming difficult for me to fully concentrate on my school with him dominating so much of my time.

The hopeless thing was I was crazy wild about him. I don't know if it was love I was feeling, but he was someone I could be with who understood something about me. He was my "person," and I was certainly impressed by his attention, and indeed, flattered that he loved me so much.

I don't actually know how I would have felt had he suddenly told me he didn't want to see me again, leave my life, but, as I look back upon all those mixed up feelings I was experiencing, I felt almost trapped, and smothered in a way, and I desperately needed counseling. There was no one back then. I had no minister. I couldn't talk to mother...no understanding there, plus she was the last person on earth to give advice. I dreamed of going back to Hartford and playing basketball.

At this point, however, Aubrey would never allow me to

leave him, and he was becoming somewhat possessive, and was showing a hint of a jealous streak that made me quite uncomfortable. He also was missing work, so was waiting for me after school so often that Ann began walking with other friends.

Aubrey parked the car in front of his parents home, under the shadows of an over hanging tree, turned off the ignition, and faced me. The street light showed through the moving leaves, and cast little lights that danced across his face. He pulled me to him, and we began kissing.

"Am, will you marry me?" His lips moved hungrily over my face and neck.

"Oh, my gosh, Arb," I breathed jerkily. "I haven't thought that far yet. I've got school and...."

"Shh, shh," he whispered softly. "We can marry anytime you would like."

His hands were seeking out places on my body, pulling clothes down, and I was allowing it. I felt he was my love, and I amazingly emerging from a dark, frightening cocoon of a very long childhood, pulled up inside myself into a hard ball. I needed out...to fly...to soar into something better.

Later, all I could say was, "Oh, my gosh, we didn't use...uh..."

"No but that's okay. I can't get you pregnant."

"You can't?"

"No."

"Why?"

"I just know'"

I looked long and hard at him, wanting to believe him at that particular time, but I knew better.

"Arb, you are a virgin too, aren't you?"

"Yeah," he said it slowly, as if he didn't want to admit it, him being the "dude" I thought he might be, and all.

We were both shaking, almost uncontrollably as we straightened our clothes.

"Am?"

"Yeah."

"Now, we are married."

Inside my head, I said, "Oh, boy, am I in trouble...and in deep trouble." And I was.

The following week, Aubrey bought me a small diamond ring..an engagement ring, and until a tender moment, slipped it on my finger.

I didn't want to make love again until after school was over but he wasn't one to stop at that. He was like an elk bull in rut, and hounded me almost constantly. If I attempted to explain why I needed this absence of sex, he would become angry, saying, "If I can't get it from you, I'll find it elsewhere!" This frightened me. I didn't want to lose him.

I was beginning to realize that he was drinking more, and his behavior was taking on a darker side, almost as if he was a small, spoiled, child.

When the realization sank into my worried mind, my poor brain wanted to shut off completely. I was feeling sick, a nausea unlike what the headaches produced, that was for sure. I was pregnant. The very word "pregnant" caused me to shiver. It was an ugly word, I had been told. Sex was a dirty word. How could I be sure? My periods were a hit and miss thing, never regular since I began them, so what do I know? I didn't feel like a woman. I felt like a dirty little girl.

I told Aubrey, and he said, "Don't worry so much. You might not be."

"How could I not be? What will we do?"

"Stop fretting Am," he answered so calmly. "If you are, we will just have a baby, then, won't we?" I could have sworn he was pleased...the look of him...his whole demeanor. He wasn't worried.

"We will find you a doctor to let us know. You know, the rabbit test."

That is exactly what I did. A blood test, inject the rabbit...if the rabbit dies...... It did.

My world was again changing, almost slapping me upside the head once more, the old way I'd always understood.

Now, I have to do some thinking....some profound thinking. Arb and I would talk, we would decide what we were to do. But, I had another source from which I could seek help. Arb couldn't be in on this appointment. I had to do this alone.. Just me, and the tiny seed I was carrying...to my Comforter...to my Protector. He would know.

As I prayed that night, alone, out on the balcony where I saw the lights in the Harbor below, I then focused my attention up into the sky. I didn't pray not to be pregnant. Strange, wouldn't you say? I prayed for help, for the Lord's help, to tell me what to do, to guide me, that I'd allow Him to make the calls.

I'd like to say I went to bed with an uplifted heart, but I can't. But over the next days, I felt the need for secrecy. Do not tell anyone. I told Aubrey that as scared, as ashamed as I was to find myself in "the family way" we couldn't tell our folks, anyone. He shrugged his shoulders in agreement.

Suddenly, there was a great need for me to protect this fetus, especially so into this early part of pregnancy when it would be vulnerable to abortion.

I didn't know the first thing about abortion, except that it was illegal, and it was being performed many times every day by doctors, by the woman down the street, even by so called mid-wives who delivered babies. For a fee it could be done, if one knew how to find them.

Back in 1943, an illegitimate child shamed the family, and was a crime against God. Most girls in trouble suddenly went to "visit an aunt in Detroit" or jumped out of a five story window to restore face to her parents. But, I didn't know what the odd strangeness was that engulfed my being; an indescribable feeling of the strong secrecy that was to take me through the entire pregnancy to the end.

I was still seventeen. Later, I would grow in height an additional half inch. Aubrey was fifteen months younger than I! He would later grow two inches more. And we were making a baby, a baby I must protect from my parents at all costs, and perhaps, from Stel.

Chapter Eleven

---

*"Oh Lord, you have seen my wrong;
you judge my cause"*
Lamentations 3:59

I had no courage in matters requiring deceit, yet I quickly discovered my deception transcended far above what I believed I was capable of. I strongly felt I could not trust anyone, and I cautioned Aubrey to keep our secret until it was safe to disclose it, or until the changes of my body alerted others.

I was thankful for Sloppy Joe sweaters and box style tops later on, but for now I suffered the agonies of nausea, and must try very hard to hide that. Mentally, I was a mess, and Aubrey spent more and more time in bars after I was dropped off at home nights, so I tried to keep up a normal routine, and a normal face.

One evening as I looked at my father's face while he was reading the News Pilot, I shuddered to think what he might do if he only knew. The consequences of my disclosure would, no doubt, be prompt and decisive. I would not be considered at all.

My appetite dropped to almost nothing, and I lost weight until I was almost too thin. Mother remarked about how skinny I was, and how the dark circles under my eyes were becoming worse.

One afternoon Aubrey picked me up at school, and I noticed he was slightly intoxicated. His eyes were red and partially unfocused, and his speech slurred.

"I've been waiting an hour for you," he said, accusingly, as I got into the front seat next to him.

"You been making out with the pretty boys, have you?" his eyes were hostile.

"Good grief, no," I replied.

"Don't tell me that," he said, as he put the car in gear and spun the tires pulling out.

He was driving too fast for the residential area, and I clutched the seat beneath me for support, a gesture he knew was my fear of fast, reckless driving. Before, he had always slowed when he discovered my uneasy feeling, but this day was different...he was different...and, he was very unhappy.

I had never been around people who drank, only that one incident in Lavaca years before, so I had no idea of the seriousness and depth of Aubrey's problem. I wondered about "drunks," and the movies depicted a falling-down-drunk as an object to laugh about, but I hadn't a clue about alcohol abuse, but I was certainly on a painful road to discovery in the following years.

I felt trapped with this mad person. There was no escape for me, and I seriously considered running away...but to where?..to whom?

The car picked up speed, was rounding corners with excessive carelessness, and he smirked at me, "How do you like that?..huh? You like that?"

"Please Arb, slow down," I remember my begging voice and hated myself for it.

He took his right hand off the steering wheel and gave me a rough push that landed me against the door.

"You are going out with boys, aren't you? Aren't you?"

"No, no, Arb, please."

"Please,..please Arb," he mimicked. "If you will let me do it, you will let anyone do it! Right?"

I was so frightened, I became weak, and I was so sick to my stomach. I recall I never had "morning sickness," always afternoon and early evening spells that I was desperately trying to hide all the time.

The car was going down Gaffey Street, a much traveled street, and he said, "I'll kill us both, now, here!"

I screamed, and ducked down upon the floor. It wasn't a wise thing to do, but at that point, I almost allowed fear to take hold of my sensible mind, and amazingly, the car slowed down, quickly. Arb must have seen a patrol car, I thought, and perhaps my screaming was so sudden and loud, he was shaken by it.

He parked the car at the railing of a dead-end street. He slumped over, his head resting against his hands upon the steering wheel. His shoulders were shaking as he quietly sobbed.

I had resumed my seat and sat stiffly as a board, stunned. What in heavens name just happened? Shock was heavy upon me, and I did not dare suspect that I was feeling as I did when dad whipped me with a belt. The fear came on. I could taste it on my tongue. Oh dear Lord, I was still caught up in another trap. I then opened the car door, got shakily out, and vomited over the railing onto a patch of weeds.

I returned to the car. Aubrey was lighting a cigarette, and looking calm. Sad, but calm.

"Oh, Am, I'm so sorry." He looked at me with almost sober eyes. "I don't know what came over me. It won't happen again. I promise you that."

One afternoon later on, I stopped by Ma's and Pa's, to bring Arb's car by before I headed on home to Channel Heights. Ma was busy in the tiny kitchen, but was happy to see me. Arb wasn't there, and I assumed he was working. She asked me to sit down, that she wanted to ask me something. She had a little worried frown on her face.

"I need to know," she began, a little reluctance in her voice," if you are with Aubrey at night...that is, late..in the morning."

"He takes me home at ten. I have to be home at ten." I waited for her reaction.

"Do you know where he goes after he takes you home?" she fussed with her apron.

"No, I don't," I told her. "But I wondered too."

"He comes in maybe two or three o'clock in the morning so drunk he stumbles all over, and can't get up to go to work 'most the time."

She obviously was extremely concerned, and I felt sadness for her.

"Now, I'd like to ask you a question," I felt brave now, and needed to know. "How old is Aubrey?"

"He's sixteen-years old," she answered, then she shrewdly nodded her head. "You didn't know, did you? He looks a lot older, because he is so tall and lanky." She put a finger to her lips. "He always manages to get liquor. They never ask for I.D.."

As I left, I wondered how much worrying she had done over her youngest son.

I rose each dawn with a good amount of trepidation, and hoped my reluctance at cheerfulness would simply be accepted as the "sulky" demeanor I seemed to wear habitually around my parents. I was becoming more withdrawn, also because I was constantly worried about my condition, Aubrey's changed behavior, and my feeling of being forever trapped.

I went through classes at school, an early morning swim class the school's athletic department required at the YMCA where I passed all requirements, except the very last one; that of swimming two and a half pool lengths. I could only mange two full ones, then as I turned to complete the half, my lungs felt full of cotton, and as I struggled to breathe, my legs ached and became useless. Weakness of my body began to pull me under the water, and with some blurred vision, I paddled over to the edge, and pulled myself up.

Ann watched me, concern on her face. "Alma, can't you

make it? You don't have but the half to go." She didn't know my condition, and was puzzled, for I had always been a good athlete.

"No I can't. I just can't do it. I'm bushed." With that I failed to receive my swimming certificate, and was given a failing grade in the class that determined my final gym grade for the semester.

I tried desperately to conceal my disappointment, and the class was bussed back to school where we resumed our other class studies. I had no problem in the regular classes, but gym period was becoming more difficult for me.

I wish I could say I was somewhat bright...with a little intellectual moxie...or, should I say horse sense? A logic born out of necessity, but I can't. I'd be lying if I did. Of course, now I know, and later I found out that Aubrey and I could have saved ourselves and our families the shameful burden of an illegitimate baby by using one of my school days and going down across the border past San Diego to Tijuana to get married by a Mexican Justice of the Peace. We could have kept that secret until I felt our baby was safe. But we didn't know, and I was too frightened to ask anyone. We were under eighteen...I had turned eighteen the following fall. This is what Arb and I finally decided to do after the baby was born, as it turned out, while Mexican marriages where still legal for U.S. citizens, and accepted by our court system. But, Arb was still under age while I wasn't.

All the thinking and decisions were made by Arb and me, mostly me, and he went along with it. Here we were, children making a little unborn baby, and we didn't have sense God gave a goose.

I was continuing to hold the flat tummy as I entered the second trimester. I didn't smoke or drink alcoholic beverages, and my appetite nagged at me enough to allow me to eat more, and most of the dreaded nausea left.

Soon, I was wearing my gym blouse outside my shorts in gym classes, and as California weather continued to be cooler up until June, especially mornings and evenings, I felt comfortable in my looser clothing, and I wondered if there were more wiser pairs of eyes out there than I even suspected. At home, no one seemed to notice my drastic taste in some clothes, however, and I was so certain Peggy would see me undressed, and point out my little tummy.

    I lay quietly in bed upon my back, staring at a dark ceiling, twisting the corner of the blanket, when the tiny stirring moved inside me, ever so faintly, and I quickly moved my hand down and laid it over the small lump just below my belly button. I'd never felt anything so amazing to me, and I lay very still, waiting, for as long as I lay upon my back, the stomach which was extremely flat, allowed the small lump to be more exposed. I waited, and waited some more, then under the palm of my hand I felt the slight movement again. My hand cupped the lump containing the fetus, and I promised it safety.

    As the lump grew, I felt more protective toward this little life, but strangely, I was carrying the baby closer in toward my back and between my small hip bones. This was to allow it to be more hidden, safe from prying eyes, I thought, and my Protector was in total charge. My belly was not bulging, and I felt comfortable, oddly.

    Running laps. I could not run more laps after the baby curled up into a little ball, the sensation so strong at it's objection, I cupped my hands over it as I came to a stop only a quarter around the track. Both gym instructors watched as I went over to the grass and sat down, allowing my breathing to even out, and the baby to relax.

    "No more," I told it. "NO more, if it hurts you."

    How does one tell a fetus you are so sorry to be so stupid, but this was a first time out of many that I told my unborn baby, "I'm sorry."

    My gym grade was final...an F for failure. Alma May flunking gym was ironic, to say the least. How would that read on a transcript into college, I wondered, but then college may never happen.

    All the high school students were in great spirits,

laughing uproariously on a constant basis, and walking more jauntily along the halls as graduation day approached. For color day, we had to wear all white, except for a touch of powder blue, our class colors. Girl's wore white skirts, and simple style blouses, and I wore my blouse outside my skirt. We all took pictures, singles, pairs, groups, and we acted sober at times, and mugged for the camera at others.

I had begun to wear a small support girdle, not too tight, only very light for comfort for me, and protection for the baby, who seemed to approve of the support preventing bouncing. The little babe was quick to show her discomfort, if I bounced her about, and I was glad of my decision to purchase the girdle.

Evenings, Arb and I would take in a movie, or ride for miles on end, listening to the car radio, and we talked. We never seemed to know what to do about our problem of marriage, but I was as reluctant to press the issue as he was. As we both felt it unlikely we could be married because of his age, we were floating along on this big supposition that soon the fates would expose our secret that we could no longer hide, and those in higher authority would certainly attempt to determine our lot whether we approved or not.

We knew, also, that our baby could not be harmed now, its tiny life abruptly stopped, but we continued to feel unsafe. We had the birth to face that would for certain cause pandemonium in both camps. We were in for a torturous conclusion to my pregnancy. Outright shame for Arb and me, and embarrassment for our parents. We dreaded it tremendously, but we must ride it out. I can't, for the life of me, believe to this day, that we kept our baby hidden from the people I lived with, and was around every painful day, that they didn't know...were not aware of! What kind of people were these, to completely ignore that, even though my shape wasn't extremely obvious? It had certainly changed. No one could have been as marvelously intelligent as to stand beside a mother, or father, or sister, while eight months pregnant without their being aware of the change. Not me, anyway. Who blinded their eyes?

Good grief, were they all in denial? I was an immature teenager at best, of course, I set out to fool them, and apparently, I did.

I wasn't feeling well as I prepared for the baccalaureate service at the high school auditorium. I felt nervous and my back was causing some discomfort. The baby seemed to find a position that suited her, so she was still.

Soon, I was in pain, and I holed up in the bathroom thinking I'd be fine momentarily. I wasn't. I looked at my frightened reflection in the mirror, the face pale, the eyes wide and dilated, the image still that of a little girl...a scared little rabbit of a girl with nobody to turn to.

Silently, I cried out to God to please help me, and protect me in the hours to come...to be with "us" as we entered a world that neither of us was familiar with and please give mom and dad some sense, and get me some help, Sweet Jesus.

I couldn't continue to stay in the bathroom, so left it to go back into the bedroom where Peggy was busy reading something. If I knew her, it probably was Archie comics...Archie, Betty, and Veronica, with their silly little problems. She looked up at me, and remarked how sick I looked.

A tearing pain struck me, and I sat upon my bed, then another. I couldn't sit, so stood, and found I could not stand flat-footed upon the floor. The pain was so severe I was raised to my tip-toes, and I walked back and forth in this position. I bit my lips to shut off the cries I wanted desperately to let out.

Peggy said something like, "Oh gosh," and took the stairs down on a noisy run to yell for mother, who came up somewhat quickly, demanding, "What is wrong, Alma? What is the matter with you?"

I still couldn't tell her...Hey Mom, I'm pregnant and in labor! What I was expecting, I don't have the slightest inclination. Why I continued to be mute is a complete mystery. And I was in terrible pain.

This started Friday, June 16th. A doctor was summoned to the house, and my vague recollections were he did not perform a complete examination, or if he did, my parents didn't take it seriously. I was given pain pills that pretty much kept me from knowing too much about anything, but I do know my pain had diminished a great deal. When the pills were wore off, I'd woke to find myself in mother's bed. My father wasn't inside the bedroom at any time I could recall, and Arb was not allowed inside the house to see me.

By Saturday, my bodily functions ceased. I'd wake, and I'd be given pills, and the doctor returned, and I was given an injection of some sort. I drank very little water, I did not urinate, and I was becoming weaker as time passed. I couldn't think properly with the medication, but later on I wondered if the baby was drugged, also. I'm sure she was, and she would be too weak to do what she must do in order to survive.

Sunday came and went, and Arb walked back and forth in front of our apartment, unable to see me. Was he silent, too? He later told me he was afraid my parents would allow "us" to die, and he was in a temper.

Monday, the doctor was back. He talked to mother and dad, then went to phone for an ambulance, and prepare Cerritos Hospital in Long Beach of my arrival, plus his diagnosis of my condition.

I barely remember the ambulance ride to Long Beach, but I do remember being put into a room with other women, and a catheter device inserted. The drugs were wearing off, even though I was terribly groggy, and the pains began again, easily at first, then harder. One of the women there remarked, "She is in labor and she is so young."

I was taken to X-ray, and the technician said to the doctor in charge, "There is definitely a baby in there," and they briefly discussed the situation. I was then taken to delivery room, where preparation was being made. I prayed again-"Oh Jesus, please let us be victorious, let us get this over with."

The birth was difficult. Even with ether. I was not all the way unconscious, only partially, I learned, because I was so weak, therefore I felt the knives. But I heard her cry. I heard my baby cry! She had miraculously made it, despite the three hard days of labor. Despite the people surrounding her who could have intervened with her life. Despite the whole, bloody, world, she made it!

The baby was whisked away to an incubator, and I was whisked down the hall to a ward of chattering women and put to bed. I was not allowed to see my baby. Why not? I was not allowed to see Aubrey, then, and I had one visitor only, my mother, Dad was not with her. Her lips were drawn into a little, straight line. Her eyes blazed. Here we go, I told myself.

"I just wanted to know why you went and got yourself pregnant with that stupid Aubrey? Why did you do this to your dad and me?" She began to cry. "After all we have done for you, and you, repay us this way. What will people say? Did you stop and think what my relations and friends will think?"

My fears had been well founded when she continued her tirade. "If you had told me in the beginning we could have prevented this from happening. Why didn't you tell me? Well?" "I don't know," I mumbled. "I'm sorry to hurt you."

After she got that off her chest, she straightened some and the fire left her eyes, and she had another little shocker to present to me. "The doctor..uh..that doctor who delivered the baby wants to adopt it. It would have a good home, better than what you can give it, and nobody need ever know...we can say you had your appendix out....and the doctor has offered money."

"Is that why I haven't seen my baby, Mom, because you want to adopt the baby out?"

"Well...well, you have been too sick to see it, and it can't be taken out of the incubator." she tried again, "You think about it."

"No!" I said to her retreating back.

The following day, Aubrey came in to visit me. Drapes were drawn around my bed, and he looked drawn, and stressed. I was glad to see him, and I asked if he had seen the baby.

"Yes, and she is cute. The doctor says she is almost six weeks premature, but is real bright." He was becoming excited now. "The doctor said as soon as she was born, she stared at the lights, and around the room before she cried.

"She is fine, though."

I was so tickled, and told him we were victorious. "I'll name her Victoria."

He grinned, and leaned down and kissed me.

"Did you have a hard time with my father?" I asked needing to know.

"Oh gosh, that old man wanted to kill me, then he made a big ruckus in the hall, tried to get me to sign adoption papers...."

"What?" I cried out softly.

"Oh, yeah, they wanted me to sign her over until they found out I'm not even eighteen yet." He grinned. "I told it loud to him that nobody is going to get my baby."

"And that is why mom came to me, then trying to manipulate me into signing, and I'm eighteen. Nobody can take her away from us. Nobody!"

It was with apprehension that I left the hospital without my baby, or even having seen her. I wondered if the doctor and my parents were still hoping I would sign adoption papers. I felt I should have been able to see her...they said she couldn't be taken from the incubator. Actually, they did not talk to me much, and I'd been forced to ask nurses to check the nursery. I was unable to walk unaided, so could not sneak to the nursery. At nights, I always imagined I could hear her cry.

Aubrey and his sister, Stel, came for me, Aubrey reassuring me the baby, Victoria, would be safe. It was my desire to be taken to Aubrey's folk's home in San Pedro. They all appeared ecstatic over this new, little, baby girl, and I felt more friendliness and ...yes love, with them. Arb was tender, and ever so gentle as he helped me into their modest home. His parents had given up their larger bedroom, and had taken the much smaller one. Stel lived next door, and began cooking appetizing meals, trying to coax me to eat. I had no appetite, was skin and bones, my once shining hair dull and lifeless. I hardly ate, or drank fluids I desperately needed, and my legs would not hold me in a standing position, but with all the help, and the great laughing, and talking, people coming and going, put me in a frame of mind that was definitely more pleasing than had I gone on to my parent's apartment. I never wanted to go back there again.

In a few days Stel and mother brought my baby home to me. My heart was pounding so furiously I was sure my whole body shook. Stel put the small...very small, little doll on the pillow beside me, and pushed the pink blanket back to show her tiny face. The room was crowded with people, and I looked up to see Arb standing by the bed, grinning.

Suddenly, I was overcome with bashfulness, and not yet having the out-of-the-womb mother instinct, I gazed at Vicki as she lay sleeping, almost afraid to touch her. I wanted to be alone with her and Arb, but curiosity was too much for the people there, so they were waiting for me to react. Most had wide grins on their faces.

"I...I...don't know what to do," I choked out. "How do I hold her?"

"Very carefully," someone said, and there was laughter.

"Babies are tough little things," Ma put in. "You won't hurt 'em unless you drop 'em."

"Go on. Pick her up," she prodded.

I reached out, and lifted her gently. She moved in my arms just as she did in my body, and I knew my little baby. An extremely small fist came to her head, an almost bald head, and her tiny mouth moved in a searching manner. She opened her eyes briefly and I saw blue eyes, eyes that would soon turn into a lovely grey.

I wondered if she was looking at me, or if she could tell it was me who held her now. As I pulled her to my body, I felt my breasts hurt, but I didn't know my emotions were completely circumvented by my baby and me, enveloping us both in this most wonderful bonding of new mother and new baby.

But, I was prevented from nursing her, for I was much too weak, the blood test showing anemia, and the milk would not be nutritious enough for her, and those were the years of "bottle babies," which was a shame, somehow. I had been given medication to "dry up" the milk, but it seemed, every time I held her close, those breasts went into fits of aching.

As soon as I was able, Arb and I took a day and went down to Tijuana, Mexico, and were married. Did I feel any better? Not really, but we could have other children, and produce pride instead of shame just with that arty, piece of paper.

At times my mother would walk down from Channel Heights to our place on Upland Avenue to check on the progress of the two of us. She turned her nose up at the small house we all lived in, making remarks to me out of hearing distance of the others to indicate her displeasure. But I wanted to tell her of all those years we lived in unheated, run down shacks, and had she forgotten? But, I didn't.

Soon, I was up and about, so thin my clothes were all loose, including my Levi jeans, but as the days passed I put on a few pounds, helped Ma around the house, and watched the quick progress of Vicki.

Aubrey had become a week-end beer drinker, and Pa, who worked hard all week, spent Saturdays at his favorite bar up on Gaffey Street. He also drank beer. The only non-drinkers in the family were the women and children, and beer was drunk freely in the home. But, the camaraderie within the family was so wonderful, and there was a constant cacophony of voices, laughter, light joking, and we always had food. Ma and I would cook, Stel and her family would come over, friends from Hartford, and relatives streamed in and out each week-end. I loved it. The baby loved it, and she absolutely thrived under so much tender care, and attention. Pa loved to hold the baby,, and rock her, and there were times he would take his walk carrying her tenderly in his big arms. He surely knew how to hold a baby.

Aubrey began to find the house too confining after a couple of months when the newness of our life change wore off for him. Our quarters became cramped, and privacy was a complete joke. He began to leave the house some nights to come staggering in late. Pa said "Oh well, all young guys go out to drink. It's just the way they are," and, Ma put in the alibi, "He is so young to have responsibilities." Then Stel would advise, "Alma, you will just have to understand him more."

I wondered what I should understand. Why did they feel I should understand something unknown to me...completely unknown to me? I felt that there possibly could be a block of some sort preventing my mind from realizing some knowledge the rest of them possessed. I was fully aware that I was "green"...that they knew I was green as a gourd, but I would watch my young husband leave the house evenings all spruced up with hurt in my heart, and confusion flooding my mind.

Aubrey did not talk to me as often as before the baby came, but he loved to tinker with his prize, a 1940, black with chrome Chevy sedan, whether he was washing, polishing, changing oil, or engage in minor repairs I would amble out where he was, sit on a wooden box, and make small talk. He always kept his quart bottle of Lucky Lager on a fender nearby.

I noticed he had a book, a manual on the 40' Chevy, that he consulted when involved in larger jobs, and upon occasion he would pull out the complete engine and fuss with it, and when he replaced the engine and all its many small parts, it purred like a kitten when he turned the ignition key. He was good...very good, and I noticed he loved it.

"You, uh, want to take a ride up in the hills later...uh, see how good a job I did?" he asked casually, without looking at me.

"Sure. Can we take Vicki with us?"

"Naw, she better stay here...just in case..." He took a long swig from the brown bottle, his throat jiggling as he swallowed. It appeared he simply opened his mouth, and easily poured the bitter liquid down his throat.

"Don't you ever taste it?" I asked, looking up at him, my eyes squinting through the sun. I was curious.

"Well, sure I taste it," he said, and laughed. He set down the bottle, and took out his pack of Chesterfields, put the pack against his lips, drew one out, and lighted it with the Zippo. He started to return the pack to his shirt pocket, hesitated, and offered me one. I took it, and he held the flame to it, and I puffed, and blew, puffed and blew. He laughed.

"You're suppose to inhale it, silly. Here, watch me take a drag and inhale it." With his mouth closed, he breathed deeply through his nose, held the smoke inside his lungs for a time, then released the smoke.

"Now do that."

"Okay, just watch me."

I took a long drag, pulled the smoke inside my mouth, closed my mouth, and breathed heavily through my nose. I began to strangle and cough, while the spent smoke boiled out my nose and mouth. I wiped my mouth, and gave him a hard look.

He looked at me, waiting for my excuse at failure.

"I know how to smoke," I blubbered. "I just don't do it this way."

He chuckled as I went inside to rinse my mouth, and wash my face.

He loved to drive, especially nights, up through Palos Verdes, around the edge of the ocean where breakers dashed thunderously against the jagged out-croppings of lumpy, urchin infested borders; great gigantic sentinels of formidable demeanor. And if the moon was full as it was that night, the silvery shimmering of the constantly moving ocean appeared to play with the moon in a dance of peaks and swells...moving...moving. I loved the sea, and I loved to stand on a beach, a lonely stretch of sand, in the coldest of weather, my face into the cold wind, and draw in the lovely smell of it, deeply into my lungs. I could camp there, bundled from head to foot, over a driftwood fire, and stare out over the tremendous expanse that thumbed its nose at my puny being. How I learned to love it, and how I miss it now.

He was driving slowly, one hand on the steering wheel, and one hand wrapped around the large brown bottle of beer he lifted to his mouth from time to time. He was perfectly quiet, appeared to look out upon the ribbon of curving road in a brooding way, and he never once looked out over the ocean, or to even notice it was there at all. I felt at this time he probably didn't know I was beside him, but I was wrong on that score.

"Am? I want to ask you," he began to speak, the words slurring. "Why do you always wear those white shorts when men are around?"

I thought Oh, boy, I'm in for another nervous spell."You hear me? I asked you a question. Why don't you answer me?" His voice was rising, and I knew I'd better answer something quickly or I was going to end up in deep trouble.

"Why..Why, gosh Arb, I don't wear shorts in front..."

"Don't give me that bull! You are a slut! You know that? You are a slut!"

The car was picking up sped, and was weaving too much around the curves. I gave out a little screech, which seemed to ignite his anger further, but I couldn't stop there. I was back into what I called my "panic zone," and whined, "Please Arb...please slow down."

He gave me a lethal look, stomped his foot down on the accelerator, and the car surged forward. "You want me to slow down, eh...eh? I'll show you how I slow down.."

As the car careened around the curves, the road fortunately empty of traffic, I let out a scream and automatically slumped down to the floor. I don't feel I was aware of the dangerous position I'd be in if we did pile up the car against the side of the hill, or over the left embankment down toward the ocean, but I do think I simply did not want to see death staring at me through the windshield.

As I lay more quietly, Aubrey took his right foot off the accelerator, and aiming it past the gear shift, kicked me as hard as he could into my slumped side. I bit my lips, but I was also working up an anger I knew I must not exhibit, for it would only fan his anger, and cause more trouble. We may end up at the foot of a steep incline, so I lay still, shuddering, waiting for his next move. He was becoming aware of all my vulnerable feelings, and he would use them, all my fears, to his advantage, and to my despair and sorrow.

Suddenly, the car came to a stop at the side of the road, and Aubrey took this time to light a cigarette, and take another swallow of beer.

"Get up, get up, and sit right in the seat." He was beginning to wind down, and I still had some hope of making it back home to my baby.

He drove slowly, without a word, and after a million years, we pulled up into the driveway. The lights inside the house were on. I let out a very slow, very long, silent breath.

Chapter Twelve

My beautiful little baby grew stronger as the weeks passed; was so healthy and bright. She laughed more than she cried, but she had so many people caring for her--the little princess of the family, extended family and friends---and it is a miracle she slept without an audience.

Some mornings I would wake up to find her crib empty, and I would rush into the front room to see that Stel had come over from her home next door, and was sitting rocking Vicki. Or sometimes my baby would be at Stel's house. I couldn't imagine the baby crying and I hadn't heard her. I slept completely tuned in to her breathing, and movements, and I'd ask if she had awakened and cried. I was told "No, I tip toed in and got her." Being reluctant to hurt feelings, I simply let it pass. After all, they were wonderful people.

Soon, it became difficult for me to have principal care of my baby without their guidance, or advice, and I was beginning to feel the frustration from their suffocating instructions from old wives' tales to the dressing and feeding of Vicki.

One evening, Arb and I bundled Vicki warmly against the damp night air, and told Pa and Ma we were taking her to visit a friend. Instantly, both began to scold us. "You are not taking her out in this damp air," Pa informed us, "She will catch pneumonia."

"She is fine," I insisted, but Pa's eyes were becoming angry. Ma came to me and took my bundled baby. "Here let me have her. You two run along and have a good time."

I stood as if nailed to the floor, tears of anger and...yes defeat...rose in my eyes. I didn't want to go without Vicki.

I'd wanted to move, to have my own little house, or apartment. I'd been harboring the need inside my heart for several weeks, now, and this particular night I confessed to Arb my desire.

"I wish we could Am, but, even with my job pay, there just aren't any available places to rent." He looked at me a bit hopelessly.

"It's impossible now," he continued. "Every housing unit has over a hundred people on lists, and---well, private apartments are not regulated, are more expensive, and I've heard, cockroach infested."

"So you have been looking into it, haven't you?" I asked

He nodded. "Yeah, I've been asking, but we will have to stay with Mama and Papa until we can find a place."

Well, I told myself, what is another stupid blow to the old solar plexus?

A couple of weeks later, there was a house trailer for rent, offered by a relative located on their property over looking the ocean. Arb and I took a look at it. It was small, but clean, carpeted and comfortable. "Let's take it," I said. Arb put his arm across my shoulder and said "Ok," and, taking a deep breath, said "but, it is going to be hard convincing Mama and Papa."

It was not a pleasant scene. Ma cried until she was ill, and later on took to her bed, and Pa appeared confused and hurt. Stel verbally yelled her disapproval.

"You're nothing but teenagers, and can't live on your own, and you are taking Vicki from us, and you don't have the sense to take care of her." This was Stel, stomping about waving her arms, her eyes blazing fire.

We moved in. Didn't need furniture except crib and high chair, toys, and our clothes. We were there two days.

The second morning the male clan came barging into our trailer, began to pile our belongings into their cars. No amount of protesting got us a listening ear.

"Your Mama is sick," Pa said to Arb. "She has taken to her bed, and she needs you there. A pretty thing when Alma didn't care if she was sick...just up and left her." He darted an angry look at me.

"She was not sick when we moved," I told him, "besides, she has Stel to help her."

He took a step toward me and said, "You--are--going--back--where--you--belong." Each word was stressed through tight lips, and I quickly backed away. Arb dared not say a word to his father.

So much for that aborted escape over the prison walls.

I became more unhappy as the days passed, and I was unfortunately adopting a defeatist attitude while I went about the mundane household chores. My new family were, while helping all they could, and with their method of assistance, diminishing my parenting role, and reducing me to a lesser personage as far as my baby was concerned.

The migraine headaches began visiting me again, especially around period time, and if I could rest during the most difficult phase of it, I could be back upon my feet by dinner time.. I was anemic, so our doctor informed me. I also had taken up smoking cigarettes, never knowing at the time the habit was dangerous, but it seemed to help me to sit out on the porch steps, and leisurely smoke, and try to rest my mind...try to gear down.

Vicki was one year old when I put on her pretty yellow dress, grabbed my purse, and announced to Ma that I was riding the bus down to a Pedro portrait studio and have her picture made. I was out the door before I faintly heard some warnings, but I was not to be dissuaded. I thoroughly enjoyed every minute with my cheerful baby, as we boarded the bus, leaving the bus on the corner of Sixth and Pacific, and taking her for her picture.

I was so tickled that she enjoyed being with me, and I hugged her happily to me as her little hand rose up to the lights and signs. This memory will be one of the best for me.

Every Wednesday night Arb spruced himself up after work, and took off for "lodge" meetings at the Eagles lodge in San Pedro. Two of his close friends had also joined, and all three eagerly looked forward to the Wednesday night rituals. With some moderate suspicions, I allowed him to leave without a word, or a question. Time passed, as Wednesdays came and went, and Thursday mornings early, it was extremely difficult to persuade Arb to roll out of bed, drink a cup of coffee to help him stave off feelings of nausea from too much drinking, grab his gear and lunch with a thermos of coffee, and go to work. Usually he was late.

I was wondering why the three "buddies" didn't carpool, considering they were going to the "lodge". I found out..quickly.

We Arkies had a functional grape vine of information, and it wasn't too long before a rumor floated in that Arb was picking up a dark haired woman under the Gaffey bridge overpass that was adjacent to the home of the original reporter. As my temperament was inclined toward believing the rumor rather than denying it, I began to examine the whole thing going on under our very noses.

As it turned out, the young woman, whose husband was in the Navy, and who was four months pregnant with his child, had been along with our crowd of friends, attending live band dancing on Santa Monica Pier at times. She was tall and attractive, a couple of years older than I, perhaps. I knew Arb was flirting with her, especially when the evenings wore on, and along with his consumption of alcohol, so it wasn't as if I'd just bumped my head on the tailgate of the turnip truck. I knew that something would come out of it, because she fell hard for him. I could see it in her eyes.

I proceeded to gather the other two wives and explained to them that the Wednesday night lodge meetings were a farce. Donna, mother of three small boys was hard to convince of her husbands's infidelity, but Beth, who had one child, apparently knew her man, and said she believed something was going on.

I picked up the phone and got the number of the Eagles Lodge, and asked for, first, my own husband. The man came back to the phone and said, "Mam, there is nobody by that name here."

"Would you find out for me please, if two more gentlemen are there," I asked in the most favorable tones possible. There was a pause, then the man came back on to inform me, "nobody by those names are here at all. I'm sorry." I thanked him, and turned to face the two wives.

"I know who Arb is out with," I said. I didn't feel as calm as I sounded.

"I know who Bob is out with, too," Beth admitted.

We both glanced at Donna, who looked as if she might be sick. She shook her head.

Later on, that night late, Arb came into the house, weaving on his feet, his eyes unfocused, his trousers unzipped, the flaps of the fly soiled and wet. He didn't have the decency to take down his pants! He tried to lean on me, to touch me, saying..."honey"... slurring his words. I side-stepped him and went on into the bedroom.

I said to his retreating back, "Get to the bathroom before you go to bed, please."

Later on when I was lying so close to the edge of the bed as I could get without falling onto the floor, staring dry-eyed at the ceiling, I heard a quiet scratching at the window. A voice was calling . "Aubrey....Aubrey." I looked out the window, the full moon casting its light onto the figure of the woman as she stood there. It was her.

"What do you want?" My question was not friendly.

"I need to talk to Aubrey," came a hushed voice. "Just let me talk to him," she pleaded.

I shook Aubrey until he finally responded and sat up in bed. "What?"

"She is out there waiting to speak to you."

He put on a pair of pants and padded out the front door bare foot. I lay there a moment, then followed Arb out to where he and the woman were standing next to his car. She was crying, and when I heard her words, I'd had about enough of this, and walked closer to the car.

"Please Aubrey," she was saying, sobs in her voice. "Let's go away, I love you." She began grabbing at his arms, and he was pushing her away. "Let's go away together. We need to be together."

I hurried back into the house, and woke Pa. "What is all this mess going on?" he asked.

"That gal is outside wanting Arb to run away with her," I answered shakily. "He has been running around with her, and they have been......"

"Been what?"

"Uh, been doing it...sex."

He put on his pants, and heaved himself up from the bed, waking Ma in the process. "I'll show him about running around," and out he went, shoulder drawn back in anger, me quickly behind him.

I ran over to Stel's, woke her and gave her the news. She was up in a split second, saying, "That stupid jerk." I'd alerted the whole of us, now, I wanted to see how all of it would become resolved, and I stood a bit back, began shaking with a chill, and tears were streaming down my cheeks.

Pa reached his son, pulled him away from the woman and around to face him. He began to shake Arb, and yelled into his face, words I can't remember, but some words were harsh, especially name calling. Arb pushed back and told his father not to touch him, but Pa slapped his face, back and forth, two times, until Stel ran up and intervened. Ma was weeping as she stood on the porch in the shadows. I could hear her.

Pa told the woman to go, and without another sound, she fled down the sidewalk, sobbing.

How in heaven's name will this be resolved? Perhaps it never was, but the following day I walked down to where the woman lived, and was greeted at the door by a mother and father, middle-aged, with worried faces. I asked to speak to their daughter, and she appeared at a bedroom door, nervously picking at her over-sized blouse. She took me to the backyard under fruit trees...apricot...and she didn't say a word. She hung her head.

"I'm sorry about what has happened," I began, picking at the grass where I sat. "I haven't come out of anger. I've come to tell you that if Aubrey wants you, I will step aside, and not cause you any trouble."

She was shaking her dark head, and she finally looked at me, her eyes puzzled that I didn't intend to claw her eyes out.

"He doesn't love me," she said, softly. "He loves you, so he told me last night."

"But you thought he would run away with you."

"Yes, and I was wrong. Today is different. I think different." She was sitting, her hands quietly in her lap. "My husband will be home soon, and I have to concentrate on that."

"You sure?" I had to tell her the truth. "Because now, this morning I feel differently about Arb. I think I don't care for him as much. I certainly can never trust him, and his drinking...it is bad."

"I'm sure," came the answer. "I'll not bother you anymore. We...mom and dad...we will be moving."

I stood, said, "Good luck," and returned home to Vicki.

This was August 1945. I discovered I was pregnant a week later.

I woke up one morning to a pounding headache, loss of energy and appetite, and a great sense of discouragement. I'd lost more weight, and it was all I could manage to get through my household chores and care for sixteen-month-old Vicki. The doctor had informed me my blood test disclosed anemia, and prescribed liquid iron to remedy this, and warned me to eat and take care of myself, at least for the unborn baby's sake.

Ma was in one of her sick spells, and had taken to her bed on the living room couch, so I had all the cooking to do, and serve her meals on a small table near her. Pa was now working on a lumber mill on the green chain, so I had to prepare his lunch pail, serve his breakfast before he left early to go to his job. I did not begrudge the long hard days I put in, for Arb only worked when he felt like it, and Pa was floating most of the bills.

Nevertheless, the days were long for me, and the best parts of my days were when I could play with my baby girl on my bed, usually around two in the afternoon, and having done this, we both took naps.

The incident with Arb and his lady friend, and our discovering of the illicit affair, only tended to accelerate his nights out in the town bars, and his drinking increased.

The terrible war was over in Europe with Germany's surrender May 8, 1945..V-E Day, and the bloody Pacific campaigns were brought to an end by the awesome dropping of the atomic bomb on Hiroshima in early August, and shortly afterwards a similar bomb dropped on Nagasaki. Both were horrifying, cataclysmic results that stopped Japan cold. On September the first, documents of surrender were signed aboard the battleship Missouri in Tokyo Bay with a delegation of allies, General Douglas MacArthur their chief representative, in acceptance to the Japanese delegation.

Herb was coming home....and, had sent a telegram to mother and dad simply, but ecstatically worded: "I'm over here from over there stop See you soon." Now America could began assessing her dead, bundle up her brave wounded for shipment home, and praise God the end to the war was over.

The heart-breaking discovery the Allies made while liberating Europe stuck in my heart like a flaming knife; that of the death camps where over six thousand Jews died in the Holocaust. As we people sat in theaters across the U.S. watching the news on the screens, seeing the corpses of the brave elite stacked as high as hills, tears streamed from our eyes that matched the tears shed by our young, unsuspecting allied soldiers, who could hardly believe this terrible crime of the attempt on Hitler's part to exterminate this wonderful race of God's chosen children. I shall never forget, ever.

I managed to hold onto my baby for eight and a half

months, and he was born May 6, 1946, a tiny five pounder, only eighteen inches in length, with lots of dark hair, and he had a big sister who couldn't keep her hands off him. She kept saying, "mine, mine," and the meaning was clear to all of us. Tommy was her baby brother, namesake for my little brother, and she "helped" me bathe him, feed him, rock him, but quickly backed off when it was dirty diaper time, turning her little nose away and clamping it with both hands. She suddenly turned into his protector, and adored him with all her heart.

Tommy had a slow start the first year, was susceptible to ear infections, some allergies, and as I was still traumatized by my baby brother's sickness and subsequent death, I was in the doctor's office often. During one period around ten months, he was showing signs of pain, fever, and some listlessness, almost lethargic at times. All of this was checked out by a doctor, but when he didn't want to stand up on his legs, yelled loudly, and promptly sat down upon his bottom, Ma thought he was afraid he would fall. That wasn't it. He was seventeen-months old.

I sought out specialists at the Torrance Memorial Hospital, who took two days of testing Tommy, then told me their diagnosis. My son had suffered Poliomyelitis, however a light case. Where obvious symptoms of severity were not exhibited, he nonetheless had been a sick baby, and his right leg was three quarters of an inch shorter than the left, and he perhaps would walk with a slight limp, but he would be fine with a dietary supplement to start helping him grow. I was so thrilled he would be fine, hugged him to me in love, run my fingers over his fine head, and watched the big, green eyes come alive. Such a precious life....so precious to me. I felt so lucky to have two beautiful children, and I prayed I could give them a good life. I prayed their father would see them as I did, pour out his love and protection for them, maybe give up his old ways and strive for a better home life for them.

One day when I felt pushed to the limit, and without realizing it at the time that another migraine was coming on, I was listening to my children play around me. They were jabbering away..at least Vicki was, and she looked up at me, and said, "A'ma, I want a drink." I got her a drink of water. Then Tommy came to me wanting to climb upon my lap, and he called me, "A'ma."

I froze and felt I must have been in a stupor all the time, or was not noticing, but I had been addressed as Alma, and they were calling their dad, "Arby." That is it, I said to myself, I've had it, and I began to re-train them; I was "mommie'" and Arb was "daddy." If they called us by our names, we quickly corrected them.

When Tommy was two, we finally moved out into our own little, bitty house. It was glorious for a while.

The next five years were spent moving from apartment to apartment, usually being evicted for non-payment of rent, and from one car to another, the beloved 40' Chevy one of the first to go. Arb couldn't manage to work a 40-hour week on a permanent basis, and went from bar to bar at nights. Only when he was flat broke, would he be home nights.

Vicki started kindergarten at Bandini Street Elementary and finished up at Pt. Fermin. I couldn't allow my children to be nomads as I had been, but I did not know what to do about it.

After we got up one morning to find another car had been re-possessed, I felt I should look for a job to help us out of our dilemma. I chose a swing shift job packing sardines and scraping tuna at a fish cannery on Terminal Island, leaving me free to care for my two children the important part of the day. Arb could care for them evenings. It wasn't what I wanted, being away from them for even a short time. I'd catch the Pt. Fermin bus down to the ferry, across the channel to my job, so I didn't need a car.

Vicki and Tommy were very unhappy and cried for me to be home with them, and when Arb couldn't manage being tied down nights, I was forced to hire a baby sitter.

The paycheck helped, but the strain was enormous, and after a short time at my job, Arb appeared one night, staggering about, and watching me. When a male employee came near to instruct me, he started shouting expletives, approaching me, his hands formed into fists.

I was fired on the spot.

I tried to work another job, and the same thing happened. I was fired. We moved again into a duplex, and Vicki and Tom started into a fine school on Bandini Street. I didn't attempt another job.

At this particular time my health took a nose dive again, and I paid my doctor a visit. There was concern on his kindly face, as he warned me against another pregnancy. He shook his finger at me, and peered at me over his glasses.

"Remember, Alma, when I injected the veins in the back of your legs, I told you then the danger of pregnancy?"

I nodded my head in understanding. Oh, how I feared what he was telling me, but he was not through with me.

"I have taken the x-rays and found your heart slightly enlarged, with possible valve problem, and young lady," he stressed this part by jabbing a pencil into the air toward me, "you have a vascular condition...uh, a vein problem. Do you know what I'm telling you?"

"Yes sir. My legs hurt some at times...my period especially...."

"So!" He stood up and walked around the desk, sitting on the corner, and crossed his hands upon a knee. "Here is what you must do...to save your health so the children can have a mother..." he took a deep breath..."is to have Aubrey come in some Friday after work, let me do a vasectomy, it will take only a few minutes, and he can go to work on Monday."

I had heard of this procedure, and felt the doctor was honest about what could happen if I became pregnant again. I sat with my head down thinking that even if I agreed, Arb would certainly not go for it. The doctor interpreted my silence as my own disapproval.

"Hey, look at me, Alma," he said "would you go for it?"
"Yes, I would, but Arb won't."
"How do you know? Has he said anything?"
"Yes, he did once, said having one of those "clip" jobs

would ruin his manhood."

After the doctor stopped laughing, he said, "Tell him to be in my office, so we can talk about it, and I'll explain that it doesn't hurt his 'manhood'."

"What, you silly bitch! You and the good old doc want to cut on me? Never! Never! Never!" Arb's face was livid, and as usual, he was half soused.
"But Arb----"
"Don't but me. It's a set-up."
"No it is not a set-up." I stood up. "It is to prevent me from having more babies, because of my health."
He stood up and pushed me back down on the couch.
"When hell freezes over."
"Arb, you won't use protection, so I will get pregnant again."
"Aw, wearing a rubber is like washing your feet with socks on."
He took a pull of his cigarette, and said in a lower voice, "Why don't you have something done on you? Cut on you?"
"I don't think there is one for women, I'm not sure."
"When hell freezes over," he said as he put on his jacket and left for the bars.

I'll tell the truth now, if there had been a shelter for woman in 1951, and a relocation program, I would have packed some bags and left. I'd truly been convinced that my doctor was right; my life was in danger. If Arb wouldn't kill me by his abusiveness, or pile us up on the road in a car, he would just as surely kill me by not using a simple condom.

I'd come to accept in a repulsive sort of way Arb's second name for me. You might call it a pet name. You must believe he put his heart into it when he addressed me...
"Stupid bitch.!"...and, it mattered not to him whether the children were present or not. He had to express himself, didn't he?

Stel came to me, and said she felt I should try to

understand her brother more, be more of a "wife" to him, and also that I should urge him to stay out of the bars, and, the kicker, that I should handle the money."

I laughed, "you're serious, aren't you?"

"Why, yes, I am," she replied.

"You want him to knock my head off?"

Her shoulders dropped, and she prissed her mouth, her gesture telling me she was talking to a silly goose. "Why, Alma, he loves you, and he wouldn't harm you, if you didn't make him mad all the time."

"How do I make him mad?" "Well he said you are always nagging at him, and that is why he drinks."

I became angry and blurted out, "Oh yeah, I nag him alright...to pay the rent, buy food for the kids, pay the payments on the car to keep it, stop spending all his money in bars and on whores. Pay his bills." I was sputtering. I slumped my shoulders in despair.

"Alma, you are getting too excited." She waved her hand. "See how you are?" She brought my attention to how I was acting.

"But, I'm so tired of it...tired of it. What I should do is take Vic and Tom and leave." I stared out the window, my eyes brimming over.

I thought I saw a flash of fear in the steel gray eyes. "That won't solve anything."

"For me and the kids, or for Arb?" I asked.

"Where would he live? He can't go back to Mama's and Papa's. They are too old to handle him. It kills mama to see him drinking so much." She came closer to me on the couch. "He never drank so much until he met you...then the baby and all...don't you see? And, you can't take the children away from us."

"Stel, you are sending me mixed messages here, and it confuses me. You either want me to understand him more, be more of a wife to him, but I'd have to force him against his will and nature to be a regular husband and father. What's it to be? A loving, kind and nice, unnagging wife, or use a baseball bat on him to keep him out of the bars?" I stood up and walked around the coffee table, stopped and looked at her helplessly.

"If you try to leave and take the kids, I will go to court and have them taken away from you." Her words came out stiffly, but firmly.

"Go...go to court? Have them taken...on what grounds?"

She stood up and started for the door. "By the time we got through with you, you would be considered an unfit mother."

"A What?" I was yelling at this point. "That will be very hard to prove, you know. I'm a good mother, and everyone knows it."

"Leave Arb and take the kids, and see how quick you become an unfit mother." She slammed the door and was gone.

> *"wives, submit yourselves unto your own husbands, as it is fit in the Lord."* Colossians 3:18

"You silly bitch! You're pregnant again! You silly bitch." He pushed me up against the wall, then down close to my eyes, staring into them, said, "Whose is it? It's not mine."

I didn't talk back. He would have no doubt slapped me, at least. He normally hit me where bruises and bumps wouldn't show. He was good at it. So I held my tongue waiting for him to demand an answer from me. He sneered at me, backed off, saying, "You slut."

The pregnancy was upon me again. Dear Lord, I prayed, if only the wind could speak, and I could have wings, and you would honor me with copious blessings of your love that both I and the seed that lay restlessly within my womb could have strength and safety. If he must, to feel he wouldn't leave his safe chamber and lose hold, allow him, please, to raise his tiny hand, reach up and touch my heart, and know I loved him and will not allow him to depart....not yet. He had a destiny to fulfill.

"Little one, take my hand;
I'll show you how to stand.

Let God be your guide-
Through a dark, forbidden land." [your mother]

    I talked to Vicki and Tommy, letting them know they were to have a little brother or sister. Vicki's big eyes were somber as she stared at me, and she wanted to know if I would be alright. "Of course," I assured her, "I will be just fine." Tommy's green eyes watched my face. "Promise?" he asked. "Promise," I told him.

    But, the pregnancy wasn't going as smoothly as I had anticipated, only placing faith in my own determination to will the strength to us both. Soon enough, though, I'd need my protector, who was in close reach, as close as the thought that dwelt in my mind. I simply did not feel right.

    Dr. Cassidy was somewhat put out with me, and I understood his feelings while I kept my eyes down in obeisance to a respectful physician, and father-figure, whose job it was to doctor people, and hopefully, those patients would live by his rules.

    "Tommy is five, now isn't he?" he asked with his back to me. He was going through my file he already knew by heart. Without turning around he asked, "Why is it you didn't become pregnant during those years?"

    "I haven't the foggiest. Maybe it was because I used the "foam", and douched quickly afterwards. I don't know." The "foam" refers to an early attempt at an Anti-bacterial agent that killed sperm on contact. Or, was supposed to.

    With a supply of his vitamins on hand, and a prescription for iron, and a whole lot of doctor advice, I walked the several blocks back home. Here I was, frightened to pieces again, not only for myself but for the little unborn baby. I felt pity for Vicki and Tommy, who would in my opinion, have less of almost nothing in order to share with another sibling. I hoped Arb would keep his job, and the hospitalization insurance it allowed us to cover the prenatal care, hospital, and any other unforeseen problems a family faces.

    Actually, I didn't want to disclose to the doctor that

during the past five years, Arb's bar activities and accelerated drinking had decimated our sexual activity by almost half, and while I despised our life as it had begun to be, I was secretly pleased of the decrease. I was, too, deathly afraid of sexually transmitted diseases my husband may become infected with on his sojourn through the red haze his private demons drove him through so unmercifully.

Through September 1951, almost four months, I was much sicker than with the other two. Also my hormones must have been constantly in flux, for I felt spaced out---the dreadful feeling of "sitting up on Cloud thirteen" I called it. I didn't cry, or scream about. On the contrary, I was quiet, I thought, almost reflectively about this pregnancy. I continued to hold onto the fear that something could go wrong. I had enough people telling me I shouldn't have this baby, and it may not be normal because of Arb's drinking, and my unhealthy condition. As Ma and Pa, Stel and Cotton, were always having to buy groceries, or have our utilities turned back on, I felt I should be grateful enough and listen to their opinions and advice. They fed my babies, and Stel was a big help keeping my two in clothes. I will forever feel gratitude to them.

The baby grew...I hoped strong and healthy, and at night I'd say a special prayer for him as I lay in bed, my hand upon my protruding stomach, and as if on cue, he always moved about or gave a little kick letting me know he acknowledged the prayers. "Now don't be dumb and kick a hole in something," I'd admonish, as I gently patted. Then I would say, "Lord, what are we to do? Stay with us and protect us."

Chapter Thirteen

In December 1951, I woke one morning feeling unwell, swimmy head, weakness in the legs which had been going on for a few days, and breathing difficulty. My lungs appeared congested, so I thought I was coming down with something not serious. It was a week-end, and the children were with Stel, who had picked them up Friday after school. It was good for them to have breaks from the disquieting home that they were becoming familiar with.

We were again without a car, but we were conveniently close to a market, the school, and about one mile from Ma and Pa, and Stel. I felt relatively safe, even though we didn't have a phone. At this point in life, I'd begun to be thankful for what we did have, although I did so want music to be part of my children's lives, and I had desperately tried somehow to begin an attempt of allowing them musical instruments. There simply was no money. It was extremely difficult explaining to them, and I felt their seriousness of needing music as I had as a child. Therefore, I did resent my inability to provide this desire for them, and blamed myself for my weakness and illnesses that prevented me from being a stronger, more assertive mother.

I lethargically dressed and put on the coffee, feeling the baby lying heavily against my back, attempted to take more air into my lungs, and asked Arb if he wanted his coffee now. He was sitting on the side of our hide-a-bed running his long, nicotine-stained fingers through his hair, the fingers shaking, as they had a habit of doing when he got up in the mornings. His eyes were blood-shot, and his long skeletal frame appeared thinner than ever. He grunted in acknowledgment to me as he lighted his first cigarette of the day. He filled his waking hours, when he wasn't working, drinking beer.

Somehow, in the past year we had acquired a television set that sat upon a wooden, swivel table, a Muntz, it was called, and the picture was perfect, so some nights Arb began staying home and drinking his beer. I was completely surprised how quickly he could finish off quart bottles of Lucky Lager. He thumbed his nose at the 6-pack cans which were somehow unsatisfactory to him. He always poured the beer into a glass, showing some class, I suppose.

This morning there was no breakfast. Arb didn't eat breakfast and I wasn't hungry, so we sat at the kitchen table drinking coffee and saying very little to each other, except he said he was out of beer and cigarettes, and wanted me to go with him to the market. The walk would do me good, he said.

It was foggy out, and a chill breeze came in off the ocean, and I pulled my coat closer to me as I managed to keep up with his long strides. He wanted to go into a little hardware store about a hundred yards past the market, then he would pick up his beer and cigarettes on the way back.

I was doing fairly well until we returned from the hardware store. My head began to spin, my eyes didn't want to focus, my lungs felt as if someone was stuffing cotton into them, and, when we got to the market I told Arb to get me home fast, that I was having something happening to me. My legs were about to buckle under me, but I managed to grab an iron pole near a flower bed.

"You are always sick...something always wrong with you...wait here, I'll be right back." He blithely went into the market for his beer and cigarettes.

I stood there hanging onto that pole wondering how I was going to get back to the house. Something terrible was going on inside of me. I was gasping to drag all the oxygen I could muster into my lungs, but the air wasn't getting past the "cotton pack" there. I felt I was not merely having a "spell," but was suffering some kind of seizure, rattling my head, blacking out my vision, and shaking my legs in tremors.

Arb finally came out, said, "Let's go," and I somehow made it to the house, and onto Vicki's half bed, gasping. There I lay for two or three days, in and out of darkness, praying real hard I would not suffocate. I don't remember eating, but I must have, because I was worried about the baby. I don't remember very much about it, except I was real puzzled about the "seizure", so very strange. No doctor was called, no one notified. Arb sat that day and the next absorbed in his beer and cigarettes.

I wasn't the same after that. Sicker, weaker, aching legs, and tingling fingers. Even my thoughts were dulled. If only the wind could talk, and it's voice direct me to safer, calmer waters. If I had the strength to tread, to pull myself to shore. If I could close my eyes, and my life as it was would fade into nothingness. If...

But, my destined bearings were here, now, and my inner thought suddenly focused upon the life inside me. I must not think of the darkness, nor desire it simply to be free of the rough road I'd so utterly abandoned myself to choose. Did I ignorantly choose this because I felt I did not deserve better for myself? I thoroughly believe in free-will, the gift of God as opposed to predestination, a fateful belief, therefore I couldn't assume that all this was planned by him and dump the guilt at His feet. No. But, now that I'd gotten my pitiful self into such a mess, I'd certainly need his help to get me out and hopefully dust me off, me and the solid, little rock inside me, who slept so peacefully my wakeful, busy hours, and moved about endlessly when I tried to sleep.

Wednesday, March 5, 1952, I'd notified Stel and my parents that I was going into light labor early in the day, but I was not ready to go to the hospital. Stel kept a close watch on me until Arb came home, then took the two children home with her. My poor children hugged me as tightly as they dared, looked at me with sad scared eyes, but I assured them the next time they saw me, I'd be bringing the kicking, bundle home. They smiled wanly as they left, hands raised in "bye".

My labor was difficult, and because I was weak and the muscles were in constant spasm, I was not completely sedated, but given only small doses to help me relax, or so they said.

When Scott finally emerged after tearing the birth canal, I cried out, "Is he alright? Is he okay?"

Dr. Cassidy had a big grin as he showed me my son who had his mouth open screaming to high heaven, the tiny fists beating the air in shock and anger. "He's just fine. Perfect boy."

The following days were spent watching the rain run down the hospital windows and sitting up in bed, pillows behind me. I was having difficulty breathing, but the doctor informed me I was having sinus problems. I could not lie upon my back, flat down, with only one pillow. I couldn't get air into my lungs, and by that time I was gasping through my mouth trying to draw in a bigger volume of air. I needed more oxygen, but the nurses didn't feel I needed it, so I had begun to try to stand and walk about slowly. It seemed this relieved the problem---until I became tired. So back into bed I went.

Arb took advantage of my hospital stay and the freedom from the responsibility of the children, and stayed inside the bars. His drinking was perpetual, and as he was unable to meet any crisis or trauma's head on as most people do, he did not feel safe when he was sober. My illness and another baby seemed too much for him. He lost his job that had provided hospitalization and paid doctor bills, and things were looking more glum than ever.

I'd go to the refrigerator and find four quarts of beer, but no milk for the children. I'd quickly walk to the market to use a phone and call Stel, asking for help for food. It then became asking money for rent, and at times, utilities. Of course, it fell upon me to beg for help.

The baby was having problems with his stomach. He couldn't keep his formula down, and I was busy walking, rocking, and singing to him. He needed a doctor. But before I could take him to visit Dr. Cassidy, I began having problems myself again.

On the 29th of March, I was down flat of my back, pains searing my right lung and my uterus. I was restricted from regular breathing, so was taking fast half-breaths, and this brought on a tremendous panic of suffocation. I prayed frantically as I took gasps. I thought of my children, my new baby, and asked God to protect them.

Stel was there taking care of the baby's needs, a frightened look on her face, and the second day was becoming hazy except for the pain. On the 31st. I was consciously fading in and out. Once, I saw Cotton's scared face, and I wanted to tell him I needed help, but I couldn't, and he was gone. I was glad Vicki and Tommy were at Ma and Pa's. I did not relish the thought of those two little kids seeing me the way I was.

Dr. Cassidy was out of town, and his nurse came to the house to bring me some sort of medication, small white pills, to alleviate the pain, but when the nurse saw me and gave a cursory exam visually, she conferred with Stel, advising her that I needed to be hospitalized immediately, that my chances of surviving hinged upon it. If I could be admitted into the nearby San Pedro Hospital doctors there would be standing by waiting for the ambulance in a matter of minutes, she told my sister-in-law.

Stel relayed what happened next to me a year or so later. According to her, a family meeting was called, to be conducted in the duplex over my bed. The members were my parents, Pa and Ma, Stel, Cotton, and others I don't recall at all. Mean while, I was riding a cloud.

I lay on the cottony-down of a breathtakingly bright, white cloud that floated high above the whole world. The gentle touch of softly blowing breezes caressed my burning cheeks as I lay back against the luxurious cloud, my comfort seemingly the only reason I was where I was. I felt no pain, but my mind was somehow aware that I was in pain. Excruciating pain. But, I only smiled, for now I was freely floating along almost merrily, with disdain for the enemy. Where was I going and why was I feeling such well-being? Where did everybody go?

The next thing I remember was when I opened my eyes to vaguely distinguish the ceiling of the bedroom, the pain was back. My back was hurting, my womb was in terrible agony, but the worst pain of all was in my right lung. My fuzzy mind tried desperately to focus inside the lung, and what I imagined, much as a child would describe an unknown feeling, a large snake, curling and writhing, tieing itself into a knot only to suddenly "slip" the knot in a spasmodic, jerking motion, forcing my body to arch in the most torturous waves of pain.

Again, I was quiet, and I lifted off the bed, ever so gently, and floated up to the ceiling to the farthest corner where there was less light until my head bobbed against the ceiling like a free floating balloon. I had no pain. I felt nothing as I looked down at the dead person upon the bed, then surprisingly, my floating self was forcefully slammed back on top of the body, and I was so sorry when I merged with it, for waves of pain engulfed me once more.

It was dark, and a lamp was on in the front room, and I lay so quietly afraid to move, The pain was quieter now. I dared not turn my head to see if anyone was there. I needed a drink of water badly, but strangely enough my bladder felt dead and without a need to urinate at all. Perhaps the kidneys were dead, too. Heck, perhaps I was dead. too. I dozed, and was awakened by a sudden voice that called "Alma." With a start I said, "What?' "Alma, if you don't fight you will die. Do you hear me?" The voice was pleasant sounding, and came from within my own self. It was a voice I continue to remember to this very day--the pleasant yet firm warning, the inflections, rise and fall of tones of the voice, simple, but I understood, and decided to give it my best shot for my babies sakes if not my own.

April one. The meeting took place according to Stel, and as I was conscious more, the members moved to the front lawn out of my ear shot. Pa took my father and mother aside, explaining, "Arb is not working now, has no insurance, but Alma has to go into the hospital quickly, if it isn't already too late."

"Yes, we see that," Mother said.

"Mrs. May," Pa went for the bottom line. "I don't have much money saved; but, my wife, Stel, and I are offering to pay Alma's entry fee they demand at the hospital, if you will help pay half of it."

My parents looked at each other, and hedged.

"Doctors are waiting for her as we speak," Pa said.

My father scratched his head. "No, I can't. We have saved for our home and our new car here...worked hard too." He shook his head. "No."

Stel told me later that Pa wanted to "thrash" Mr. May, but didn't want to make a spectacle of himself.

It was the county hospital I was taken to. Mother had taken Baby Scott, after Stel informed her she must help with the children, and that the baby was having health problems, a newly discovered hernia, plus the stomach problem. Mother was not happy.

One of my first bad experiences inside the county Hospital on Carson Street in Torrance was the awkward handling of the gurney that was banged against the double swinging doors to open them with no regard for me lying cringing in pain. My moans oblivious to the white-coated nurses and interns. They talked, laughed, joked about their last night's date, and chewed gum. They barely looked at me at all....until I was completely nude, lying shivering with only a sanitary napkin to keep my crotch covered, but soon that, too, was taken from me.

I wasn't in and out of a coma, but I was still very sick. I was taken to a "waiting" room, with a thin sheet over me, thankfully. Soon, a young dandy, also in a white coat, jaunted up and began testing my lucidity by asking questions. He started with my name, age, and jumped to what day it was. I told him April fools day, and he proceeded to try and trick me with what year is it? Where do you live? But when he asked me, "can you tell me who the president of the United States is?" I choked down my irritability, raised as far upon my elbows as the pain and gasping allowed, looked him straight into his arrogant eyes behind the glasses, and said, "My gosh, don't you know?"

He stared at me long after the snickers of the other white coats subsided, said, "Take her away," turned on his heels and left.

I was lying naked while being probed, gouged, taken for x-rays, told to sit up, which I couldn't, answered a lot of questions, perused intently, and told to take "a deep breath" by seemingly impersonal voices that applied cold stethoscopes. Their hands were almost as rough as stevedores', their demeanor practically indifferent.

It was time for me to rest. I felt like I could bear no more of them. I was certain hours had passed. I couldn't rest. They wouldn't allow me that. Doctors and nurses paraded in and around me, and blood samples drawn. All of my tormentors talked medicalese, thereby, not allowing me to distinguish their varied diagnoses, apparently so tickled to be able to hear themselves pour out all their technical terminology they had recently learned. Oh, they meant well; only doing their jobs.

I was taken to an examination room, a small room, and from what I recall, dark, without the glaring overhead lights. I was becoming weaker, pushed my head back so I could breathe better by stretching the esophagus, and started the small gasping breaths. My attendants duly noted this, asked me if I frequently arched my neck back, and I said yes.

I was then told they must draw fluid from the spine to test for meningitis, whereupon I told them I didn't have spinal meningitis; my problem was in my right lung, and my womb. Of course they didn't listen to a hundred pound, young woman who hadn't a chance in Hades of surviving, and the painful procedure was performed, my jaws being massaged to better promote the flow of fluid. Later, I was left alone where I laboriously turned upon my right side and discovered that in this position the pain lessened.

I was in quarantine until test results determined I did not have meningitis, and was promptly rolled out to one long quonset-style building, where the sick were housed in large wards. I was immediately given a blood transfusion that seemed to take forever to complete. Hours later I was on bags of saline solution and dextrose. Tall doctors in white, and in suits, came by to check on me, and requested more x-rays. Sulfa drugs were given by mouth along with pitchers of water I had to drink. I was rudely introduced to the fantastic penicillin. That is, I suppose the penicillin was fantastic, maybe result-wise, but in 1952, the serum wasn't thinned down yet, so a very large needle had to be used to force the thick, almost waxy serum into soft part of the buttock. I was to have them every two hours, but after two days of torture, and a couple of permanent lumps on my bottom, I decided I'd not have any more. I was too nervous to continue those treatments.

After a few days, and doctors' round table discussions, they finally made a diagnosis; not only infection in the womb that wasn't any secret, but I had developed a blood clot in my lung. Ah, hah! Then they went about my problem with more aggressiveness.

My family hadn't made an appearance, except Arb, and as he was usually "in his cups", I would react in a negative way; one of agitation, so noted the nurses on duty. They began taking my blood pressure immediately after he left, found an unfavorable rise, reported to the doctors who then restricted visitation to him.

I think Peggy came by once to visit, and maybe mother once or twice, but I can't be sure. My dad never visited, who complained hospitals made him sick, Oh, well....

I lay upon my right side, breathing faster and more shallow. What day was it? I couldn't be certain anymore. I struggled, desperately needing the oxygen, and with each movement of my body, the lung screeched out in protest.

I looked at the woman in the next bed. I've...I've got...to...take a ...deep....breath. I have...to." I told her, gasping.

"You be careful girl. They said you had a lot of fluid in your lungs," she warned.

"I know...I know...but I have to...to have air."

I rolled carefully over upon my back, gasped a moment,

then breathed in deeper. Instantly, there was severe pain and I was choking on my own fluid. "Oh Lor', Oh Lor'," I managed to moan, as my friend in the next bed yelled for the nurses.

Immediately my bed was surrounded, and a slender hose inserted into my mouth, down, down it went and the hissing of the small hose as it vacuumed out the fluid was loud in the ward. All the patients lay quietly, waiting for my reprieve.

They drew more liquid, if that is what it was, for it was a sticky mess, almost viscous, and finally they withdrew the tube and listened intently to the lung through their trusty stethoscopes, nodded sagely, and withdrew back into their busy netherland. I was left with my head and torso upon another pillow, almost in a sitting position, and given more sulfa and a fresh pitcher of water.

I was perspiring, but I felt relief! I felt better! Not as much pain, and I could breath more deeply.

"Gee, I thought you were a goner," remarked my friend. I grinned at her and felt a kindred toward her. She was black, and she was beautiful....and she was very ill.

As I lay there panting, I thought of my children. I was convinced Vicki and Tom would be fine with Stel, but I worried about my baby, Scott. He needed a good pediatrician, and I prayed that my mother would care for him better than she had her own children. If Scotty was as strong as I felt he was, then he would certainly hang in there until I could care for him again. A sick baby could drive my impatient, high strung mother to distraction.

After twelve days at the hospital, I wanted to get upon my feet and seek out bathing facilities. I know I was in desperate need, and it could make me feel alive again, but the uppermost reason was that I felt the water would speed my healing, and I could see my babies again. I had to try. It wasn't easy.

Very gingerly, I put my legs over the side of the bed to test gravity. I was extremely light-headed, but after a minute or two, I slipped my skinny rump off, and stood upon the cold floor. Immediately, I experienced a sensation of great pressure in my entire left leg, a sensation I'd only felt in the veins of my neck when I was having a migraine. I looked down at my thin legs, and my heart leaped up into my throat. I swallowed, and closed my eyes thinking, "Now what?" I took another peek, cautiously. Yes, it was a bright pink color while the right leg was normal. Wearing the hospital robe of dark blue, I padded my way ever so carefully into a door that said "Showers". Perhaps, the shower would tone down pressure and pink color.

Extreme weakness prevented me from being in the vertical position as long as I would have liked, but I had allowed the water to cover me fully while I stood revelling in its tingling wetness...from head to toe.

I padded slowly and shakily back to bed, and I combed my hair and toweled it while I waited anxiously for a nurse to appear. The nurse came, and I stepped off the bed to show her the pink leg. She said she would see if a doctor was about. One never showed up at my bedside. They were too busy, and I was forgotten.

I spent a semi-restless night, sleeping only quietly in the early hours, and when morning arrived, I felt feverish and couldn't turn my body over. Something was weighing the lower part of my body down, and I slipped my hand down underneath the blanket, and discovered my thigh was bulged like a huge sausage, was hot to the touch, unlike my right leg that was normal, and I hastily withdrew my hand. I lay there scared half out of my wits, and slowly raised the blanket to take a peek.

The leg, indeed, was swollen beyond anything I'd ever seen, and it was white now, not pink anymore....white like a sheet of paper. Oh boy, if I was ever in trouble, this certainly was going to top all of them. I was going into some sort of shock as I asked a busy nurse just coming on duty, if she had time to take a look at my leg. "As soon as I have a chance", she said to me, and hurried on.

Another nurse went by heading for the exit door, and I asked her to please, come take a look at my leg. She didn't acknowledge, except to give me a slightly scornful look as she departed. Okay.

I tried to move the leg, but it was lying there like a dead log, and there didn't seem to be any feeling in it at all. I felt my hot face. My mouth was awfully dry.

Nurse number two drifted in again, and as she passed the end of my bed, I hailed her once again to take a peek at my leg. She rolled her eyes, and said, "Oh, alright. I'll look at it." She threw the blanket back, took one horrified look that made me think her eyes would surely pop out of their sockets, dropped the blanket, and headed for the doors, yelling names, and "come quickly."

Soon, I had young doctors, old doctors, tall doctors, fat doctors, and a contingent of white dresses, all there wanting to take a peek. I was so frightened. These were the big guns, and they are going to talk among themselves, say, "uh-huh," "ah," rub their chins, and almost never meet my terrified eyes with their own calm, curious ones.

"Phlebitis," one doctor announced.

"For certain," another said.

"She just have a baby recently?" asked another as he perused my chart. Someone nodded.

"How long has she been here? Says here admitted April one," and this older doctor looked up, arched his brows, and pointedly asked, "Why wasn't she more carefully monitored?"

"She didn't show signs of this coming on," a nurse spoke up.

"She had uterine infection and a blood clot in her lung. How many signs you people need?" The older doctor was becoming inpatient with his staff, began ordering left and right the procedures to attack the problem. He spit out to the nurse as he left, "and keep on top of her temperature. I'll check in later."

I began to feel panic rising, and I asked what happened here. One red-headed doctor who had lingered, looked me straight in the eye. Finally, someone noticed I was here, and he said, "Your veins are inflamed, some breaking down, and possibly this leg is where the blood clot came from."

"Will I ever be normal again?" My lips quivered as I probed his eyes, watching closely for signs of lying.

"Uh, well, maybe, uh...sure, but it will take time, and ..."

"Take it off!" I screamed out. "Cut it off!" I was slapping at my bloated leg. He caught my hand, and called for a nurse to get me a sedative as I went into the sobbing of utter defeat.

Where was my Protector all this time? Why did he allow this to happen to me? I'd had so much, I just wanted to die. Didn't he love me anymore?

I didn't pray that night, the next, or the next.

I lay quietly in my bed after the lights were out, thinking back upon the singing Bettye, Peggy, and I had done for churches in San Pedro, and Wilmington. Bettye and I were parents, but we would practice our songs at various houses while our little ones played at our feet. My favorite time was the Sunrise Easter service one cool dawn at Channel Heights. We girls had sung at the tent revival the night before, lifting our voices in praise, but this morning with our voices almost hoarse, we sang our favorite "The Old Rugged Cross" as the sun broke the sky in deep orange, then yellow.

Tears rolled onto my pillow as I remembered the music; tears of sorrow that my Lord didn't love me, so I thought he had abandoned me, too, and I wasn't worth much to anyone. I felt so alone, couldn't see my children. I didn't have visitors to speak of, and my father did not visit at all the thirty-one days I was there in the hospital only three miles from his home.

I'd lost my Protector, and my Comforter. There was no one left for me to hold on to.

I had completely lost my sense of humor, and spent the remainder of my thirty-one days with a wire cage containing a lamp over the hot wet packs that draped my left leg. I would catch glimpses of the lumpy "thing" when the packs were changed, and was completely repulsed by the sight.....the gray-white, clay look of it was to me a dead attachment that should be cut off. My toes were stretched wide, spread far apart by the swelling, and unlike the leg, the foot showed liver-colored broken veins that encompassed the entire foot, and large hematomas bulged about them. It looked as if all the veins in my leg and foot had burst, flooding inside the skin at random. I felt nothing. It simply laid there, a grotesque horror from some evil planet. I kept hoping that one day I'd wake up and find it was all a horrible nightmare, and I'd look and see my normal leg again, but it didn't happen. The awful monster was there; a thing of disgust, and the worst fear was for all the world to see and be repelled by it, too.

Every time the young, red-haired, Doctor Grace passed my bed I'd ask him, "Are you going to cut this off?" He would stop and try to encourage and cheer me, but I would have none of it.

"Think of it this way Alma, you will be able to walk."

"Seems remote," I snorted, and would then ignore him by picking up a magazine to put in front of my face.

The first time I stood was by orders, and a couple of nurses practically had to haul me up. I was still in a trauma situation, shock I could not shake, and I certainly wasn't going to cooperate, or make it easy for them. I screamed out, then ground my teeth together as gravity rushed all fluids down into my leg causing further misery for me. Well, the leg certainly wasn't dead. The nurses, one in particular whose name was Nancy, urged me to take steps. I couldn't lift the heavy lag, so dragged it along as my right leg, weak in itself, worked hard to pull it forward.

Day by day, day by day, I struggled up, inched along the floor, dragging that leg. I was so damaged I couldn't think normally anymore. I was hostile, and my eyes showed nothing but hate for the world and this hell I was in.

Dr. Grace sailed by, yelled. "Hey, Alma, that's remarkable progress there."

"You know where you can put this remarkable progress, don't you?" I flung back.

He stopped, and faced me. "I think you will be going home day after tomorrow. How's that?"

"Oh, I dunno. I'm beginning to like this place."

"I'll call your husband today and let him know. You want to see your kids, don't you?" He grinned widely.

"Of course I do. I just hope I can care for them. I'm different, now. I'm a cripple." I looked down at the leg.

He put a freckled hand on my shoulder, gave a pat, and said, "You will do great. Just fine. You have guts." What else could he say? He knew he couldn't lie to me. I knew him too well. Besides, I wasn't the person to be flip with. Not anymore.

I took long, hungry looks at my beautiful children, feeling I hadn't seen them in ages. Scotty was eight-weeks old, and stared at me long and hard, and began to fret at my unfamiliar face, and mother cried as we packed the bassinet, tote bags, diapers, and bottles of formula into the car. I did hug my mother, cried with her and told her of my gratitude. I had no money to pay her.

Vicki and Tommy both, seemed taller than I remembered, and while Tommy was tanned, Vicki's face sported a smattering of cute freckles. They were very shy, and I noticed my daughter was the leader over her younger brother. She was a mite bossy, but he didn't seem to mind. He was trying to see my legs through the wide-legged slacks I wore, and I knew that Vicki would quietly survey the situation and make her own conclusions. Tommy was literally bursting with questions. Scotty cried a good portion of the night, but having Vicki and Tommy about, he began to acclimate quite well the following day. I would be visiting Dr.Cassidy shortly, and I wanted to take him for an examination. He appeared to be over his stomach problem, but the hernia was becoming a problem. I was trying to concentrate my efforts on the baby, and the other two were doing fine, and they helped me a great deal. I loved having them with me again. Meanwhile, Arb worked throughout the days, was more quiet and pensive at times. He never went to bed nights sober. He never asked me questions about my hospital stay, and ignored my leg, but there were times when he would be helpful in the house....if he was sober enough.

Chapter Fourteen

Back in generations past discipline and punishment were harsh, principally dealt out by the husbands and fathers, and the teaching from the Bible, *"spare the rod, spoil the child"* did not deter the fathers of families to go beyond the mark the quote was intended, stepping further into brutality that maimed not only bodies, but minds, too.

Many times a wife was punished along with the children, no better than cattle, and decades ago women were termed "Legal Chattel" in legal documents, and "owned" by the husband. And, you know what? Women accepted it. They were forced to. And a women seldom divorced a brutal husband. It was unthinkable. The other outcome to brutality other than injury or death, was hate for the brutish man, and a life of complete fear and sorrow for the ones caught up in the life where there was no escape until the sod was laid over them. The male children who survived went on to pass the hateful legacy down, generation after generation.

Many women ended up quite mad and were shipped off to an insane institution where the abuse continued by other hands; some women chose spinsterhood over life with a man and droves of children. Then, some women were stronger-willed and survived, but until the rights of women and children started to be recognized, obedience to the man continued.

It was a man's world, and women were not worth a

2-cent stamp. The all-male courts were not a place for women to plead for mercy from abusive husbands. Domestic violence, as we call it today, appeared condoned by the courts. It was simply that way.

It took a lot of years after the women received the right to vote to start off into a whole new direction, and we began to change the completely, new concept of the women's role in our society, and, especially, in relation to rights to be citizens up there with the men, and to take our rights as voters and citizens to push us farther ahead as anything except chattel. We ceased to be bond servants to an all-male voice of opinions and rulings.

However, as the years pass, and society makes its big leaps and bounds, the 1990s are proving to be inundated with domestic violence and abused children in our courts in all cities of our country, especially as the population grows. Jobs are difficult for the poor and uneducated, and stress fills our lives with drug and alcohol abuse, and crime. The problems appear to be absolutely insurmountable, and unsolved.

Where did we women stand on selective careers and marriage and children by the end of World War II? How would I know? I was already caught up in a disastrous situation that not even Gabriel could get me out of. It was too late.

When Scotty was five months old, I could not locate a surgeon who could correct the hernia. Their claim was flimsy, to say the least, conveying to me a reluctance to cut on a baby that young. They told me to bring him back when he was eighteen-months old. The baby couldn't wait that long.

I was forced to find ways of relieving Scott's pain. At times the intestine looped down through the opening into his scrotum, and I worked as gently as possible to manipulate the intestine back up into his lower abdomen where it belonged. I tied a knot in a cloth and fitted it closely against the groin much like a truss. As this was a hot season, and the Tehachapi earthquake gave us southern Californians a good jolt, I felt everything coming apart at the seams. To put it mildly, I sweated and swayed while consoling my sick baby.

When I could no longer help Scotty, to ease his pain, the situation became more precarious when the hernia strangled and hydrocele was evident. Arb and I took the lifeless baby to my mother's home to inquire of her private physician. It was Sunday, of course, and late afternoon.

She quickly put in a call to his residence, and when I talked to him, informing him of my son's condition, he said, "Meet me behind my office. I'll be there as soon as I can. I'm on my way." He hung up.

Arb and I raced to the car praying the doctor could break the speed limits. I believe my sister Peggy was with us during the frightful time. I can't remember. I was so worried.

We chewed our nails as we waited; one minute seemed an hour. Soon headlights headed our way, came to a stop parking next to us. The tall doctor in casual clothes hastily got out of his car and said, "Come," as he took keys and opened the back door to his office. We followed, and he switched on lights to an examination room, told me to lay the baby down, quickly stripped off the diaper, and I watched as slender fingers probed the area of the hernia.

At this point the baby was hoarsely crying, plaintive and not as loudly as earlier. He was exhausted, and my dread for him was on the edge of panic.

The doctor told us he would have to draw fluid from the area which would promptly relieve the pain. The baby was weak, but after the procedure was finished, and I held a quiet, sleeping baby in my arms, I asked him if he would operate, so this would not continue on. "Yes," he replied. "In one week. He has to gain more strength first. But, yes, call me tomorrow, and I'll set it up."

Arb and I were so grateful to this hero of ours, this doctor, and soon Scotty was in peak condition after the surgery. What can I say about unsung heroes such as he was? He had come to a little baby's aid, and no doubt saved his life. I interrupted his Sunday evening meal with his family, but I like to think that he felt good about it. Thank you, Dr. Newburn.

I could now turn my attention upon my neglected condition....the abominable leg. It hurt viciously, especially in all the sweltering heat that only August and September in Southern California can put out, and I soon discovered another enemy.......fatigue, that would come with the vascular disease. The pain was with me day and night, and the least bump would bend me over, and I thought about how the leg had no feeling in the beginning. Well, that changed quickly enough. When I could, I would apply hot, wet towels as hot as I could possibly tolerate, and wrap that in plastic sheets.

When I thought of going out in public in a dress, I became agitated, wanting only to hide my ugly limb underneath slacks or jeans. I refused to examine my naked body in a full-length mirror, and I forced myself to walk without the "drag", as I called my limp, but I was sad about the condition. Each morning as I woke for another painful day, I tried to focus my attention upon my children......only, for crying out loud.....do not allow anyone to see the leg and pity me. I couldn't stand that. Seeing pity in people's eyes, much as I used to react to a crippled person when I saw him. Did I show pity in my face to those people?

I never cried for myself anymore. Life had been lousy to me and I was angry about it. I hurt inside....terribly....and I truly felt God could have spared me this. Why didn't he? I'd care for myself, the leg, and I'd tell myself that it was something I could not change, or turn around, so I'd best get myself a workable plan of therapy, plus a plan of disguise. I was still athletic looking despite my slender build, but I could try to dress where the offending limb would be less noticeable. Lets face it; legs were in to stay and my bikini would never, ever drape itself around me, except in my secluded back yard while I worked on tans. No more white skin, and the injured appendage received a double rub of sun tanning lotion.

In the fifties woman simply do not wear pants or jeans to functions. Only dresses were allowed, and the helpful panty hose had not been invented yet. So, I became a type of rebel who crossed the barriers of dresses and skirts by showing up in pants. I looked good in Levi jeans, so I wore them. And I waited for the day when something less revealing than the nylon sheer stockings would break through and aid people like me. Leg make up wasn't a new idea, and Helena Rubinstein made a bundle off me later on, even though it would not alter the Elephantiasis, or unsightly swelling.

While I pondered on this, I started the hot water-ice water therapy sessions in my bathroom, a daily routine that would pay off for me in the long run. I'd fill the bathtub with very hot water, put my leg into it, holding it as long as I could tolerate it, then switch it to a large bucket of ice water with floating cubes of ice. I'd repeat the procedure over and over. The leg continued to be a clump of grey-purple clay, and could easily be molded with the fingers. A small push of a finger would leave an indentation that lasted a while.

Arb was back bar running, but managed to hold onto a job of sorts, and we still had the same car we had two months before. But, our bills were not getting paid, and I was never allowed to handle the money, and to suggest a budget to him meant I was overstepping my boundary, and that set off another bad scene.

I was hounded by Arb's parents and sister to try to gain control of the money. Did they actually belive I could? I don't think so. My parents were bickering with me about what to do to better my situation. They suggested I leave him, but they didn't have a clue where I would go with my children. All this unrealistic advice was causing more turmoil for me, and I certainly didn't know what to do.

We were forced to move two more times, Vicki and Tommy in and out of two more schools.

It was with uneasy trepidation that Arb and I allowed ourselves to be persuaded to pull up stakes and move to Wichita, Kansas by my brother, Herb, whose argument was to eliminate family interference by getting completely away from it. He was involved in a career of police work, had been a Christian since youth, and so drew upon his expertise in the field of helping his fellow man; in this case, a sister and her dysfunctional family. But he overlooked the important fact that he knew absolutely nothing about alcoholics.

I, knowing my husband on the one hand, and harboring feelings of unbelief in rehabilitation, but on the other hand, hoping in miracles, was willing to try to save my family and all the time feeling unsafe getting that far away from Arb's family and the help they had always provided.

January of 1953 was cold in Wichita with snow and dipping below zero temperatures made me uneasy. We started to church, and Arb had taken tests for fire fighter for the department there, scored high and was accepted to a station in the suburbs close by. We were all so proud of him, and he settled in to change his ways and focus upon new, more constructive behavior patterns.

Arb became restless with his relinquishment of alcohol, and the desire must have been demanding upon him, yet he stuck in there, wanting desperately to succeed.

The cold weather did great wonders for my swollen leg. The pain and swelling were being relieved, and I kept right on with the hot water-cold water therapy. But, I had noticed another disturbing complication to my ongoing battle with the phlebitis; my right leg was becoming involved, and varicosity of veins was worsening with time. It was difficult to consider that at any time I could repeat with it as I'd had with the left leg. Blood clots were evidently becoming a life threatening reality.

Somehow, we managed to get through the following summer. I was missing California, but did not voice my opinion in the presence of my children, or Arb. Arb was still trying. The children were trying, but I knew Vicki, who was nine, missed her Aunt Stel and Ma and Pa, so was homesick. Then, when school started in September, she and Tommy were more cheerful.

One day in November, I knew I was pregnant again. This time I cried tears of discouragement....tears of doom....my doom. I couldn't think of the fetus yet. I was in trouble with keeping my life. The darned legs! What can I do with the stupid legs, the clots that nestled there that could break loose and wander up to my lungs again? These clots could also travel to my heart, or my brain. I was warned.

Reluctantly, I went to the office of an OB-GYN man for a complete examination. He was stunned when he discovered my complete condition. I was truly pregnant, would deliver in June of 1954, if I lived that long. I needed leg surgery, a "stripping" procedure that would take out the offensive, infected veins which harbored possible blood clots.

Herb acted nonchalant about my being pregnant again, and the possible consequences, and quickly hunted up a reputable surgeon, and we consulted with him. After his examination of the damaged legs, he told Herb and I, "Let's do it as quickly as is possible." We promptly agreed. No hesitation.

The complete inside lateral veins of both legs were stripped out from the groin to the ankles. Other cutting was necessary to remove isolated ruptures. It was a lengthily process, and both legs were bound with elasticizied bandages....bandages I'd have to wear throughout my pregnancy, and later. I suffered from thrombophlebitis, or as so frigheningly was told to me later, thromboembolic disease syndrome. How very impressive. And, scary. I was completely and utterly shocked down to my discolored toes when Tommy, my lad, came home from school with a high fever and pain in his neck and jaw. He had the mumps! I felt so sorry for the little guy and made him as comfortable as possible in his bed. The swelling had already begun. I wasn't too sure about the disease, except males should be careful about exercise and exertion. I wondered about Scott, the baby, who had undergone his second hernia surgery there in Wichita, but was doing wonderfully. He was full of life, grew into a beautiful, blond, curly-headed imp with more energy than all of us put together. He certainly had his share of pain, and I had no doubt that he would be infected and be sick again.

There was one other dread hiding in the back of my mind as Vicki helped me with Tommy, and we talked of the possibility of Scott coming down with the mumps.....I had never had mumps! Although, I slept in the same bed with Bettye, and was exposed to the disease by Peggy, I had never caught the disease. I was uneasy. If I did get them, what would be the effects on my baby?

I called my doctor, and while he was quite concerned, he advised me to keep in close contact with him, and for me not to worry. Oh, yeah. In the meantime, I kept busy with my little brood, and we celebrated when Tommy's cheeks and neck were once again normal. Actually, I was counting down days.

I was resting with my legs upon a foot-stool in the early evening. Arb was on his 24-hour shift at the fire station, and the children were occupied with their varied games when Scott walked up to me and announced, "No feel good, mommy," and a chubby hand he placed upon my arm was hot to the touch. I said, "Oh, no," as I lifted him and felt his head. He was definitely feverish. I called to Vicki, my little trooper, who stuck her blond head out of the bedroom . "What is it Mom?" I said, "I hate to say this, but I think Scott has mumps." She was still as a statue. Tommy's eyes stared broodingly up at me holding Scott. "It's okay Tom," I told him. "You couldn't help it."

"Yes, I did too," he said in his low, quiet voice. "I'm to blame."

"No way," I told him. "Someone had to give them to you. Right?"

He flashed me his great smile with one front tooth partially in, and no sign of the other one at all. "Yeah, that's right huh?"

Arb was off the week-end, so we settled around the kitchen table playing Parchessie, the coffee pot always ready for Arb, and soda for the rest of us. Tom and Vic were having loads of fun, and were becoming quite proficient with the game. Other times we played Rook, not as much fun for the kids, but they were learning.

Scott had been sleeping, and I must say, he was taking this mumps craze very well. If he made a peep, however, one of us immediately jumped to the call. I began calling him "Mighty Mo," not only because he had weighed thirty pounds at the age of nine months, but, because he was such a stalwart, gutsy little boy. He wasn't feeling much like Mighty Mo now, but we were there to comfort him.

What would be the next worse scenario you could conjure up? You are correct. I got the flipping mumps. Gosh, I hurt on that one side...one side only. What is this with taste buds that can cause havoc if you merely think of a lemon, or a sour pickle? Being so ill, I couldn't take care of Scott, who still needed attention. It was disturbing to me, and Vicki was forced to miss some school to care for him while I wallowed about the bed. A couple of times I imagined I felt cramps. I was four months pregnant, and I was worried. I also spotted some, too.

Spring came along, and I was feeling fine even though I was forced to wear the bandage on my legs, both of them. I had also been fitted with the elastisized stockings, but they felt too tight, so I used the bandages I could loosen when I felt more swelling. I was active enough, I suppose, preparing meals for my family, cleaning house, laundry, and ironing, and my legs were working with me more as long as I didn't stand too long, or bend them into a position that lasted very long.

The baby was growing inside me, and as I thought back upon the small body I had....almost invisible....while carrying Vicki, the fourth pregnancy was a "poocher," that was for sure. But, the infant was alive and kicking, and I would know about the middle of June if my having mumps left any marks upon him. I hoped not.

I had been attending church and Sunday School for my children more than for myself. Arb could not attend with us every Sunday, because his 24-hrs on duty, and 24-hrs off duty did not allow every Sunday visits. But, I was simply not feeling right with my faith. I was somewhat bitter since my bad experience began, and had escalated to a point that when it culminated into the blood clot, the hospital, and legs, I was thrown in with a pack of dogs, it seemed to me, where there was no God; no help from my Protector, that the constant bombardment to my body and mind, of the pain, and the fear, not to speak of the reduction of my built-in courage, was decimated to nothing.

The definite puzzle to me was that as a child in trouble, in a troubled atmosphere, I found something seeking me out that I hungrily grabbed for, to hold dear, to tell my troubles to, to pray to...my Jesus, and feel comforted. My dream that God would certainly allow one of his little ones to find peace if I but fought, and later, when I looked around for Him when terrible things were happening to me, he wasn't there. I couldn't find him. He was ever so quiet. I missed him.

Six months pregnant, I decided to iron clothes while watching some T.V. Scott was asleep and the other two in school. Now was a good time I told myself. Vicki's dresses, Tommy's shirts and pants, and Arb's clothes waited to be pressed, and so I began my chore. I'd been standing for sometime when suddenly I began to feel unwell, so I told myself I should take a break. Turning off the iron, I felt my mind wandering away from me. I cannot properly describe what happened next accurately enough to make it clear to you, but I will try.

The news was on the television. At least, I think it was the news, and the voice, the commentator's male voice, began to speak in words I could not understand. I was hearing the voice, but it made no sense. The words were garbled. My mind was telling me I could think alright, but external stimuli were not being conveyed properly to my brain. I was terrified. What in the world was happening to me? Was I losing my flipping mind?

Following that, the left side of my body started a numbness that covered my whole left side, basically. My tongue and lips were becoming numb, and I wasn't seeing exactly as I should. I went to the phone, and becoming more frightened, and for the life of me I don't know how, dialed the fire station. The captain's voice came on, and I thought I asked for my husband, saying that I was ill, but he kept saying to me, "Lady, is this a joke? I can't understand a word you are saying. You are talking gibberish." He hung up the phone. I was told this later.

I was becoming less lucid, except, I could talk inside my head, and I attempted to dial a neighbor with no success. The attempt to the doctor's office resulted in the same lack of success. I was now unable to dial the rotary phone at all. This told me I was getting worse.

It wasn't time for the children to come home from school, I thought, "Oh gosh, I think I read somewhere....yes, yes....I'll get to the bed and prop my feet upon a pillow."

I dragged into the bedroom where Scott was sleeping, and managed to lie myself prone upon my back. The numbness was almost complete, and the T.V. kept yelling out mumbo-jumbo I couldn't understand. Was my life going out? Desperately, I tried to concentrate, and I wanted to speak, but I couldn't. I could not open my mouth, and I could not move my body. What is this? Am I to go through yet more of the seemingly obscure sicknesses that the doctors can't cure?....again? What have I done so wrong that there is no let-up for me?

The headache began, charges of pain stabbing; a different type of headache than I'd ever known. It pounded my skull with its fists of iron, then slowly settled down to a tolerable level and continued there in the dark recesses of my mind.

I was drifting again up above the earth, and there were clouds. But, these clouds were terrifyingly scudding with tremendous speed across the wide expanse of a gray sky.... somber....threatening....casting me off. I wanted to float again upon a fluffy cloud of white that comforted me. No, these clouds were in extreme disharmony, crashing through one another, and I yelled so loudly to them to stop, that I could no longer bear to see them, so I drifted in a descent ever so slowly, and I whimpered with tears streaking down the sides of my face, "Oh, My Lord of Heaven, do not allow me to die, please. Do not let something else happen so disabling that I cannot care for my children. Please help me."

I became quiet, andwaited for something else to happen. The bedside clock was ticking and I heard it. I began to count with the second tickings and happily noted I wasn't dead. But, what kind of state was I in?

Two hours passed. I looked up into the puzzled, freckled face of my daughter standing by my bed. Tommy noisily came in and began playing with Scott, who was sitting up in his crib playing with a toy.

"You okay, mom?" Vic put her hand upon my left arm, and I felt it.

"I am f-fine," I replied with words slurred.

"You don't sound fine," she said almost accusing me.

"Give me time," I managed, and my little daughter, a precious child, reached out and helped me to a sitting position.

"And, you look awful," she decided.

My head was still hurting and would continue to do so for almost two weeks. My one eye was a little blurry, my tongue not very adept, and my arm extremely weak as was the left leg. I felt as if I'd had a dread disease.

I called Dr. Crowley, who ordered me to his office immediately. He called in his colleague and my surgeon. They poked and tested, then sat me down and explained to me that I was a very fortunate young woman. I'd had a very light stroke that shouldn't leave me with disabilities. Also, the baby was doing fine. I was duly warned that with my leg and vascular problems, I should never stand in one place for a lengthy period, that I should begin moving about more and take short walks while I was pregnant. The blood had become stagnant in the lower part of my legs, and because the valves had collapsed, the blood could not be pumped properly back into my body. My blood pressure had soared upwards dangerously, before settling back down. The stroke was a warning to me, and I certainly did not want to die, and worse, I did not want to become a vegetable. So, I must be careful about living habits.

I was monitored closely by the doctor while I was still carrying the baby, and when Chip was born I had no trouble at all to speak of, and after four days in the hospital, I took my healthy son home to introduce him to the children.

Indeed, Chip was a fine child, wide shoulders and

muscular arms and legs, who sported a birthmark on the back of his head, the white hair standing straight out in a patch of light brown hair. The other outstanding feature about him was the eyes. They were aqua color, and very slightly, almond shaped. He resembled his grandfather, Pa Pickle. He was the easiest baby to care for out of the four.

There was one very important matter I was milling over in my head that was not going to give me rest, unless I had the opportunity to bring it to fruition. It dealt with my being a mother, or more strongly put, I felt cheated! There I said it.

I had not had the beloved opportunity of breast feeding my babies. None of them. I was too anemic....I was too ill, and when Vicki was born "Bottle" babies were the majority rule. Even so when Tommy was born, very few mothers breast fed them. I was too sick to nurse Scott, and this time I was given pills to dry my milk producing glands.

Well, pooh, on that, I said again to myself. I'll refuse to take one of the pills--stave it off for a bit so I can have the pleasure of nursing Chip at his 2 AM feeding for as long as I can before I follow doctors orders. I did just that, and I was thrilled that I had the privilege. It was a wonderful feeling to hold his sweet little body against my breast in a ritual of bonding since the birth of dawn. And, I thanked God.

I must explain that when I was urged to get back on the path of the interaction and closeness to my Comforter and Protector, I opened myself up to Him as I lay there upon the bed when the stroke came, and knew I'd always have a line open to Him. He proved He would help me if I but asked. He swept away and forgot my many sins by responding to my cry for help.

If winds can blow
And, trees can sway,
I'll love you Lord
For Eternal's Day.

If I could but scan
a thousand seas,
I'd bow my head
To you; fall on my knees

If I could climb
To your hiding place,
I'd reach out my hand
For your saving grace

If, by my fault
I've pushed you away,
Please take me back
For Eternal's Day

    I wrote this especially for the book. It is a poem of surrender I wish to share with you. First, I make a vow of love, then ask forgiveness, make a vow of veracity, and lastly, a plea of entreaty. May I dedicate it to you, the reader?

Chapter Fifteen

I was doing fine after the baby's birth, having more to do, but with the assistance of Vicki I got through each day a lot better. Effects of the light stroke would gradually blend in with the leg problems, but ultimately would cause short memory blocks that would clear only with time. As an example: I would ask one of the children to please bring me a....a....[I could not remember] a....a....[I struggled to put a name on the object] a....tissue.

As late as the sixties, if I became nervous, I would have a slight stoppage in my speech. After college, speech, voice and diction classes, and being with active people involved with organizations demanding constant verbal interaction, I began to come out of the troubled area quite well. All effects never really disappear, however.

At the current time, as I grow older and become tired, my mind wants to stop thinking, and I limp without noticing, whether it be caused by vascular situation or having had a slight stroke I don't really know. I try not to think of it too much. In writing this book I am forced to dwell upon unpleasant things, and soon I hope to be living in the present, and put these uneasy memories in a dark closet with my worn out shoes.

My husband, the fire fighter all of us were so proud of and who rode the very rear of the big, red fire truck clutching the typical headgear with one hand while hanging onto the safety rail with the other, was becoming unhappy. We were so eager to run out into the front yard to wave to him as the screaming truck raced to a fire. Although he couldn't wave to us, he would give us his biggest grin. Later on, we would crowd around about him and congratulate him; let him know we were proud. The kids' daddy a firefighter....wow.... that was something. Scotty always clapped his chubby hands in glee.

I knew very well what was wrong with Arb. His nervousness was completely unmistakable to me. I knew the signs. I waited with a frightened heart, and knew without a doubt he would fall "off the wagon" or ladder, so to speak, and my apprehension was building as his unhappiness built. On his 24-hours off, he would leave the house, only to return later with the pronounced odor of beer about him, and a slight slur of speech.

Oh, dear Lord, why can't Arb stay sober? He had so much to look forward to, a challenging job....but wait! He had a challenging job with all the accouterments attached for achievement, and even though he was bright and qualified for fireman first class, he must stay in there and advance grade by grade into higher rank. Herein, I felt, lay his weak spot: he couldn't go on competing, struggling in a world of many competitors, examinations, spit and polish, and marching to a band of good behavior day and night. The stress was too much for him. Poor, lost lamb. What demons did he fight? Our world subsequently crumbled. My heart broke to see the tears in Vicki's and Tommy's eyes. Their daddy refused to take the next grade test.. Scotty's chubby hands didn't clap as he ran outside to see the fire truck pass and daddy was not riding the back.

The children and I made a half-hearted effort to play our games at the kitchen table, and we continued our prayer circle with Scotty sitting in the high chair, his small hands clasped in front of him. In the small apartment we seemed to huddle, or group together. Chip was a good baby, and slept most of the time in the beginning, so he wasn't present at the table with us.

Uncertainty began to crowd rapidly into the faithful heart of my daughter. Her prayers became toneless, and her enthusiasm for Sunday School classes dropped into silence. The poor child was struggling with her own faith, as I found out soon enough. She finally took in a deep sigh and sat back in her chair. I couldn't stay silent any longer as I watched the change in her.

"Vicki, would you like to share anything with us?" I asked.

She took another long sigh, shrugged her thin shoulders, and said, "I just don't see the use of it."

"Of what?"

"All the praying." She dropped her eyes. "Mom I've prayed for daddy. Remember what the Bible says about having the faith of a small grain of mustard seed?" She held up her finger and thumb so close together to signify the smallness of a grain.

"Yes of course," I answered her.

"Well, I've had that much faith when I've prayed for daddy for so long, and....and, it doesn't work. It just doesn't work, so I am not going to pray for him any more." She got up from the chair and went into the living room.

I looked at Tommy, who had kept quiet throughout all this, and he only nodded his head in agreement.

"We can't stop praying," I told them. "we must continue, not only for his sake, but for ours. We don't know what God can do, but we can't give up."

We continued our grace before meals, but our prayer time was lacking in faith, even my faith that had sustained me for so long. I had no answers for my children, but tried to encourage them as the weeks passed, and things were getting bad again..

It was November 1954, and the winter was upon us again. Our apartment was cozy enough, but for how long I could merely speculate. Arb was back in full swing with the drinking, and he began to frequent a place a few blocks from us that served beer, and offered table shuffleboard for gaming interests. He spent most of his time and money there, coming home only to change clothes and sleep.

There was this one night I shall never forget as long as I live, that retaught me the awful thing called fear. Just in case I had forgotten, you understand, from the "good old days."

Something was wrong with the car, Arb was at the bar, the kids needed food, and I left Vicki with the boys, donned my coat and headed out to the bar. It was night, and the bitterly cold wind was rising making my walking more difficult, but I plunged on.

I had some very unwise notion that somehow I could salvage some money we needed desperately at home. Did I actually think I could approach him as he sat upon his trusty bar stool, say to him, "Come with me," and he would meekly say "Yes dear," and follow me? He scowled when he saw me, and held the glass of beer to his mouth. He lowered it and said, "What ya doin' here?" I sat on the stool next to him, suffering the inquisitive looks of the other patrons, mostly men, mostly in their cups . "I thought I'd come walk you home." I tried to sound light and breezy. "Sur' ya did, sur' ya did," he remarked as a dark moody look flooded his face.

Whether it was close to the time for him to leave, or that the other men continued to openly stare at me, I don't know, but he drained that last dregs of his beer, got up, and said, "OK, ya wanna go, les' go," and he pushed me roughly toward the door.

It soon became a nightmare for me as we walked into the freezing wind. He began kicking out with his feet, aiming at my injured left leg. I tried to keep ahead of his stumbling strides and yet close enough to watch him, thereby moving quickly out if his way. But this game was completely frustrating him.

A car passed. Arb was oblivious to it. He aimed another kick, then began yelling obscenities as anger engulfed him when the kick missed again. Soon, the fury took over full control of his being, and he began striking out at my head with his fists--both fists, one after the other, hard blows I was desperately trying to block, for this sudden action change surprised me and left me open for assault.

Another car passed and I screamed out, "Help me, help

me," then it sped up and disappeared. Another blow sent me to the ground; dry dead grass between the sidewalk and the street. I was upon one knee, holding the trunk of a leafless small tree, struggling to pull myself up. Finally, I was up and running for my life. Running against the blinding wind, gasping, with tears streaming and my coat billowing out and away from me. My knees felt numb from the cold, and I was aware the silly left leg didn't want to cooperate. It was holding me back.

As I approached the house, I knew that if I went inside, not only would I be trapped, but the children would be crazy with fear. Arb was in the strongest peak of his anger, and he would kill me if he caught up to me now.

Quickly, I crouched under a bush and squatted there, my breathing sounding so loud I was sure to be discovered. I watched as he entered the unlocked front door, and I prayed he wouldn't harm the children. I'd wait and listen, and perhaps he would go to sleep.

Time passed, the frantic heat I had built up quickly dropped down, and I shivered, my teeth rattling in my mouth. I surely had myself in another mess. How to get out of this one? I prayed, tears dropping down upon my cold, ungloved hands. Here's another one for you Lord, that I haven't a clue how to solve.

The bush was too confining, and my legs began to cramp, so I stole quietly upon the little porch and tried the door. It was locked! He had locked me out! The feeling I experienced then was panic. I couldn't get to my babies. My babies needed me. So, I moved out into the yard where the dead grass was softer, wrapped the coat tightly about me, and laid down. Being this close I could hear what was going on inside the house. Perhaps soon Arb would cool off enough to unlock the door.

I dozed, unfortunately.

I awoke to sudden, searing pain in my right side, and my surprised mouth opened in a yell I couldn't control. I looked up clutching my side. Arb was looming over me. I couldn't see his face, but the dark outline of his body was completely threatening. He had kicked me viciously with his hard soled shoes, and aimed another that, as I turned, the blow landed on the side of my head. I was stunned, but managed to roll aside. He reached down, grabbed me by the arm and roughly jerked me to my feet. I could barely stand.

"Get inside! Get to bed, you bitch," he hoarsely spoke. "I'll take care of you tomorrow."

He pulled me ahead of him, still clutching my arm, and shoved me onto the bed. "Get undressed and into bed."

My children were unharmed. Vicki and Scott slept on the divan in the living room, Tom on his half bed, and Chip in the crib. I knew Vicki was awake, but the boys were sound asleep.

Arb did not continue his physical or verbal abuse the remainder of the night, although I slept with one eye open to the possibility of more unwelcomed surprises.

Aubrey woke the next morning with an air of contriteness, which wasn't unusual at all for him, as with all abusers, even though I wasn't aware of it at the time. It wasn't until four years after that I would acquire knowledge of the correlation regarding behavior patterns of abusers. All I knew was that I felt Arb could stop drinking, the stimulus for his abuse, when in reality he couldn't stop drinking.

When I thought back upon the years with my father, his abusive nature, as also with the others, there was no alcohol involved to provoke abusive natures, so I felt puzzlement, complete confusion in my dealing with my husband. Basically, I didn't know what to do. What I could do to help our situation?

This day I asked myself, was I in such a precarious position that I was standing upon a precipice and a huge grizzly bear was barreling down upon me with the ferociousness of a speeding locomotive? Probably not, but I was in a completely unpropitious situation where the odds for my life weren't worth two hollers in a high wind. I figured the final outcome could be identical, but I felt helpless and useless in matters of making serious decisions.

Arb was hung over as usual, too, and drank his morning coffee with unsteady hands while I silently moved about the little apartment caring for the two babies. We had to talk about other serious matters.....a job for him, because our money was gone, the rent due, food for the children.....bills to pay. The worry I felt was near hopelessness, because our future depended upon him, and he was incapable of properly caring for us. But, I could not, dared not, stress him to a complete breaking point by bringing up a discussion.

I kept thinking about Herb, and what he had said to me recently. He had taken a lucrative job as Police Chief of a small city in Kansas a short time before, leaving the vice squad there at the police station in Wichita. He had come by the house before he moved stating his extreme disappointment in Aubrey and, also in my lack of effort to control the drinking problem. Therefore, he felt embarrassment to him to the extent he needed to distance himself and his family from us. I was crushed.

We desperately needed Arb's family; to be near them and the protection they could provide. But, here we were stuck in a state we weren't familiar with, no friends or relatives, in the dead cold winter coming upon us fast, and not a dime to get us back safely in California where help was. I was in a panic.

Finally, Arb decided to grace me with his thoughts, which went something like this: "I think we need to try to go home....don't you?"

I was so relieved that he brought up the subject instead of my being forced to do so, could only humbly nod my head, even though I felt another failure against us. I experienced some releif. But, how could I help keep him sober? He always had money for that, it seemed.

A call to Stel was hastily put in where we admitted defeat and needed advice and money to get us through until we could sell our home furnishings and the little car.

We were going home. The children were ecstatic to the point both Vicki and Tommy cried tears of joy. Scotty was happy because we were happy, and the horrible pall they felt was lifted. Chip was six months old. I would never again see Wichita except to pass through. I was not happy there. Except for the very brief time Arb was on the fire department I was in constant state of uneasiness.

> "Why do we do the things we do?
> Why are our happy days so few
> It's all a mystery to me
> Why our minds can't think it through.
> why can't you tell me?
> why can't you tell me?"

Back in California I felt quite relieved of the burden of being adrift in an unfriendly place that Wichita had become for all of us despite being forced to unload another problem upon the families; getting us settled into a place that would be convenient for us. The huge worry facing them was the same as before--trying to keep Aubrey sober and working to support our growing family.

By this time I feel Arb was all too aware of his incapabilities, but was forcing himself to learn another trade, using air tools in construction work under the protection of the union with very good wages and health coverage for the family. If he lucked out on a job, he simply kept his dues up to date, and put his name on the bottom of the employment list at the union hall, to eventually be called back on another job.

He continued to drink, and sometimes he would be late coming home after work loaded to the gills and with faint wafts of cheap perfume clinging to his work shirt. Other times he came straight home, ate dinner, showered, dressed, and left for his favorite bar, never uttering a word. It appeared he was constantly waiting until he could drink; waiting until the night came after a hard day's work as if he owed himself the best the night's drinking could award him.

It was to my utter dismay that Arb began yelling at the children, and freely lashing out at them with a long arm. He mostly aimed at the boys, leaving Vicki out of his frequent slaps across the head. He "cowed" her, however, and she learned to stay away from her father, or at times blended in unobtrusively in order to keep the attention off herself. I can still recall her large, scared eyes, if Arb was especially stressed. Her manner of complacence as quietly as possible was to her safe benefit, also. Actually, I do believe after careful observance over the years that he loved his daughter very much. The bond developed surrounding her birth and, he was genuinely reluctant to harm her. But, psychologically and emotionally he quickly alienated her, and she eventually lost respect, and I'm afraid, most of her love for him.

The boys, being so full of energy, were sources of irritation that quickly grew into anger that Arb could not control, and it was obvious to me that he soon learned that to bring peace and quiet he desperately needed, the calm, he would reduce them to tears by his "punishments" and send them to bed.

Tommy was his dad's buddy, and constantly sought his father's approval and support for his athletic abilities, his ambitions in the Boy Scouts that subsequently led him to become Eagle Scout and Explorer, and acquired week-end jobs that earned him extra money. He needed his father, and wanted him to be present at games and functions--to be there for him, to receive a pat upon the back and see the pride in his father's eyes. And Arb was proud, and he would be at the games, watch Tom's progress in all he accomplished, and give him that pat upon the back regardless if he was so drunk he could barely stand. At this point, Tommy became Tom. He was tremendously loyal...to us, to his friends, to coaches, scout leaders, teachers, and to adults in general.

Scott was a nervous lad and so bright. He learned things quickly. By age four, he tied his shoes, learned to tell time on the hour and half hour, print his A-B-C-'s, and work the basic first grade math. Being as nervous as he was, he also learned the "Dodge Syndrome" almost as well as I could, and no doubt he saved himself some pain for it. I worried about him. He was soft-hearted, loving to me, adored his sister, and he needed love and comfort. He needed a stable environment. His interaction with his father was somewhat strained, I'd say; but, he desperately needed his attention and approval.

Scott also was active in childhood sports. His greatest talent, I felt, was running, whether it was in track where he excelled, or going for the goal with the football. He put his nice head back, pistoned those long legs in the most graceful running I'd ever seen except for my idol, Jesse Owens. Scott ran as much like Jesse, a thing that could have been set to music, and the times that I watched him, my eyes held tears that could only brim up when seen by something so lovely.

When Scott was thirteen I listened to his clarinet solo bit from "Greensleeves" with his junior high orchestra that Christmas, and I was thoroughly proud. Later on, he played a cornet in the Caballeros Marching Band in Carson, California, and was a Civil Air Patrol Cadet at Ft. McArthur in San Pedro.

I am compelled to tell you of the accomplishments of my children so you can understand somewhat as I do, the reason behind why they deemed it necessary to drive themselves, to find something more real and acceptable to their characters than sitting about participating as victims and audience to the constant, dysfunctional behavior they were born into.

Of course, I helped push them along so they could experience a good feeling in the heart, that they could recognize their own potential, and, the foremost important aspect of life, to make choices of higher standards allotted to us all. I desperately wanted my children to stay one length ahead of the pitfalls of what they so easily could inherit....alcoholism, abuse, and the terrible fear of what living on this planet could mean, the stress; all can cause if their personalities are weak.

I must tell you about Chip. How must I describe him to you as he functioned as the youngest in our family? Strong and husky, calm and methodical, intelligent, an artist, a musician, a mathematician. A staunch believer in never using the "Dodge Syndrome". This little guy would not lower himself to be degraded by acting afraid of a swift blow without external reaction. He had gall, I will say for him, but I was afraid that he may be injured if he didn't attempt to dodge out of the way.

Chip did not like his father. He tolerated his presence by ignoring him altogether. When it was necessary and expedient for him to interact with Arb, he did so as quietly as possible with no emotion whatsoever....except, perhaps the aqua eyes showed attentiveness with a spark of something similar to dislike. He was forced to respond in a discreet manner to the authority he had no respect for. This is what I observed, and even if I felt pain for my young son, I knew exactly what he was feeling.

In 1956, I underwent my second leg surgery that was advised by my current family physician, and the results were unsatisfactory. By that, I mean, I actually needed a specialist in the field of vascular surgery.

While I was waiting to heal, Arb and I spent an evening out with another couple we had recently became acquainted with, and we sat chatting while sitting at a rather small table near the center of the room.

Something happened to change Arb's mood, and I felt he was becoming jealous upon occasion when the young man looked my way. To me it was conversational courtesy only when he spoke and looked at me as well as his wife and Arb. However, Arb read it completely wrong.

I noticed my husband took a look under the table, and feigning an adjustment of his body upon the chair, struck out a vicious blow with his hard-soled shoe which hit its mark upon my left, inside ankle. It landed at the place where I'd had both surgeries, and immediately I slumped over with the pain, reached down and closed my hand over the injury.

I rose, and haltingly made my way to the ladies room, excusing myself as calmly as possible. When I reached the empty room, I allowed the tears to flow freely, I couldn't hold them back. I inspected my ankle, horrified to see a swollen hematoma rising at the area and spreading in broken veins and capillaries. The area was rising in temperature, and my ankle was exhibiting the beginning signs of swelling, or edema.

I repaired the ravages of the tears, noticing in the mirror the paleness in my face, then made my way back to the table.

"Are you alright?" the young woman asked.

"For Pete sake, Alma, what did you do?" Arb asked so

innocently. "I bumped a tender spot on my ankle," I answered.

Returning home that evening was another trip of accusations from Arb, of how I should keep my eyes off the men and straighten myself up. He did not apologize to me when I soaked my ankle in cold, ice water to relieve the swelling and pain.

Soon after that I returned to the hospital for more extensive surgery. The injured ankle was given close attention, the bone scraped, and the outer skin was so damaged a portion was removed, and the wound stitched with fine wire. Eighteen incisions I later counted on both legs, some new cuts criss-crossing older incisions. I was swathed in elastic bandages from the groin to my toes, both legs. I was a mess--another painful mess. I not only resembled a mummy, I walked exactly as a mummy. It would take time and therapy before I could comfortably put my left heel flat upon the floor. I don't think I ever fully recovered from the blow. I inwardly cringe if that ankle bone is exposed, always having the fear I could reinjure it. Believe me, I have bumped it over the many years, but every time I look at my ankle I think of that night, and bits of anxiety force me to move about and think of something else.

It wasn't long afterwards that Aubrey became involved with a woman he had met in a bar near where he worked. Things were getting bumpier as the years passed, putting me in relatively expectant acceptance of his behavioral pattern although I continued to feel territorial, even threatened by a possible love interest on his part. But my reasons were, no doubt, familiar to many women in my same situation. I was ill, considered disabled at that point, with four children, all of whom needed me to care for them as best I could, so I felt I needed Arb at that time despite the abuse.

I also thoroughly believed my own saying that an "alcoholic father is better than no father at all", so I needed to protect the homefront until I could gain much more physical and emotional strength. I also needed to "outgrow" the obsequious, servile attitude of the abused victim before I could work on the difficult task of gaining courage, guts, I call it, that would permit me to rise above all I have ever known, and push forward to a worthwhile life.

Therefore, I tried to discourage Arb's women friends without too much ado, my mind planning on a better future for my children and myself.

My own major fear at this time was the real possibility that Arb would pass on a sexually transmitted disease to me, and with the luck I'd always had, it wouldn't have surprised me one bit. His accelerated intake of alcohol was beginning to dramatically slow down his sex drive to my thorough relief, and at other times when it was necessary, I would cajole him into using a condom. I did feel the situation was important enough to begin asking questions about protective solutions with germ killing properties, and I was cautiously faithful in applying them. I certainly theorized that I would be less embarrassed in asking a pharmacist for a preventative medication than be forced to hand him a doctor's prescription for a cure.

Chapter Sixteen

Dear Pa Pickle had passed on with pancreatic cancer in 1957 leaving all of us heart broken. I felt the family was swept up in a vortex of confusion by the loss of the revered patriarch for a time, but his death appeared to push Aubrey beyond what he could properly respond to, only making his mind seemingly less able to cope with every day life.

By 1960, we were living in a respectable enough housing project adjacent to schools and an athletic park area. All four children were constantly involved in outside school activities, including Vicki, who was a lovely pom-pom girl in the San Pedro YMCA Marching Band.

I became involved in civic affairs, coached teenage girls' sports at the park, and was taking college courses nights. All this activity allowed the children and myself to vent our frustration during the summer days, making our lives more tolerable. The nights were different, indeed.

When we all arrived home for our dinner and end of the day chores, we were apprehensive, harboring deep dread after the good day's high, fully aware we would be thrown into our area of battle always hoping Arb would be "better" this night and the battle not so bad. The tendons in the back of my neck were taut--stretched to a fine filament--so I expected the children were experiencing the same thing.

We seldom made it through the evening meals without the argumentative voice of Arb, the cursing, the offensive words aimed at all five of us, the generous slaps to the boy's heads, and usually ending up with his throwing food against the wall. The children would be sent to bed without watching television, and certainly Vicki could not play her 45 records.

I have never been able to analyze my husband's typical behavior for an abuser by allowing me to attend college, and he was quite proud of the children's accomplishments. This has always been an enigma, or rather, a deviation from the usual alcoholic abuser's pattern, so I go on wondering.

When I attended college, I would warn the kids to please stay out of their father's way, and what ever they did, never turn their backs on him. Tom didn't move fast enough one night, because he didn't hear the sudden approach, and for his inability to be on alert, was harshly hit in the back of the head with his dad's fist.

Another symptom of Arb displayed was to start an argument with Tom, then try to draw him out into the yard for a fight.

"C'mon, ya chicken," Arb would yell, his fists drawn up in front of him in circular motions. "C'mon. What's the matter, ya chicken?"

Hurting to the core and tears in his 14- year old eyes, Tom would attempt to placate his dad, who was struggling for a decent foothold in the yard. "Aw, dad," he would say. "I can't fight you."

"No!" came the yell from Arb. "Ya do as I say! C'mon out! I'll sho' ya wha' a man is." The words were very slurred.

"Come back in the house dad. I'm not going to fight you."

"Ya think you are a big strong guy....got all the girls. C'mon."

Arb was unable to coax Tom out, came and pulled him out by the hair, and proceeded to push him and punch him. Tom, humiliated and completely unable to fight his drunken father, would strike out in a run toward the park, tears rolling down his cheeks.

By nine o'clock Arb would be passed out in his chair,

and Tom would silently enter the front door, gently skirt his father's stretched-out legs, and go to his room.

Poor Tom. He was everything his father wanted to be and never could be. Arb was so proud of his son in one part of his brain, and envy in another part of his brain.

By the time 1962 came along, Arb was unable to work at all. I'd get up early in the morning to get in some college study time, fix Arb's coffee, make his lunch and fill his thermos with coffee, and send him on his way. By 10 AM, he would be back home so intoxicated he would be compelled to sleep in the chair.

One day, instead of coming back home, Arb drove up into the Palos Verdes Hill where he was pulled over by a patrol officer and ticketed for drinking while driving. This was not news to me. It was becoming a habit. The bitter part of this placed me in a precarious position, very illegal position, I might add. Because of the ticket, another DUI to his police dossier, and entering private roads , Aubrey was due to appear in front of a judge in a crowed court room in Redondo Beach.

"I'm not going to court," exclaimed Arb's voice adamantly.

"This is serious stuff, Arb," I said, trying not to bring my voice up high. I'd yelled at him too many times, and got "what-for" for my troubles. "You can't ignore this."

"Yes I can, and I will," he took a long sip out of his glass.

"If you don't, you will be arrested and spend time in jail."
"Oh yeah? Well, Jus' watch me."

I called Stel and told her about the problem to try to get some input of value, I hoped. Perhaps she could talk to Arb. I wasted my breath.

The end result was that I ended up appearing in the court in Aubrey's place. He drove me there, parked so nonchalantly in the court's parking lot, sat in the car with his brown paper bag upon his lap and told me, "Go do it. And, hurry. I'm out of beer."

When Arb's name was called out, I stood and walked

down where I faced the scowling face of a dour, old judge. He glared down at me. I couldn't keep my hands from shaking as I stood in that empty area. "Who are you ?" The judge growled. "I called an A.C. Pickle. Are you A.C. Pickle?"

"No, sir....I...."

"Speak up! I can't hear you. State your name, please"

"My...my name is Alma, Mr. Pickle's wife," I managed to say.

"Where is your husband, Mrs. Pickle? And why isn't he here?"

"He..he is, uh..sick, your honor, and couldn't appear."

The judge stared daggers at me, looked down at the sheet in front of him. A flush came over his face, then he looked up.

"What was your husband doing up in a private residential section on this day, aimlessly driving about..?" he looked down at me again,"....and drinking?"

"I..uh..don't know, sir except his construction site is close by."

My palms were sweaty as I stood, not moving, my left leg swelling. I could feel it. The pressure and tightness.

Then, the judge stated his demeaning lecture that lasted only about fifteen minutes, but by the time he finished I was so humiliated, I couldn't look anyone in the eyes as I left. The set fine to be paid within five days, more money than I had, would have to be met by that time limit or a bench warrant would be issued for Arb's arrest, and I felt, for me also. I was now a co-dependent. And, I had lied to the court.

All this took place while Arb sat several feet from the building drinking the balance of his beer, impatiently waiting for me.

I sat up on the bleachers at Scott Park, a chill breeze forcing me to pull my wind breaker closer. The night afforded me some privacy even though the lights that shone throughout the dark hours relieved me of total darkness that I do not like. My thoughts were jumbled as I pulled my legs up, and leaned my arms and chin upon my knees and I stared across the expanse of the two baseball diamonds to the houses beyond.

I had slipped out quietly as my family slept, past the outstretched legs of Aubrey who was completely passed out in his chair. He was drooling on his shirt front, wheezing snores beginning as he fell deeper into sleep. Later, he would have intervals of apnea, a sleep disorder that previously had frightened me, but not tonight. Not anymore.

This night had been extremely difficult on me and the children, especially sixteen-year old Vicki, when after a period of ranting and lashing out venomous unspeakable phrases, Arb had hemmed me in one corner of the kitchen bent upon "Keeping me in line." His hand was raised back ready for a blow across my face, when as quietly as lightning Vicki had placed her slim body between us in a protective action for me. The blow struck her face dead center, causing her nose to spurt a stream of blood. Her body was thrown against me, and I grabbed her, screaming out at Arb, my strident voice that of a wild animal. "You drunken ape! Don't you ever, ever hurt her again!" I was shaking with seething anger as I shook my finger at him. "You touch her again and I'll kill you!...kill you! You hear me?"

"Shut your stupid mouth, bitch!" He was slowly backing out. "Just keep her out of the kitchen."

Vicki had protected me without a single thought for her own safety. How long could she take this abuse.

I wondered what I could do to speed up my plans for leaving Arb and taking the children. They must be protected.

Sirens in the distance, mingling with the sounds of the late night traffic on the freeway nearby gave to my uncertain mind a sort of reality, or stability. It was soothing in a way. There was normal activity out there, and the children and I desperately needed a vacation from Aubrey. We were all exhausted with him, of dealing with his madness. He was similar to an autistic child who needed constant attention, and went on wild rampages, exhausting the parents. It seemed ludicrous.

When Aubrey discovered somehow--maybe it was only

a fear of his--that I was planning on leaving eventually, he threatened me, saying almost calmly, "If you try to leave me, I will kill you." He meant it.

With each passing day we noticed Arb was becoming more erratic in behavior. He didn't have the old spark left to stay out in bars, or strike up friendships with the women. He left the house each day with beer and cigarettes, but seldom stayed long enough to allow us to rest.

When money became tighter, Arb replaced the beer with cheap red wine, which I felt reduced him down a level with the lowly "wino." When he drank the wine, he had less control of most of his functions, less willing to acknowledge life around him, refused to eat, and his habit of cleanliness tapered off.

It was as though my will to be free was in complete captivity to a force that was determined to refuse relinquishment, for in doing so, the force would surely be destroyed. It would have no food to sustain it. I was a sacrifice of broken bread and thrown-out wine to the force of destruction that I had been rendered so helpless from the age of six and throughout my life. I was molded as a young sapling to break under the fierce winds. I honestly did not know how to break the bonds that held me captive.

Somewhere across the park the screeching tires of a fast moving automobile taking off echoed with determination, and my thoughts faded.

My leg began to ache. I stood up, drew in a long sigh of dejection, and undercover of darkness gave in to the pain and allowed myself to comfortably limp back to the apartment. I would return again to the force that bound me. My children were there, and I needed rest.

Vicki couldn't endure anymore, and it appeared to her that I was locked so tightly into this interminable grid of absurdity that she hated so desperately, she chose a hasty marriage and moved out. My heart was broken, and I felt so guilty, adding more disheartening baggage for my mind to deal with. My baby girl was now making choices in the only way she felt offered to her, and I prayed her choices would eventually lead her on to a more successful future than mine did for me.

She was my baby that I protected from the world when I carried her beneath my heart. Now, it had come to this--to the crossroad when I was incapable of protecting her.

One day Stel's husband came by to check on us and to take inventory of our financial needs....the food situation....rent, utilities, and I told him of our need to take time off away from Aubrey. Rick was a pleasant man who was all too aware of the problem Aubrey had been to the family from the time he was a little boy; how disciplinary measures had no effect upon him.

"Would you be willing to take him home with you....for just a couple of days?" I asked him, hoping he would see how desperate I was.

He was shaking his head before I finished the question.

"No, oh, no. We can't Alma. We simply can't."

"Rick, the kids and I are going crazy, we can't sleep....no rest at all....just two days....to get some rest." I was pleading.

"No way. I will not have him in my house, the way he is." He got up and paced about in agitation. He slapped his hands together in futile gesture.

"Arb needs help badly, and I'm hopeless to do anything about it." I said, as the tears welled up in my eyes. "I called an attorney about hospitalization and rehabilitation, but I can't sign him in. He is an adult, and must seek help himself. And, he certainly won't agree to that."

I watched Rick pace, his florid face pained, but stern. "We, Cotton, Stel and I, will keep your boys fed and the rent paid....other needs....as long as you stay here with Arb. If, on the other hand, you choose to leave him, we will not help you." He stopped pacing and faced me. "Know what I mean?"

"Oh, I know what you mean, alrighty," I murmured. "But, one of these days you will find Arb on your doorstep. Then, I just bet you he will be in a hospital fast enough."

"Now, come on Alma," he glared at me, and for emphasis, slapped his hands again.

I stopped my pacing, and threw my head back staring at the ceiling. Softly I said to him, "Arb is very sick, the constant drinking, and he doesn't eat, Rick, we are suffering abuse from him. We are afraid of him."

I looked back at him, my hands stuck down in my jeans pocket. "Another thing, I'm sleeping on the couch. Have been for about eight months now. I sleep facing front. I never turn over. I don't want my back exposed to him."

Rick watched me as I took another few steps across the worn carpet. He seemed hesitant to believe what I had just told him, decided I was being truthful, said, "Gee whiz, it is bad, isn't it? Worse than I thought."

"Is that honestly all you have to say? Does Stel and Cotton have any idea how serious this is?" I said this through clamped teeth, turned around to take more steps.

"I'll tell you this Rick, I'm glad Pa is not alive to see Arb becoming a vegetable, a brutal vegetable, even though he and Ma felt I could somehow prevent him from drinking. Alcoholism is like a slow cancer, and Arb is getting closer to writing his own ticket to death."

"Rick, I also sleep with a kitchen knife handy," I added. "I may not use it if he gets rough with me, but I will use it if he goes after the boys....if I am forced to." I concluded.

"I'm very sorry, Alma. I'll try to talk to Stel and Cotton. See if they can help." With that Rick left.

I was angry with the seemingly uselessness of it all. I held no animosity toward Rick, but I felt certain that Aubrey with his problem was all too real for his family, and they knew absolutely nothing about helping him, either that, or they were aware that there was nothing to be done for him. I also felt that I was being paid to stay with him....accept their charity to keep food in my sons stomachs, and to have a roof over our heads. They certainly didn't want the heavy burden of caring for him.

What made me think I didn't already live in a surrealistic world when the awful day of reckoning came with such ineffable movement that at last forced my hand? This was definitely different. I even woke up to a different feeling that something dreadful, but necessary, was to take place. I was not to be selected as the receiver of Aubrey's attention that day. Tom was the quarry.

Tom had been busy from the time he was ten, and at seventeen, along with Boy Scouts, a star pitcher for his high school and Scott Park, he worked after school at a local drive-by dairy up on Avalon Boulevard. Instead of accepting all cash for his work, he would bring home milk, butter, eggs, and bread each week, supplementing, as was his own decisive wish, for his brothers. With his heartfelt deed, his dad began to brood, and his resentment for his son grew heavier until one day his jealous rage exploded.

Arb began with stinging remarks as Tom moved about the house busy with his own chores. The mere sight of the handsome Tom was a motivating factor of his rage. Tom did his upmost to ignore the escalating insults profusely peppered with profanity.

Quickly, the tirade turned into what abusers use so often, attempting to tear down the confidence, attacking the self-esteem, setting up the victim in his vulnerability before losing control completely, and move in for the physical abuse. Tom continued to move about, and wasn't swallowing all the offensive expletives, yet he was becoming uneasy, as I was, as I worked about in the kitchen.

As Arb's voice raised in threatening slurs, Scott and Chip surreptitiously came to the living room door, and staring out of frightened eyes, recognized the severity of their dad's behavior. They didn't dare enter the room bringing attention to their presence.

At this point, I believe Tom decided to leave, go to the park, or somewhere, and avert a deadly show-down, for he made a motion to reach the front door. Arb, who was standing at this time and flexing his hands, a warning that he was ready for physical contact, blocked Tom's way of escape. Tom, I believe, recognized his mistake in approaching too closely, couldn't correct himself quickly enough, and Arb reached out with both hands to grab Tom's neck, applying pressure in a forceful manner.

I was watching from the kitchen, and horrified, glimpsed my son's ashen face, the eyes rolling to the top, and the hands that were bent on choking the life from him.

I do not remember picking up the sharp, butcher's knife, but I was standing behind Arb with my arm raised, the knife poised to descend into the back.

Suddenly, there was this tremendous streak of lightning in the form of Scott, the young face pale and frightened yet determined, his small fist raised in front of him. He struck up into the face of his father with all his strength, causing a surprised Arb to release his hold upon Tom's neck.

Tom fell into a heap upon the floor, and without stopping, Scott raced to the screen door as Arb turned, his attention diverted to Scott. Arb raised his fist, striking out for the back of the younger boy's head, but the flashing target ducked so speedily and so successfully, he made it to the door to vanish like a shot, and Arb's fist was driven into the door facing instead.

I observed this woodenly, as in an irrational dream, the incongruity of it all rendering me almost completely unable to refocus my reflexes. As Arb stood swaying, nursing his right, injured fist, my spell was broken as I looked up at my own right hand, still poised, as frozen in time, the knife blade steady, aimed for the back of my husband who would harm my son.

Slowly, I lowered the knife, and knelt down beside Tom, who was struggling to breathe. He appeared to be choking, but was attempting to raise himself to a sitting position. His face was white as a sheet as Chip and I helped him to the couch where he began gulping great gasps of precious air, and began rubbing his injured neck.

Arb continued to watch us, no expression on is face. When he saw Tom would be alright, he sat back down in his chair, and lit a cigarette. He would calmly wait for the police.

Scott raced for Vicki's apartment where the police were notified. He ran back to us, but was afraid to enter the house until Vicki was there with him.

This was the denouement....the wrap up of the twenty years of love, pity, hate....who knew?....and I was facing a big change of a fearful nature, but there was no going back....ever. It was September 1963.

Each time I was abused by my alcoholic husband, I lost respect for him. In my eyes he became less of a man, and by the time I took my sons and left him, to me he had become a sub-human; a deranged piece of humanity of pathetic nature.

Whether his abuse was physical, or verbal, his basic problem was not addressed by him, for it lay within himself protected, yet must be exercised to give him the vent he needed.

Being the coward he became, he chose the weakest person closest to him to express his frustrated feelings of failure. Only then could he feel powerful. Through continued abuse, he thought he would command complete obedience. Constant abuse kept us terrified, and kept us in line.

I did endure it, often feeling the way he acted was my own fault, until after twenty years I knew that not only I, but my sons, perhaps my daughter, were in danger of losing our lives.

Why did I <u>really</u> stay with him so long? Why do any of us?

I do not know when I stopped loving Aubrey and pity crept in. The transition was so subtle. But, I certainly knew when pity ceased, and hate took its place.

My son Tom told me shortly after we moved out and things looked bleak, "If you had not talked back to dad, and had tried harder to get along with him, maybe all this wouldn't have happened." Of course this was an angry and wounded seventeen-year-old's words, but there again were the same old words of frustration--the words of misplaced blame I can't let go of coming from a child who lived it.

A Reflection: My children

It is that I must behold the boundless beauty presented so caringly to me--the children of strength--for I was a weak vessel indeed, my lips deficient, my breathing faint, and God so graciously kept the wounds of my heart sealed so I could present them to the world. And, they go out from me and never look back, as it is the custom, and the wounds in my heart are opened again. I see them no more; only with a worried mind.

Aubrey died of alcoholism in September, 1991, alone in a hotel room. I can remember his smile of long ago, and I ask, "What happened?"

Conclusion

You can always hear me singing this song.

I could hear the choppers coming in close overhead just skirting the tops of the trees, and the loud slapping sound of wet leaves and brush against khaki legs as the runner kept up a pace, never speeding up or slowing down. Just keeping the pace. The runner's breathing was geared to the rhythm of his strides, giving an indication he was a master of what he was now doing--running.

The choppers were not chasing the runner, but keeping pace with him. There were no other runners in front of him, and none behind him, and he could see in the pitch blackness of the jungle on a moonless night. He detected no enemies near who could very well end his young life that night.

Suddenly, the runner's breathing labored, and his steps faltered....I couldn't see his face it was so dark there in that Alien's jungle. I reached out my hand to him....before....before the loud explosion sounded, and the fire lit up his youthful face under the streamlined helmet.

"No! No!" I cried out.

I sat up in bed, awake now, but my eyes were still blinded with the exploding light, and the sound of the choppers faded....both light and sounds faded. Where? Back into the jungle blackness somewhere, and there was nothing. Except the terror in my mind, and my heart was breaking.

"My son! My son!"

God gave Scott the speed of a cheetah, the lovely, flowing grace of a gazelle, and the courage of a grizzly bear. He ran as I had never been able to run. He ran to banish his pain and his frustration.

He ran until he could run no longer.

I am a lioness stalking the dangers to her cub, trying to circumvent that danger without discovery, and I hear my cub cry out in surprised bewilderment, and my padding efforts become intensified, laying all caution for my own safety beside the paths in a foreign, unknown forest. My eyes glint at the rumbling anger boiling up inside my heart as it beats wildly. My speed accelerates, discarding all covert noises I had chosen in the beginning to obliterate my presence, but my cub is crying out to me, and I must reach him before it was too late.

Suddenly, a strangling cry of frustration arose out of my throat as man-made nets of capture ensnared my hind legs drawing them tightly about rendering me helpless, and I lay ever so still, immobilized, the realization of the fate of my cub was set.

These two dreams I experienced a few nights previous to November 23, 1970, upon different nights, however close. On the anniversary of the assination of President John F. Kennedy in that year 1970, my eighteen-year-old son, Scott, a medic for the 101st Airborne Army Division, was seriously wounded as a land mine set by the enemy Viet Cong exploded killing his sergeant and wounding another Non-Com soldier as they were scouting out a camp site for the night.

Scott's bright future to attend the Los Angeles Police Academy and a subsequent career in law enforcement was dashed to pieces in a moment, a blinding moment, and, hopeless disappointment enveloped him. My brave cub. My wounded Eagle.

I did all the acceptable and proper whinings. I had a bad and strange feeling about this, I saw my son stagger and fall in all my imaginings; and I did not want to give him my cheerful blessing; give him the old high sign, and say, "Give 'em hell son." No!

I was against the Vietnam War and all it stood for, and to me, our involvement over there where we were not wanted was simply to enhance the prowess of political figures, and escalate big business, for starters. The old brainwashing blather about nipping communism in the bud before it had a large wordly control didn't soak in on me.

To me, the war meant the daily announcement of body counts, and we here in our country kept watching with horror as year after year passed, and there didn't seem to be an end in sight. Did we send a whole one-third of our young men over there? And, if they returned without a scratch on their physical bodies, the scars within, the wounds slautered their hopes, completely altering the beautiful phyches that started out being bright-eyed with carefree innocence, then if you don't believe that, just take a look into the eyes of the returned and tell me what you see.

I met my second husband in 1964 as I was ending my college classes, and received my associate of arts degree from Los Angeles Harbor College, and we were married at Lakewood, Ca. January 26, 1968. Bruce was a fine, gentle man, thirteen and a-half years older than I, an athletic person who loved the outdoors, and who took me on with my many problems, helping and encouraging me to break free of my monsters.

I watched his deep grief over the loss of his lovely 21-year old daughter, and grieved with him. He held me, and his blue eyes brimmed over when we watched Scott, my wounded Eagle, limp home in a state of defeat from the Vietnam War. He consoled me after Vicki took her two little sons and left to raise them in Missouri. He accepted Tom's little children as his grandchildren, and always tried to stay neutral in Chip's fiascos, but was there to help me when things became rough.

He was my stablizing force, my lover, sweetheart, and my friend, and when he passed away in January, 1990, in Flagstaff, Arizona, I was devastated. Although we were trying to prepare for his death...he needed a new heart, but he was nearly 77-years-old, so he left me. I'm thankful to him for sharing his life with me for twenty-six years. I will always miss him. He could calm my fears, romance me as I'd never been romanced before; he touched my life forever.

I'm positive some will say, "Oh, all that never happened," or, "That isn't the way it happened," but I will feel secure that it happened, and that was the way it happened for me. Let them write a book and tell the way it all happened for them.

All the times I would look around after a particularly difficult episode for me, there was nothing but silence, no sad sympathetic eyes observing, no touch upon the shoulder in love and understanding. Nothing. How could they be absent and then say it didn't happen? Because, they didn't remember it?

Some will ask how could she have such a memory for detail? I do feel it is because I know how to put my feelings into words. And, how can she remember some things and not others, they may ask? The same reason they can't remember some of my memories....because they either weren't there, or it was not impressive enough to register for them. Perhaps, they should be glad I did not write about <u>ALL</u> my memories.

I am truly hopeful that as I wrap up this book, when I can stop the difficult concentration upon the painful aspects of my life, then perhaps I will be able to relax and work again to heal my mind, and my heart. I would like to find peace, or a proper and effective way to put the pain and heartache behind me.

When my father died I did not cry for him. As I stood over his casket, looking down upon the Abe Lincoln-type face without the beard, I couldn't squeeze out a tear. I couldn't control the lack of emotion that would produce tears. This was duly noticed by the minister conducting the service, and he approached me, and gently asked, "Are you all right?" I gave him a calm look, and answered, "I'm fine." If the reverened had thought I was possibly in denial, he was wrong. But I'll allow him his assumtion. I was fine. To me, an enemy was gone.

I wonder, oh how I wonder, if my mother dies before I do, how long will I live on, for I will have no purpose to go on. And yet I ask myself also, what was <u>her</u> purpose to live on and on and on? These are questions I have no right to ask, because only God has the answers, and I am not supposed to question Him. But Dear Lord, what is she?--and why is she so important to you that she is allowed to destroy her daughters, and her son died without her love, and she hurts so many people each day that she breathes?

I come from my visits with her feeling she has taken yet some more of my strength; some more of my spirit. I drive the twenty-five miles back home in so much pain I almost cannot breathe, and I pray I have sense enough to dodge the 18-Wheelers on the two-lane I-71 highway.

The drive is lovely in winter as well as the nice months. Cattle graze lazily, oblivious to my pain as I pass the placid creatures. The huge rolls of bailed hay lay out in the sunshine drying in the fields mile after mile as my little car picks up speed when the highway is clear ahead. And sometimes I barely see at all, and I react to curves and hilltops by rote.

And, I can't stop myself from thinking of her.

She dominates my thoughts. She will not turn loose of me.

*   *   *

Notations of feelings

It isn't until everything is all over that there is interpretation, and interpretation has no place in the victim's life until after the fact. Then the therapists take over and make much ado about something that can't be fixed.

Complete, solid prevention is the only answer to avoid child abuse, or spousal abuse, or any other abuses.

Frustration and life's pressures, broken dreams and bitterness, alcohol and drugs, and patterns of behavioral dysfunction going back generations--all spawn abuse and keep it going.

To really know someone, there should be extensive observances. Relatives and neighbors sometimes never find out until after the fact, then they are incredulous and remark, "You must be mistaken. He is _so_ nice." After all these years when I am winding down, I can see how my present day conflicts were formed from the cradle on through nonceasing abuse patterns. I continue to victimize myself by being unable to make decent choices for my life. I deserve better, but I didn't believe I'd ever have the best.

Abusers are people who need to be in control, and often feel no importance out in the mainstream of society. It is not only a matter of control, but the fear of being unable to control those closest to him [her], which naturally are spouses and children. They are easier to control, so he uses the worst of fears against his victims--physical, verbal, and sexual molestation, all keep his victims in frightful panic at all times even though he may not be present.

Perhaps terrorizing the family allows the abuser to overtly act out the actual seed of his fear, that of having a lack of control out in the world, or in his competativeness outside the home.

However, some abusers, especially of their own children, and family pattern abusers, are stressed for various reasons, are not equipped with a high tolerance for coping. That is, they are nervous and impatient individuals incapable of enduring chaos within their private worlds.

But, I am surprised, surprised again and again, over and over at the positions I just happen to find myself in, but the surprise is that it <u>never</u> stops. I do say to myself after another laborious bout of dealing, oh, well, that really doesn't surprise me in the least. And, mechanically I try to put the pieces back together again.

These bouts are ongoing, year after year, dealing with people who are most hurtful to me. I remind myself of an Ant who is never done. Everything is, as we know, in a constant state of change, and I am changing, much older now with more wrinkles, and if I was Cotton Top when I was a child, now I would be lost in a cotton field altogether.

My biggest surprise is yet to come; that of becoming completely free. No more antagonists, and, I'll check in with the Lord, who will say to me, "Welcome home, but I do wish you would have trusted me more."

EPILOGUE

I keep thinking about life and things, perhaps too much so, but to me there is a beginning and an ending, a future and a past, and we are the players, or more specifically, the pawns, in an ongoing saga.

I was a little girl, and even though I remember her and am imbedded with her memory, I am no longer that little girl.

Where are my babies?--I ask. Where did they get to? Oh, they are not around anymore. <u>They</u> are adults getting older now, and I carry only the memories of the little babies that were the focus of my life. Should I grieve?

I must have sat too long up in the oak tree, but I muse on life and its being a circle, and we players; what happened to us? Did we race toward the future with lightning speed, carrying only a memory bank, or did we actually race <u>back</u> toward the past so fast we become dizzy, only to meet at a time we have no concept of, to merge eventually in an explosion of beautiful re-birth? I don't know.

One thing, I am not going to search back for is that little girl who was supposed to be me, even though maybe I should, and want to do a much better job of it, so she can fly backwards on happier wings before connecting with the future's more experienced being. What a splendid reunion that would be, don't you think?

Where to write for information-

Help for Abuse:

National Child Safety Council:
1-800-3275107

A 2 Z Alcohol Abuse-Addiction:
1-800-2742042

Child Help/National Child Abuse:
1-800-4224453

Domestic Violence Hotline:
1-800-7997233

Alma, a sensitive child, struggles with a poor family's abuse in the Mid-West during the Depression era when day to day survival was a constant battle. As she grew, she turned to her "invisible friend", her Protector, for comfort, even though abusive situations abounded and there was no one to turn to. Sickness, distrust, and hoplessness became dark companions early on, and strengthened as she grew older. The painful memories and how she attempts to overcome the bad forces are set down in this auto-bio, narrative-novel. Some frightful consequences of long-term abuse continue to walk through her life as ghostly guides of fear only to be temporarily dispelled to allow her to use reason and the protection of her "Friend" for healing. Today, at age seventy years, is her spirit broken as remaining members continue to attempt the old ways of abuse? Find out why she calls her abusers "victims" of their terrible need to control others.

AGS '96

TO OBTAIN MORE BOOKS, SEE LOCAL BOOK STORES OR ORDER FROM:
RABETH PUBLISHING COMPANY
ATTENTION: SALES DEPARTMENT
P.O. BOX #171
KIRKSVILLE, MO. 63501
ENCLOSE $14.95 + $2.50 S & H